MEISSEN CHINA
AN ILLUSTRATED HISTORY

DR. K. BERLING

EDITOR

DOVER PUBLICATIONS, INC., NEW YORK

MF

Published in Canada by General Publishing Company, Ltd., 30 Lesmill Road, Don Mills, Toronto, Ontario.

Published in the United Kingdom by Constable and Company, Ltd., 10 Orange Street, London WC 2.

This Dover edition, first published in 1972, is an unabridged republication of the work originally published in English in 1910 under the title *Festive Publication to Commemorate the 200th Jubilee of the Oldest European China Factory, Meissen.* The original publisher was the Royal Saxon China Manufactory, Meissen (Königlich Sächsische Porzellanmanufaktur Meissen).

International Standard Book Number: 0-486-21958-5
Library of Congress Catalog Card Number: 72-75580

Manufactured in the United States of America
Dover Publications, Inc.
180 Varick Street
New York, N.Y. 10014

RESPECTFULLY DEDICATED TO

HIS MAJESTY
KING FRIEDRICH AUGUST OF SAXONY

BY THE ADMINISTRATIVE BOARD OF THE
ROYAL SAXON CHINA MANUFACTORY
MEISSEN

PREFACE.

une 6th 1910 is the 200th anniversary of the day when the Saxon china manufactory which arose from Boettger's discovery was removed to the Albrechtsburg in Meissen, after having existed in Dresden for hardly a year. These two hundred years have been a series of continual ups and downs, the factory has experienced many changes of fortune, its life has been toilsome and full of energetic striving after success; it shows hard battles fought and won.

In the first years of its existence it can not be said to have met with success. Although its productions soon astonished the whole civilised world, still it did not attain the pecuniary success which had been so ardently hoped for. A certain space of time was required for overcoming the technical and commercial difficulties which stand in the way of every factory in the beginning of its existence. Then it reached the acme of success and kept to it unflinchingly for decades arousing the envy of the half of Europe. Want of potency has several times brought the affairs of the factory to a low ebb; this was owing to disturbances of war and other particularly unfavourable political circumstances which the competitors — who had grown strong with time — knew how to make good use of. But again and again the Meissen factory found the strength to keep above water and to reach so flourishing a state as to regain the first place among its contemporaries and — faithful to its old traditions — to bring large sums of money into the royal treasury.

The rare and auspicious occasion of the celebration of the 200th anniversary of the works gave rise to the idea of publishing a memorial in its honour in which everything concerning the factory is particularly dealt with. Very willingly did I agree to write the text, I only regret that so little time has been granted me for preparing for this task. I have had to renounce the idea of revising the most important china collections and all the archives which I thought necessary. If ever another edition of this work should be required, this may perhaps be added to it.

In writing the text, I have made use of my book published in 1900 "Meissen china and its history 1709—1814" abbreviating or extending its contents as proved necessary in this case. I had to leave a good deal out, as only what concerned the Meissen factory could be considered and the illustrations could represent only such chinaware as was made at present and such as could at any time be produced by the factory out of old forms or according to them, with painting that was as like the old models as possible. I have made the work more exhaustive by treating the 19th as well as the 18th century and by describing the commercial, technical and artistic investigations made by Privy counsellor Gesell, Counsellor superior of mines Dr. Heintze and Professors Hoesel and Achtenhagen. I made use of the knowledge gained through the literature* since published about Meissen china and through exhibitions and auctions.

The memorial is addressed, in the first instance, to the public at large. Its aim is to simply give a concise description of the origin, the existence and the change of fortune experienced by the factory, as well as to give an idea of the great and precious store of forms and models at the disposal of the factory. The book may, in many instances, prove of interest especially to the expert. I mean, above all, the table in which most of the models are connected with the artist who made them. Through this many views held up to this time are altered. The art of Aciers, for instance, appears in a much less favourable light than

---

* Besides short articles in periodicals:—Sponsel, Cabinet pieces of the Meissen china factory, 1900. — Bruening, European china, 1904. — Bruening, China, 1907. — Doenges, Meissen china, 1907. — Zimmermann, Discovery and early times of the existence of Meissen china, 1908.

has been the case to the present, while Kaendler's admirable creative powers and rich fancy are seen in all their greatness, although many works are proved to belong to his assistants. These assistants of whom up to the present precious little has been known, now step clearly forward in their work and an attempt has been made to ascribe to each man his individual character and style.

I am greatly indebted to Professor Hoesel with regard to the last mentioned work. I frankly own that without his help I could not reckon with success. For this task a thorough knowledge of the old forms in connection with investigations of the Meissen archives as can only he gained by years of practical work is essential; this knowledge can only be possessed in a sufficient degree by the manager of the plastic department in Meissen.

The illustrations have been chosen by me and Professor Hoesel with the approval of the Privy counsellor Gesell. The execution of the illustrations has been supervised by the Professors Hoesel and Achtenhagen; the latter directed the drawing of the cover vignettes and the first letter of each chapter which were executed by Paul Richter.

A historical treatise of the chemico-technical working of the factory by the director of the working Counsellor superior of mines Dr Heintze and a sketch of the organization, financial management and social statistics of the royal china factory, as well as a description of the celebration of the 200th jubilee on June 6th 1910 by the director the Privy counsellor of commerce Gesell have been added to the general part treated by me.

In this manner it has been sought to give a complete picture of the development of the factory during the 200 years of its existence. It may serve to put before the reader not only what fortune it has met with during all these years, but to show that it has been able to prove itself technically and artistically justified in asserting itself worthy of its old renown to the present day.

Dresden, June 1911.   **Dr. K. Berling.**

TABLE OF CONTENTS.

A.

THE MEISSEN CHINA MANUFACTORY FROM 1710 to 1910

by PROF. DR. BERLING.

B.

THE DEVELOPMENT OF THE CHEMICO-TECHNICAL MANAGEMENT FROM THE BEGINNING TO THE PRESENT TIME

C.

ORGANIZATION, FINANCIAL MANAGEMENT AND SOCIAL STATISTICS

D.

THE CELEBRATION OF THE 200TH ANNIVERSARY OF THE ROYAL CHINA MANUFACTORY ON JUNE 6TH 1910

LIST OF ILLUSTRATIONS.

I. ILLUSTRATIONS IN A NATURAL IMPRESSION OF COLOURS AND DOUBLE AUTOTYPE.

[The Tables marked ⊕ are in full color and are all to be found between pages 36 and 37.]

II. ILLUSTRATIONS OF THE TEXT.

THE INVENTION OF SAXON CHINA.

It is over a thousand years hence since china has been invented. It is, as its name implies, the invention of the Chinese. Excellent raw-materials and practise stretching over centuries have enabled them to reach a technical and artistic perfection which we admire in their works dating from the fifteenth century. Afterwards they shared the knowledge of their art with the Japanese, a people which not only comparatively quickly learnt to make use of many of the Chinese tricks of technique, but decorated their productions in a charming and peculiar manner of their own so that, in a certain sense, they could compete with their masters.

It is probable that in the middle ages only occasionally single pieces of china came to Europe. Only when, after the circumnavigation of the Cape of Good Hope, the sea-way to the East Indies was discovered, the Portuguese opened the market for these goods to European peoples. But the china trade began really to flourish in Europe only after the Dutch had founded their East Indian Company in 1602. Now the China-Japanese porcelain went through India to Holland and other countries; owing to which circumstance the use of the false terms "Indian china" and "Indian flowers", even to this day may be ascribed.

The beautiful, white, symmetrical paste (largely consisting of Caolin) was transparent, clear-sounding and to a certain extent fire proof after the burning. Its firmly adhering glazing which threw such effective lights and shadows offered painters and modellers a good opportunity of showing their art. Its smooth, white surface its brightness and beautiful colour were the cause of its victorious entry into the market. The demand for these highly decorative but very frail goods went further and further, until some princes who had given up whole rooms in their palaces to their collections of china, began to vie with each other in acquiring it.

Enormous sums of money went out of the country in this manner and that was the cause, of ways and means being sought to make it possible to manufacture the goods at home instead of importing them. This tendency may explain the attempts made to make china in the 15th century in Venice, in the 16th in Ferrara and Tuskany, in the 17th in France, Holland and England. The end of imitating the Chinese in manufacturing porcelain was not fully attained at any of these places, moreover it can be said to have remained without lasting keramic influence.

After so many useless attempts they succeeded, at last, at the beginning of the 18th century, in solving the problem i. e. in manufacturing real, white china. This discovery was made at the court of Dresden and it was an event of incalculable importance. The prince at that time reigning there surpassed all others in his fondness for the Chinese goods. He was the Elector of Saxony Friedrich August I known as the Polish King August II and generally called August the Strong. Although he went a little too far in this passion of his, still he left a treasure in the shape of the Dresden collection of china to his people, a treasure which in its beauty and abundance stands unsurpassed in the world.

August the Strong possessed a great thirst for knowledge and a refined taste for the beautiful. Besides, his economical policy was thoroughly mercantile and he took great pains to protect home industry from foreign competition[1]. So that the invention by Boettger of Saxon china is due indirectly to him.

Johann Friedrich Boettger[2] was born on February 4th 1682 in Schleiz. He was the son of the Reussian mint-warden Johann Adam Boettger. His parents moved shortly to Magdeburg where he received good teaching at the hands of his father and after the death of the latter at those of his step-father Tiemann. He early showed a particular fondness for chemistry, as the result of which he was sent to Berlin in 1696 to the apothecary Zorn as a pupil. He made the acquaintance of Johann Kunkel (who did a great deal for the glass industry) of the Greek monk Lascaris[3] and of most of the people who occupied themselves in Berlin with alchymy at that time. He was young, clever and fortunate and the acquaintance of such distinguished men seems to have incited him to seek the philosopher's stone and to attempt to create the gold-making fluid, the Tincture, the Liquor or the Arcanum.

With time the most adventurous reports as to his mysterious powers spread: so that at last King Friedrich I wished to see proofs of them. Boettger fled and reappeared after some time as a student of medecine in Wittenberg. Even here he was persecuted by Prussia which demanded him to be delivered up by the Saxon authorities. But these last could not be moved to deliver him up, and reported the matter, as one of importance, to their sovereign who did not miss the opportunity of winning such a promising personality for himself.

On November 25th 1701 Boettger was brought to Dresden and held in strict custody first here, then in Meissen, on the Koenigstein and then again in Dresden, where he was informed that he should have to work for the Elector. He proved himself incapable of making gold out of baser metals, as he was at first required to do. Still everybody will admit that he has through exertion and energy, which accompanied his discoveries, done more for Saxony than had he really discovered the philosopher's stone.

As assistants he received besides the Privy cabinet secretary, later Council of the chambers and mines Michael Nehmitz who had fetched him from Wittenberg, Pabst of Freiberg, later on Council of mines, who, in his turn was assisted by Dr. Nehmitz, a brother of the first-mentioned Nehmitz. Afterwards he received the miners and smelters Koehler, Schubert and Wildenstein as helpers. All these seem not to have had any influence to speak of on Boettger's work. This is different in the case of Tschirnhaus whom Boettger managed to captivate by his great erudition and pleasing personality at their first meeting.

Ehrenfried Walther von Tschirnhaus was born on April 10th 1651 in Kieslingswalde in Upper Lusatia. By able teachers he was made fit to enter the university. After having completed his studies at home, he went abroad several times and returned as an able mathematician and clever natural philosopher. He was in close relations with Leibniz and was highly esteemed as a man of letters, so that he was a member of the Academy of sciences at Paris in 1682 and later Counsellor of the Saxon court. He was perpetually occupied in raising home industry besides doing the same for science. His optical experiments and discoveries brought him into connection with glass manufacture which led to the foundation of three glassworks. His chief merit is considered to be the manufacturing first of metal then of glass burning reflectors having a lensdiameter and power hitherto unattainable. It was Tschirnhaus who (probably encouraged by the King) from the year 1698 made attempts to get from homely materials a produce similar to chinese porcelain. These attempts did not bring the desired results. He is however supposed to have made white vessels out of a sort of milky glass, as well as several articles in brownish-red and black-veined glassy flux; but Tschirnhaus has not, (as we here particularly mention, notwithstanding assurances lately circulated to the contrary) discovered china. But it was he who probably early recognised in Boettger his great knowledge of chemistry and induced him to continue his own (Tschirnhaus') attempts of imitating chinese porcelain. We find them now working together and Boettger seems to have been more fortunate than his master in working with the burning-glasses of the latter. On the Koenigstein he succeeded in making Dutch ware, a sort of Delft fayence, and in the last months of the year 1707 he brought forth in Dresden red stone-ware.

The King's joy at the final success of Boettger's work must have been great. On November 20th, as Boettger stepped forward with a succession of plans for the future, the King gave him the right of founding several factories and supported him plentifully with money and concessions.

Boettger however did not cease in his attempts to make white china, although the manufacture of red stone-ware alone was an amazing achievement on his part. But after the death of Tschirnhaus in 1708 he must have attained what he had aspired to reach. This is proved by his report to the King March 28th 1709 where, among other things which he prided himself upon having discovered, he mentions firstly: that he knows how to make "the good, white porcelain with finest glazing and painting in such perfection as to at least equal, if not surpass, the East Indian (i. e. the Chinese) production"[4]. It is probable that at that time only a few articles could have been made by way of experiment, neither is it possible that these articles were faultless. Only much later could colours for painting on china successfully have been used.

According to Böttger's wish the King called a commission to examine what Boettger proposed to have done. As the commission had not enough matter on hand to go by, it dissolvet without having succeeded in fulfilling its mission. Nevertheless the King, in a paper[5] which appeared on January 23rd 1710, represented most of the things which Boettger had only promised to make, as already completed. At the same time the foundation of the china works was proclaimed, further arrangements for factories in Saxony designed and artists and workmen called upon to participate in the work.

With extraordinary strength and much ability Boettger dedicated himself to the manufacture of china, as the undertaking was now mostly called. This may be considered as his great merit not only with regard to Saxony but with regard to all Europe; because this factory founded by him became the starting point for European china manufacture.

THE MISNIA (MEISSEN) CHINA MANUFACTORY.

I. PERIOD:

BOETTGER (1710—19).

Deep investigations founded upon the study of archives[6] of the Counsellor superior of mines Dr. Heintze in Meissen have given us explanations of the technical part of Boettger's discoveries. He comes to the conclusion that chance could have played only a small part in these and that Boettger must have acted in a thoroughly systematic manner, building one experiment upon another; also that it must have required long and serious labour before the desired end could have been reached. Heintze describes how Boettger (at first in collaborating with Tschirnhaus) tried with aid of the large burning reflectors, first the co-relation of metals, then of various stones and lastly of coloured earths. When he ascertained that the latter proved to get more or less liquid in the baking and that loam proved to be a medium for liquefaction, the idea struck him to combine a mixture which turned into a stone-like mass resembling porcelain. According to Heintze this mixture consisted of about 88% of red bolus, red Nürnberg earth, a yellow argillaceous earth from Zwickau, Borner earth from Berggiesshübel and later red clay from Okrilla mixed with 12% of washed loam. The red Nürnberg earth had already in the 16th and 17th century been introduced into the Pharmacopoeia under the name of "terra sigillata" and originally consisted of red bolus from Lemnos, which was probably already in Boettger's time cleaned red bolus found in different parts of Germany and at any rate exported from Nürnberg. The red bolus contains about 42% of silicic acid, 20—25% silicate of alumina, 20—25% of water, the rest being oxyde of iron.

Before the end of the year 1707 on the strength of this discovery of Boettger's, to which he from the beginning attached great importance, a factory was built on the Venusbastion. Counsellor of chambers and mines M. Nehmitz acted as director of the factory, Tschirnhaus guided the technical part while Dr. Bartholomaï who was appointed as assistant to Boettger owing to his chemical and technological knowledge took care of the composition of the paste. Since the 24th of January 1710 the staff of direction consisted of Nehmitz and the secretary later Counsellor of commerce Matthieu, but the administration was given over to Boettger. For the biscuit-baking of the vessels Peter Eggebrecht, a Hollander was brought, while at first, the potter to the Dresden court Fischer had to turn and form which work later on was done also by Eggebrecht. The latter had had the opportunity of gaining more experience in this at the Delft factories. After having taught three or four potters[7] this branch of the trade, he withdrew from here in order to devote himself entirely to the Fayence factory[8] which had also been called into existence by Boettger.

The arranging of the factory was entered into with great assiduity. Large kilns were built, a pit for storing the prepared paste was made by the Superior board of works and a large quantity of material was procured. As the space soon proved insufficient a more suitable place had to be looked for. It was found, isolated to a certain extent and yet near Dresden, in Albrechtsburg in Meissen, which at that time harboured the Court of procuration of the country. On the 6th of June 1710 the rooms were delivered for this purpose, the King having ordered the transferring of the works there March 7th before. The whole year passed, however, before removal could be effected. On 3rd September it was still reported that only the "factory for producing the red paste" was in a working state, and that, as the Chapter of the Cathedral raised difficulties about some of the buildings, they found it impossible to work as they would have liked to do.

Still already on the Easter fair of Leipsic 1710 an attempt was made to bring to market a large quantity of the stone-ware, while only a couple of trial pieces of white china were included. These goods did not receive the expected reception. Although it is attempted to explain this by outward circumstances, I believe, that the real cause of the failure was, first of all, the defectiveness of the goods themselves. I do not think it probable that during the first three years particularly high class work could have been turned out. The documents can not in this respect always be taken literally. When it was a matter of one's own merit being put in the right light, the truthfulness of the statements made was not at thing very particularly considered.

Boettger, Bartholomaï and Nehmitz[9] were novices in the field of keramic fabrication and the fitness for independent work of the artisans-proper could not, at that time, be particularly depended upon. The potter of the court Fischer who must be the first to be here considered was doubtless a good master workman, but he was hardly a match for higher expectations. His place was taken by Eggebrecht for a short time. But, I greatly doubt, if the latter rapidly and completely made himself familiar with the technique.

As far as the forms in these oldest times are concerned, I believe that first of all cups, teapots, vases and such-like articles which were as simple as possible and could be made on a potter's wheel could only come in question. Then the King who had always paid attention to all single details in the factory, seems to have stepped in himself. He probably saw that with the men at hand alone not much could be attained, so he ordered the goldsmith of his court Joh. Jak. Irminger (verbally) to assist the factory in the work of shaping the articles and "to think of such inventions as to enable to produce especially large or other kinds of well and artistically made vessels".

It seems to me that Irminger must have been the one to whom the credit of having done a great deal to further this part of the industry is due. Although he continued living in Dresden, he not only constructed a large number of models himself, but instructed the potters[10] of the factory, by pointing out and correcting faults, to go on working independently yet in accordance with his own ideas.

At the beginning the chinese models were followed as closely as possible with regard to shape; some pieces seem to have been faithful copies. This manner of copying did not give satisfaction for any length of time, shortly the Barock-style, then prevailing in Germany, came forward here as well. The ornamentation with masks and acanthus leaves, the decoration of pipes, the eaglesheads and lambrequinpatterns distinctly shew a familiar style. Most of these articles are strongly and pithily modelled with firm hand and artistic eye. Not only all possible parts of table utensils, but a great variety of vases, dishes, candlesticks, then reliefs, busts and even entire figures were modelled and made. As the forms became more varied the finish had to be differentiated accordingly. They became acquainted with the polishing and engraving particularly suiting this material, by means of which they were able to produce peculiarly charming pieces. Other articles were furnished with a glazing on which occasionally "patterns in gold and silver, in lac and enamel colours were painted"[11]. In this way an incalculable quantity of different articles in stone-ware was produced; articles of such technical and artistic perfection which were not only (in the first years of their manufacture at least) very popular, but were soon successfully imitated[12].

At the beginning of the year 1709 Boettger, as above mentioned, succeeded in finding, what so many had vainly sought before him, the secret of making real white china.

The Counsellor superior of mines Heintze, to whom my thanks are due, has made deep studies[13] on this subject, which I here mainly follow. When Boettger found in earth dug up in Colditz, a very fire-proof clay which turned white in the baking, he combined it with a medium of flux i. e. calcified alabaster (baked sulfate of lime) the paste which after being sufficiently well baked gave forth china. Colditz clay played, at first at any rate, the principal part. Still, at an early time already, the earth dug up on the property of the hammersmith Schnorr at Aue was added to it.

Records that must have been written about 1730 give us an explanation of the sort of raw materials then used in Meissen. The porcelain-clay is spoken of in the following manner: "That one found on Schnorr's ground, not far from Schneeberg, near Aue and that one of Bockau (near Zwickau?) remain the best, although some to equal them may be found at Raschau close to Schwarzenberg. Still there are some not unserviceable clays at Geyer, Zschopau, in Silesia and other places". Then the other materials necessary for making porcelain paste are spoken of and it is added: "The proportions of the compositions may be changed, still if one wished to stand on firm ground the following recipe might be recommended:—1. Schnorrs clay 4 parts. 2. Colditz argillaceous earth 2 parts. 3. Fine silicious earth 1 1/2 parts. 4. Alabaster 1 1/2 parts. Further in order that the principal material should not be too lean no alloy is required. Even if the paste so combined appeared a little yellowish". Silica was thought to be necessary to make the paste capable of retaining the glazing[14]; alabaster was used to give it transparency.

Several recipes were found for glazing which was also discovered by Boettger. Here it is also mentioned that many attempts had to be made and that first of all, the glaze must be adapted to the material used. A recipe of this kind runs as follows:—100 lbs silica, 10 lbs Colditz clay, 20 lbs rough borax. Lime afterwards took the place of borax.

Taking into consideration the great difficulties connected with the manufacture of china at that time when that sort of production was a "terra incognita", it is not surprizing that during the first decade hardly more then attempts were made. On June 28th 1710 it was already possible to send to the King to Warsaw a glazed and unglazed china article which were both richly ornamented in as many colours as possible. Still it was considered necessary to beg pardon because the colours did not flow on the glazed piece and because the glazing seemed dusty on account of the cracks of the saggers.

Although Boettger took the greatest pains from the very beginning to colour his china, still, at this period, mastery in the art of colouring can not yet be spoken of. The preparing and baking of colours is combined with many technical difficulties, the knowledge of which had to be gained very gradually. Attempts were continually being made, but nothing really satisfactory was arrived at. Even painting in blue under glaze, although great pains were taken with it, remained in a state of imperfection throughout this period. Only painting in gold and silver seems to have been produced to a greater extent[15]. The principal aim was, at that time to produce a white and faultless china and that aim was probably reached in 1715. Certainly it was not yet of the desired milky whiteness, but had a tinge of yellow or grey, while the glazing was rendered rough and otherwise irregular by insufficient washing of the clay. The baking, especially of the larger pieces, was also connected with difficulties, as we can gather from the many cracks and distortions so evident in them.

As far as the modelling is concerned, it is similar to that of the stone goods. Sometimes even the same forms seem to have been used. The simplest models were preferred. It was thought to make chinese porcelain more pleasing to European taste by the addition of some suitable ornamentation. A part of it was ornamented by chinese flower-wreaths or by masks and garlands of leaves, in Barock-style, while a part was left without embellishment at all. The ornamentations were made seperately and then joined to the main article before the glazing was put on. Then china-ware was produced which came out of the forms ready-ornamented and lastly the walls of the vessels were made quite plain and over them a filigree work of geo-metrical ornamentation was made. In single instances they might have ventured at small round plastic works in which case not only china served as a pattern, but independent models must have been produced. Such were the so-called Callot-figures[16], the statuette of August the Strong and many others besides[17].

Although it has not been possible, at this period, to bring the Meissen china out of its state of ex-perimentation to a certain stage of perfection, still the more or less successful attempts to improve in shape, colouring and in matters of technique were the necessary preliminaries for the flourishing state into which the Meissen factory was to be led in a very short time.

Table 2

Pages 11, 16, 17.

1. Cup with applied flowers, *107*.   2. Tea-caddy, □2.   3. Vase, H *128*.   4. Sugar basin.
5,3 cm.   9 cm.   22 cm.   9 cm.

5. Cup with applied flowers, *51*.   6. Vase, I *103*.   7. Tureen, M *201*.
14 cm.   20 cm.   29 cm.

8. Goblet with plastic acanthus leaves. R *162*.   9. Tureen, *8,3*.   10. Plate, E *181*.
15 cm.   12 cm.   23 cm. diam.

11. Goblet, *6*.   12. Cup with plastic acanthus leaves, *107*.
7,5 cm.   5,3 cm.

II. PERIOD:
MAINLY UNDER THE INFLUENCE OF HOEROLDT
(1720—35).

GENERAL WORKING.

fter Boettgers death in 1719 a change had necessarily to be made in the management of the factory. The King called a commission of three members, whose duty consisted in reporting upon the defects which had, of late years, made themselves felt and to make suggestions for improving them. The earnestness and skilfullness, with which the commission set to work, were the cause of the whole management soon being given over into its hands. In this way the hopes, of Counsellor of mines Nehmitz (who had up to that time acted as director) as well as those of the General Postmaster of the crown Holtzbrink, of obtaining the entire management of the factory, were shattered. The latter had, by order of the King been inititiated into the secrets of the arcanum. Steinbrueck who had up to that time acted as inspector was appointed "administrator". As such he had to superintend the workers and to keep the accounts in order his duties were, after his death 1723 taken over by Reinhardt who was called the "inspector". Dr Nehmitz who had for many years worked under Boettger took over the management of the technical part of the works.

When the commission dwindled to one member in 1729 the management of the factory was given over to a board of chambers under the leadership of Count von Hoym. On May 19th 1731 August the Strong himself took over the direction of the works which he carried on, with the assistance of three commissioners[19], until his death on February 1st 1733. Under his successor the Cabinet minister Count von Bruehl was the mediator between the King and the commission.

As a result of this orderly management the factory soon showed a series of improvements. As the position of the management was put on a solid footing, the discipline which had become lax was made firm and the sale of the goods was regulated. From this time the sale of china-ware in the Dresden store under the supervision of the manager Chladni began, although it had already been opened in 1714. In Leipsic a shop in Auerbach's Court was rented for the sale of goods during the fare. In 1731 in Warsaw a warehouse was established. But above all things it was sought to improve the china itself in all respects. The paste itself, the glaze, baking and ornamentation.

The baking, especially of larger pieces, left even now much to be desired. So in 1720 the baking caused a great deal of trouble, "as the ware often came crooked or cracked out of the kiln and of 24 dozen cups often hardly a dozen was fit for use". The damage done in the final baking by grains of sand and other small irregularities were sought to be removed by grinding off. As there were many inferior goods turned out, already in the years beginning with 1720 they began sorting the ware into good quality, medium quality and garbage[20]. In 1723 a new kiln for biscuit baking and 1729 two kilns for final baking (white heat), double size of the former, were built. In 1729 the discovery of the turner Rehschuh came into use. This discovery consisted of using the tin stencil at the potter's wheel and through it the work was made easier and could be better regulated.

At the time of Boettger's death it was still the principal aim to manufacture different colour especially cobalt blue under glazing and to apply it to china. All those who sought to succeed Boettger, and there were, besides those above mentioned, several others promised to give the King satisfaction in this respect. Mehlhorn jun. who had been called to Meissen for the sake of the blue colouring, produced, in company with his father (the Inspector of polishing mills) blue-painted china which was of a whiter colour and was less cracked and distorted than was at that time usual. A perfect application of blue colouring under glaze could not in their case be spoken of either. Still the two men who knew too much about the arcanum were ordered to remain attached to the factory. The attempts of the master workman David Koehler (one of the oldest arcanists) seem to have given better results. He had directed his principal attention to a paste which blue colouring adhered to better than to the one used before. On March 5th 1720 the commission sent several pieces of a tea-service made by Koehler and a tea-pot produced by both Mehlhorns to the King. They mentioned that, although the blue colouring was not altogether perfect, they hoped that perfection would soon be reached especially "as soon as the knowledge of a competent artist were here applied"[21]. An artist who not only knew how to make on artistic use of blue painting under glaze, but who, with time, imprinted the influence of his own personality on all the productions, was soon to be found in the China Factory of Vienna.

Although, from the very beginning, great pains had been taken in Meissen to preserve the secret of the arcanum; although the workman were carefully supervised and their work kept away from the prying eyes of the uninitiated, still these precautions proved almost useless. For the extraordinary popularity of the Meissen china naturally brought with it the desire of many countries to take the industry into their own hands. For this purpose they sought to bribe those who knew, or professed to know the trade secrets, to entice them away and thereby be enabled to found factories of their own[22]. Besides the arcanists-proper a few more people had to be here considered. Those were the ones who had managed to gain Boettger's confidence and so worm out the secrets from him. During the last years of Boettger's life this was probably not a difficult task.

So in 1718 with the help of the enameller and gilder Konrad Christoph Hunger the Vienna factory was founded. Hunger was born in Weissenfels in Thueringen and came in his wanderings as a goldsmith from France to Dresden where he had the opportunity of obtaining Boettger's confidence by cunning. He was then not employed in the factory but Boettger persuaded him to busy himself with the blue colour under glaze. At the end of the year 1717 he is supposed to have gone to Vienna. In this vicinity he, working together with du Paquier, sought vainly for a porcelain paste. As du Paquier soon noticed that Hunger's knowledge of the arcanum was not worth much, he himself travelled to Meissen returning to Vienna in company of the arcanist Samuel Stoeltzel whom he had enticed by making thee most brilliant promises. Even now it was for some time vainly attempted to combine a good china-paste at home, and only after the importation of Schnorr's earth from Aue was it possible to produce pieces of china fit for use. As the factory did not at first prosper the promises made to Hunger and Stoeltzel could not be kept. As the result of this both flew from Vienna the former in 1719, the latter in 1720. Hunger went to Venice, where he, for five years, produced china out of Schnorr's clay. After having led an irregular life he was, at his own request, employed at the Meissen factory for "enamelling in gold". He did not, however, remain here for any length of time, but left the factory because he had business-dealings in company with Stoeltzel. In the record a note is found to the effect that he was in Stockholm in 1731[23].

The founding of the factories in Vienna and Venice was looked upon in Meissen with well-deserved suspicion, and as Schnorr's clay had been used in them, it was prohibited to sell it to any but the Meissen factory. Notwithstanding this prohibition it was still, as reported by Hunger delivered to Vienna and Venice in 1727 by a lace-dealer from Schneeberg. It was packed in small barrels and labelled "blue starch". The interdiction for the exportation was therefore severally repeated.

While Hunger went to Vienna, Stoeltzel returned to Meissen, as the King on January 16th 1720 pardoned him his flight and treachery. At first he was treated in Meissen with suspicions care. He had to work separately from the other arcanists and had no admission to the workrooms for clay-washing and glazing. At any rate he quickly regained the confidence placed in him before and fully satisfied the expectations put on him. At the death of the principal master workman Koehler he was appointed to succeed him as the other two arcanists Schubert and Hoppe seem not to have been over intelligent. He was particularly admired for having in 1725 succeeded in gilding china "in colour and brilliancy just as well as Funke" and that he was able to fulfil a many-times-expressed wish in making larger pieces of china such as dishes, vases etc. This he was able to do by improving the technique of baking[24].

Although the Meissen factory has much to thank Stoeltzel for, the painter Johann Gregor Hoeroldt, brought by the former from Vienna, was fated to play a more important part in its developement.

It has been above hinted at that at Boettger's death the art of colouring was not far advanced. Except gilding hardly any coloured ornamentations worth mentioning had probably been made[25]. Shortly after his death blue painting under glaze was brought to a certain state of technical perfection, but it was not understood how to make an artistic use of this knowledge which had so long been sought for. At that time there was no real painter at all at the Meissen factory[26], nothing could so please the commission as the fact that Stoeltzel had in his flight from Vienna brought Hoeroldt with him. The latter was a man whose abilities gave rise to and fulfilled the brightest hopes.

The trial pieces which the commission set before the King on May 22nd 1720 were commented on in the following manner[27]. "Hoeroldt's work proves that he is able to trace on china not only in blue but in other colours as well, that the china is not scratched in the process, that each pattern is artistically drawn and retains its colour and outlines in the baking."

It was Hoeroldt to whom the flourishing state which the Meissen factory now entered into was due. As he was, first of all, a painter, it is a matter of course that this period which was so greatly influenced by him was characterized by the painting. It soon became evident that he towered above the other employees so far as energy and technical knowledge were concerned. He was not only considered an able painter and a good draughtsman, but was so far experienced in the chemico-technical part of the manufacture that he was able to take an active part in any part of the works. To show the ability and quickness of his judgement we shall mention a case in point: when only very few plates and dishes remained straight in the final baking, he gave such order as made these faults almost entirely disappear[28]. Besides Hoeroldt is said to have been an able administrating official and a man easy to get on with. It is not surprising that, possessing so many good qualities, he was soon appointed manager of the factory. This position was filled by him with skill and address until such a time as he had to allow his place to be taken by younger workers whose taste was more in keeping with the ideas then modern.

His rapid rise points to the fact of how greatly Hoeroldt was appreciated in Meissen. Johann Gregor Hoeroldt was born, or christened, in Jena on August 6th 1696[29]. He was the youngest son of the second marriage of the master tailor Johann Wilhelm Hoeroldt. He worked for a short time in Vienna and came in May 1720, as an ordinary painter, to Meissen. In the pay list of 1723 he already figures as "painter to the court". On November 6th 1725 he married the only daughter of a relation of high-standing in Meissen named Keyl. In 1731 he probably was inititiated into the Arkanum and was created Commissioner of the Court, in 1749 he was made Counsellor of mines. On September 18th 1765 he wished to be pensioned off and died in Meissen January 26th 1775.

Hoeroldt, as may well be imagined, had enemies. The appreciation which was in full measure meted out to him by his superiors and his energetic actions with regard to keeping order among the mostly frivolous painters must have been the cause of much envy and hatred. At one time he even feared that his enemies would triumph and make him lose his position.

This was at the time when the factory was under the supervision of the Prime minister Count Karl Heinrich von Hoym who acted as its chief manager 1729—1731. Under him the Paris merchant Rudolf Lemaire who is described as a connoisseur of porcelain was priviledged in a striking manner. Rudolf Lemaire had made a contract with the factory on July 22nd 1729. According to this contract he had to deposit the sum of 1000 talers yearly and could then receive a large quantity of goods to be disposed of by him in France and Holland. These goods were to be only partly after the fashion of those manufactured in Meissen generally, many of them had to be especially made according to models and drawings sent by him. It was his wish that the factory should concede him the sole right of dealing in the last-mentioned goods. This wish was however not acceded to. He only received a promise that those goods would not be sold elsewhere for a year. His desire for unpainted china was not satisfied either; he received only painted and ornamented china. Hoeroldt seems from the very beginning not to have trusted this dealer and to have feared that the factory would suffer some damage at his hands; that he would have the china painted himself or palm it off as chinese porcelain. For this reason his wish to have the goods bought by him stamped with a chinese or any other mark was not fulfilled either. The articles were not only marked with the swords under the glaze, as was then customary, but another hardly perceptible mark added without his knowledge[30]. Lemaire seems to have gone still further, as he made use of every opportunity of gathering information about the working of the factory. And, even if he was not successful in fathoming the secrets of the arcanum, still he, by order of Count Hoym saw the process of turning and baking. In other instances also a certain preference was shown to Lemaire. For instance his orders had to be executed before any others, although he received everything exceptionally cheap; he is also supposed to have received articles without the mark of the swords[31].

It is possible that Hoym, possessing a preference for France and french taste wished to make Lemaire manager of the works; reproaches were afterwards made to him on this subject. The appointment of Lemaire as manager of the works would have been synonymous with Hoeroldt's fall. This was not fated to happen however. When, in March 1731, in Saxon political affairs a friendship with Austria was formed, Count Hoym who was head of the French party fell. The King himself overtook the chief management in Meissen in his stead. In the case made against Hoym and his creatures the favours accorded to Lemaire played a large part. We are made more closely acquainted with the actions of Nohr, the keeper of the Meissen goodsstores by the reports of this case[32]. In this matter he was found guilty of many offences and severely punished. Lemaire was arrested as well, then he was banished from the country. Naturally at the same time all business connection with him was broken off. Only in 1734 his partner Jean Charles Huet of Paris was successful in obtaining china again in Meissen.

Hoeroldt had another enemy in the face of Reinhardt the inspector of the factory, who is described as an avaricious and intriguing person. This man was probably envious of Hoeroldt's rapid rise and Hoeroldt was therefore a thorn in his eye at any rate, he sought to do him harm whereever possible. So he set the sculptor Kaendler and everal others against him and sent, together with the first, a long denunciation against him to the commission[33]. As a result careful examination of Hoeroldt's actions was entered into, it did not, however, show up anything detrimental to Hoeroldt. In this case he proved without reproach as well, while Reinhardt was punished by imprisonment and dismissal; others were only warned.

Hoeroldt now became the soul of the whole undertaking and met with astounding personal success. Every year the factory rose in every respect, and as the china improved in quality, the profits increased in quantity. Under Boettger the factory had required pecuniary assistance while now it brought profits[34] which grew with each year; that is, the mercantile part of the business had greatly improved. In 1733, 104 dealers in 32 towns stood in continual business connection with the factory[35]. Among them, besides the above-mentioned Lemaire, the turkish merchant Manasses Athanas took up a peculiar position. In 1732 he ordered not less than 2000 dozen small cups[36] so called "Turk's cups", in 1734 he made a contract with the factory by which he bound himself to take "as many tea-cups of all sorts as could be turned out by the factory according to his models, even when the quantity reached 3000 dozen; this on condition that such were sold to no one else[37]. His request, uttered in 1732, not to stamp the goods intended for him with the swords, seems to have been fulfilled. Instead of the swords the staff of Mercury with a dot was used[38].

The King however remained at all times the best customer. He continually kept the factory working for him. His plan, which will be particularised below, that of furnishing the Japanese palace in Dresden with east-asiatic and Meissen china lavishly, required the manufacture of many extraordinarily large pieces. The execution of these orders caused great difficulties and required many years after the death of August the Strong[39].

Through this a great deal was required of the factory and as a result a greater number of officials and workmen had to be employed. So for instance in 1723 there were 36—40, from 1731, 92 from 1733 174 and in 1734, 194 people employed at the works.

A that time two kinds of paste were used at the factory: the blue paste which was so-called because it was blue before baking and the white or ordinary paste. Out of the first clear white china was made, while articles made out of the second were yellowish, often bore small holes and were not fit to be painted in blue painting under glaze. After many attempts they were at last successful in 1734 in making the ordinary paste of a whiter colour and were able to paint on it in blue under glaze.

The improvement in the state of affairs of the factory proved an enticement to quite a number of adventurers to attempt to put forth their real or imagined knowledge of the fabrication of china. Isr. Aug. Schueler, formerly an apprentice of the chemist' shop of the Court of Dresden, offered his services in improving the paste and glazing[40], a certain Dr. Müller professed to have invented a way of putting different shades of red colour under glaze[41], these and many more requested to be taken into the service of the factory. These offers were seen into in Meissen by competent men, but seem to have given no results to speak of. The former inspector of polishing mills Mehlhorn, whose attempts in blue-painting I mentioned above, seems to have molested the factory most of all. He had been dismissed by Count Hoym without a pension. After the fall of the latter he made many offers of his services to improve the factory[42]. At last he and his three sons were given employment[43] on it, but only through fear lest they should do harm to the trade by making use of their knowledge elsewhere. Even now the Mehlhorns kept coming forward with new "inventions", which were always useless and sought to extort larger salaries by threatning to make use of their knowledge abroad. It is probable that they had offers enough. In 1735, by chance, a Cassel factory is spoken of which was probably organised by Mehlhorn senior[44]. In the same year a complot was discovered, the members of which — the painter Thausend and six other employes including Mehlhorn's three sons —, had decided to flee to Bayreuth for the sake of making china in the factories there. The painter Thausend was ready to do this although he had been employed at the factory for eight years. They were all arrested in the nick of time and had to expiate their treason[45] in the prison of Waldheim. Last of all it was rumoured that the Commissioner of commerce Meerheim, one of the largest spungers in the factory had fled from Meissen in May 1735 and wished to establish a factory in Potsdam in company with a certain Kirchner or Krieger. Gotzkowsky in Berlin confirmed the rumour[46].

THE MODELLING.

Among the china articles of the years between 1720—1730, breakfast services took the first place. These comprised at that time six cups and saucers, slop-basin, tea and coffee-pot, a tea-caddy, a sugar basin and in some cases goblets for chocolate, which were made with one or two and sometimes with no handles at all. Jugs for chocolate were not spoken of; probably the same pots as for coffee were used, milk or cream-jugs I did not find mentioned before 1731.

To satisfy a wish the King had many times expressed great pains were taken to produce larger articles such as vases and dishes. The difficulties met with in turning and forming and the still greater ones in the baking allowed only of a slow progress. Stoeltzel and Hoeroldt were greatly praised because at the beginning of the twenties they succeeded in making some few improvements. Attempts were continually being made to get at least single large pieces unharmed out of the kilns: these attempts were rarely crowned with success. The large articles were mostly intended for the King. We find dinner-sets with large dishes on the general market only in 1734. At the end of 1731 I find a dinner service first mentioned. It had been ordered by the Chief-treasurer Count von Friesen and was not to be painted but to be ornamented with a sort of engraving[47].

Most of the articles were plain in their foundation (Table 2, H 128)[48], some were, however, striped i. e. consisted of four, five or more circular parts or were sea shell-shaped (saucer Table 3, 80). The ground was either without plastic decoration or with leaves ready-pressed in the form (Table 2, R 162 and 107) or covered with vine-leaves, roses, jasmin or fancy leaves or even lizards. Besides breakfast sets, chimney-piece ornaments in the form of vases, urns, goblets or bottles which were made in sets of five or seven pieces were, at that time, much sought after. Also pagodas with firm or shaking heads (Fig. 1, 2884)[49], wine or beer-jugs, salt-cellars, knife-handles, soup-tureens, salad-bowls, ink-stands, snuff-boxes, pipes etc. were in great demand.

The people whose duty it was during the first years of this period to do the forming of articles in Meissen had formerly been potters. They had been taught by Irminger and were even now occassionally controlled by him. There must have been some capable men among them, such as Fritzsche, Wildenstein later Mueller, Schmieder and Krumpholz. They modelled, formed, turned and finished and may have even invented some new forms. Principally however they kept to the shapes and forms of the Boettger period as they were not really sculptors. At this time when a new model came their way it was generally sent from abroad. In January 1725 for instance the Dresden manager Chladni sent 161 pieces of plastic figures as models which he got from a certain Augsburger the like of which were to be produced in china at the factory in Meissen. There were "models of different peoples in their national costumes and other figures". It is reported that in 1728—29 snuff-boxes were made according to french pattern and a plate with a cover like a Vienna model. August the Strong sent drawings for several large "epergnes" to be used for sweets, Lemaire sent models three times and a Regensburg merchant and one from Augsburg sent models for clock-cases. For forms wooden models were preferably used and this is particularly noted. In 1725 chess-figures which were painted in purple and gold, a pagoda and a winged dragon which last was intended as a support

Page 11.

Fig. 1. PAGODA, 2884.
31 cm.

for a coffee barrel were all made after wooden models which in their turn had been formed by the sculptor Gottfried Müller in Meissen[50].

As the factory came into a more flourishing state it was necessary to construct new forms within the factory itself. So a report to the commission dated 22nd of March 1727 speaks of the necessity of sending a sculptor to Meissen as follows:—"a good sculptor who makes different models and several capable boys should be engaged". The forming of models has, so far, been practised by Fritzsche who was able to make some independently but was better at copying other models; he is however too much occupied with the ordinary work "to think of forming new-shaped utensils".

In fulfillment of this request the sculptor Johann Gottlob Kirchner (born 1706 in Merseburg), living in Dresden, was engaged at the Meissen factory at a wage of 220 talers yearly. He seems only very slowly to have got accustomed to the work, the technique of which was strange to him. In January 1728 a complaint was made that the models formed by him of clay and gypsum, as well as those cut in wood,

did not adapt themselves to china and that he had not had sufficient practise in handling the material. It was added that Fritzsche was the only one who knew how to manage the porcellain paste properly. Of the articles made by him at this time a clock-case is often praised, ewers and basins being mentioned as well. As Kirchner, who is described as very frivolous brought little use to the factory and sometimes left his work altogether undone, he was again dismissed in the middle of April 1728[52].

His place was taken by Johann Chr. Ludwig Luecke a sculptor appointed by the King himself. It is probable that he at first made a very good impression, he is spoken of as "master of models". He proved industrious and modelled "all sorts of handles and figures for large epargnes, models for tobacco-pipes and snuff-boxes". Then he was once sent to the Leipsic fair in order to "gather a few drawings of the Augsburg silver-plate and all sorts of steel engravings" and was deputed to teach the apprentices drawing in the evenings. In September complaints against him were heard already; he is not supposed to have fulfilled what had been expected of him. It was also said that he had only done trivial things which would just as well have been done without him. He could not even be compared with Kirchner. A model of a richly decorated big drinking cup which he had begun at that time seems to have proved a failure; from a ten-days' stay in Dresden he only brought a few bad drawings (executed in goldsmiths' shops) with him to Meissen. Shortly, he gave so little satisfaction that he was dismissed in February 1729[52].

After this place had remained vacant for over a year, it was again taken by Kirchner who had in the meanwhile lived in Weimar. He was engaged at a higher salary (300 talers yearly) than before. He seems to have given satisfaction, was made a model-master and manager of the modelling department. It was also his duty to see to the teaching of drawing and modelling to the apprentices. In the same year he was ordered to get a book into which drawings of all the models whether those already existing, those to be executed in the future, or such as were sent ready to the factory-were to be entered in reduced form[53].

Another Luecke, Karl Friedrich by name, came to Meissen as finisher in October 1731. His duties consisted in helping the sculptor by finishing the already formed large vessels and working out the decorations on them. He was employed here for only a short time as in March 1733 he tendered his resignation. In October of the same year his resignation was accepted as "he", to quote the words of the commission, "had become very dissolute and could not be influenced for the better, he also had many debts". Before taking leave, he had to spend four weeks in prison[54] for fighting with town soldiers.

The factory kept extending and more was expected of it. The principal difficulty consisted in executing the King's order for the Japanese palace in Dresden. This order will be spoken of more particularly further on. This led to the employment of Kaendler the man who did as much for the factory in plastique as Hoeroldt had done in painting. He was summoned to Meissen by the King himself who expressed a wish that Kaendler and Kirchner should collaborate in making the large vases and animals[55]. From the very

Table 4

6 by Kirchner, the rest by Kaendler.

Pages 13, 33, 64, 65.

1. Pointer, 1124. 2. Parrot, 20*. 3. Ure-ox, 2687. 4. Cacadoo, 1780. 5. Wild pig, 742. 6. Wagtail, 58*.
17 cm.   29,5 cm.   13 cm.   32 cm.   7,5 cm.   23 cm.

7. Parrot, A 43. 8. Bologna dog, 2841. 9. Pigs hunt, 739. 10. Bologna terrier, 333.
36 cm.   23 cm.   24 cm.   20 cm.

beginning the relations between the two modellers seem to have been strained. Kirchner, naturally, saw in Kaendler a rival who he feared would supplant him. Besides his salary was lower than that of Kaendler, although his position that of modelling master-workman was higher. He therefore in the beginning of the year 1732 demanded higher wages and free quarters—as this was not fully granted he tendered his resignation. It was not accepted; but as he again tendered it in February 1733 it was accepted, as it was taken into consideration that he had lately been carelessly carrying out his duties. As Kaendler had already got well-used to the work and had useful assistants in Krumpholz and Schmieder, no new man was put in Kirchner's place[56]. Certainly at the beginning Kaendler was unable to deliver any perfectly made models, as it required a certain time for him to familiarize himself with the peculiarities and difficulties of working in china. In the opinion of the commission Kirchner was still the more capable of the two. It reported that "he understood his work well and was very useful and that he surpassed the other modeller, Kaendler, in his inventions and other ways"[57].

Fig. 2. KRONOS,
the uppermost figure of
a clock-case, 132.
14 cm.

We know very little about what Kirchner had created for Meissen. Sponsel[58] and I[59] attempted to trace some pieces to him as their originator, some others may be here added.

It was particularly noticed that the animals which Kirchner modelled for the factory were less true to nature in colouring and position than those modelled by Kaendler. Taking this circumstance into consideration, it seems to me that the wagtail (Table 4, 58*)[60] and the parrot (Table 1, 343) which the factory has fashioned after the original one in the Dresden collection of china must have been Kirchner's work.

The Kronos shown in Fig. 2, 132 was intended for the uppermost figure of a clock-case decorated with many statuettes[61].

Judging by the records, the following may be proved to be Kirchner's works:—In 1731 he created a Saint Peter who was nearly 1 1/2 metres long in baked china and, after a model with a pedestal which was given to him he made a holy Nepomuc 56 cm long. In 1732 he modelled not less than three large religious representations:—"the holy Wenceslaum, on a pedestal, ornamented with accoutrements of war and other figures", a large image of the Virgin with the Infant Jesus in her lap, with other decorations on it, and the so-called holy Anthony of Padua on a pedestal with various ornamentations[62]. Who made the large vases red lacquered and phantastic (Fig. 3) remains doubtful to the present. They can hardly have been made by Kirchner[63].

Of Chr. Luecke's Meissen activity I have till now found no trace. On 25th September 1728 it is said of him:—"The master of models Luecke goes slowly about his business. What he has made is trivial. He understands little of drawing and nothing of architecture". Hardly half a year after this he was dismissed as unfit for the work. It is therefore hardly possible to suppose, as Lessing does, that the statuette of August the Strong[64] is the work of Luecke. To-day I should sooner believe that it was made by Kirchner. The latter had modelled a small model for the King's statue in August 1732, in September he made it of a size of three yards. Of this model no signs have up to the present been found. It is, however, probable that the little model was also executed in china or in Boettger's paste.

It can be in no way proved that, as is often thought, the lid of a hunting vase is the work of Ludwig Luecke. The hunters and dogs seem clumsy and heavy in comparison with those by Kaendler shown in the same illustration. The cause of this may be that Kaendler only commenced them letting Ehder execute them. Such lids showing various hunting scenes belong to vases which were supposed to have been made for the castle of Hubertusburg. Later on they were used not as lids, but after removal of the grove constituted independent groups[65].

Fig. 3. CAN-SHAPED VASE.
71 cm.

Kaendler's first work in Meissen was the modelling of animals. In the first month (June 1731) three models were ready, among them was a large eagle. The year after he made a large ape of a particular species, a large heron, and in 1734 a cacadoo[66] (Table 4, 1780). He attempted to make a still larger St. Paul as "pendant" to Kirchner's St. Peter, but the attempt was

Fig. 4. PADUA ROOSTER, B *144*.
76 cm.

Fig. 5. VIRGIN, *136*.
67 cm.

not successful. Kaendler himself speaks of his works at the end of the year 1732 in the following terms[67]:—

The list of what I have fabricated from June 22nd 1731 to this day at His Majesty's Royal china factory runs as follows:—

1. A large eagle (on a pedestal) whose outspread wings measure 2 yards less 3 inches.
2. A fish-eagle or fish-eater 1 yard high which His Majesty have already received.
3. A sea-mew on a pedestal ornamented with all sorts of sea-shells, of which also divers are ready.
4. Another fish-eagle in the act of tearing a carp to pieces.
5. St. Peter (with two keys) 3½ yards high, dressed in Roman style.
6. A large owl on a pedestal which His Majesty has received as well.
7. A hawk on a pedestal which is partly ready.
8. A water-fowl sitting on a pedestal ornamented with rushes and other things. At present I am at work on a statue of His Majesty on horse-back which has been graciously ordered by His Majesty and on a ure-ox destroying a wild pig.

Whereas most of the articles here mentioned are to be found in the Dresden collection of china[68], no trace has up to the present been discovered of the figure on horse-back.

During the first years he made the rooster (Fig. 4, B *144*) the model of which was renewed in 1750. Then his statue of the Virgin with an angel (perhaps the group on Fig. 5, *136*) and a "clerical history" of the Mother of God with Jesus in her arms, the last-mentioned group was copiously decorated with ornaments and figures. He had also begun the construction of an organ to be modelled after the instruction of the Dresden organ-builder Haehnel. It was to consist of 964 pipes and 51 bells made of china[69].

Kaendler had in his time modelled many forms which were like the china models (although this copying of chinese models was peculiar to Hoeroldt). Of these two Indian busts of a man and a woman[70] each 85 cm. high, an epergne in the shape of a sea-shell with Japanese figures[71], a tea-pot in the form of a rooster (Table I, A *44*) and the "Platmenage" made in 1737 for the minister Bruehl of which the mustard pot and the oil or vinegar jug (Table I, *607* and *608*) as well as other articles serving similar purposes (Table II, *150* and *476*) formed a part.

THE PAINTING.

When Hoeroldt came to Meissen in 1720 there was, as above mentioned, not a single painter employed at the factory. But the gilding was done by the worker in gold Funcke till the year 1726; after that Hoeroldt overtook that work as well. The china articles ornamented with his painting soon gained great popularity, so that in order to meet the demand, he was obliged to employ more and more assistants. In the first year of his work in Meissen he already took on two boys Heintze and Horn. The first was so good at the work that Hoeroldt mentioned him in 1731 as one of his best journeymen. In 1725 Hoeroldt was working with 10 journeymen and 5 boys, in 1731 with 25 journeymen and 11 boys and 2 colour-grinders. At first he employed painters who had already been working in the keramic line, but this plan did not work well. Out of conceit they would not allow their faults to be corrected and did the work entrusted to them slowly and not sufficiently well. He than went to work another way and employed people without considering their former trade at all, they might have been weavers, glovers or carpenters. The only thing he put

Fig. 6. PLATE.
New cut. Corn-ear pattern.
25 cm.

Fig. 7. PLATE.
New cut. Flying fox.
25 cm.

stress on was their ability for drawing which he made sure of by examining them before hand. So his own brother-in-law Keil, whom he employed to his own satisfaction not only as an artist, but also to take his place in superintending the other painters, had formerly been a hunter.

Most of them had to begin work with Hoeroldt as painters' apprentices and those who showed themselves fit for the work were, after six years' apprenticeship, "given their freedom as fellow-craftsmen with presentation of the sword or absolved from apprenticeship in the usual manner".

The painters were entirely under the management of Hoeroldt. He could employ and dismiss them as he liked, paid them weekly wage according to his estimation, as the factory settled accounts with him only. This was altered when the King himself took over the chief management. Hoeroldt now received a fixed salary of 1000 talers. His duties consisting in overseeing the painters, preparing gold and colours and, as far as his time permitted, the painting of the particularly dainty china articles. Most of the painters had to work by the piece and received payment according to a price-list fixed up by Hoeroldt. Only a few were made exceptions of and were paid weekly wages for practical reasons. From the enumeration of the duties of the latter it is evident that the division of labour among the painters in Meissen was greater than is generally supposed. It was thought to make a wholesale disposal of painted china possible. The pieces which were more richly-painted were usually decorated not by one, but by several artists. So for instance one could have painted in blue under glaze, another chinese figures a third flowers and a fourth gold cartouches.

Fig. 8. TEA-CUP.
Partridge pattern.

It can, however, be supposed that the patterns were principally designed by Hoeroldt and that the invention of the drawing and the selection of colours, as far as either were not directly copied, must be ascribed to him. In many cases this is directly confirmed. So for instance Hoeroldt, when in 1731 he was

Fig. 9. PLATE.
New cut. Butterfly pattern.
25 cm.

no longer paid by the piece, asked for payment for single pieces of china described, which he had himself, by order of Count Hoym, prepared as models for the painters[72].

The beautiful stately decorations in gold dating from Boettger's time were certainly kept up by Hoeroldt as well, they were only made more perfect in an artistic sense. At first in many cases whole articles were gilded and only afterwards single parts were

Fig. 10. PLATE.
Newbrandenstein. Butterfly pattern.
25 cm.

Pages 16 and 26.

Fig. 11. SALAD-BOWL.
Yellow lion.
21 cm.

Pages 16 and 26.

Fig. 12. PLATE.
Sulkowski. Yellow lion.
23,5 cm.

accentuated by gilding, also gold edging was used.

However Hoeroldt had not, been called to Meissen for painting in gold, but as is explicitly mentioned, because of his knowledge in dealing with coloured paint especially red and blue. After many zealously contrived attempts he was, in a surprisingly short time, able to paint in a great variety of colours. For colours under glaze cobalt blue and brown[73] were successfully made use of. He however made use of a vigorous-blue, sea-green, iron-red, lemon-yellow and purple as vitrifiable colours, i. e. colours in which oxides of metals were combined with a vitreous flux which became fluid in the baking. These bright, transparent colours combined with the white glazing in producing a very decorative effect.

As East-asia was an authority for these colours and their combination, so at the beginning its models served for drawing from. In many cases the Meissen artists so well understood the art of copying, that at first sight the origin of some things may be doubted. Certain patterns seem to have been particularly popular and were continually copied in Meissen. Such are the patterns showing ears of corn or stiles (Fig. 6 and 7), patterns of branches (Table 3, 32) that with two partridges (Fig. 8), with the butterflies (Fig. 9), with the red dragon (Table 3), with the yellow or green lion (Fig. 11 and 12), with the black-thorn (Fig. 10), with mythical animals (Fig. 13 and 14), rock and bird (Fig. 15), buckled ring (Table 1), further the little table pattern (Table 3) and patterns with every possible kind of flowers, among which chrysanthemums and peonies (Table 2, □ 2) played the principal part.

Some of these designs pleased King August III, on a visit to the factory, so well that he ordered them in future to be made only for him. Probably the yellow lion and the red-dragon patterns were of those chosen, as utensils with these patterns were then made for the court-confectionery in Dresden, Warsaw and Pillnitz.

Painting in blue under glaze was at this time not only, as will later be particularly spoken of, used as a decoration in itself, but was now and again used like Aritachina in connection with enamel painting. This had a very effective appearance.

The China with a coloured ground showed a different kind of painting which was also copied from Chino-Japanese models. Here the outside, all but small patches, was painted all over in any one enamel colour (with the exception of brown). The patches left white were ornamented with many-coloured painting. A yellow ground is written about already in 1725. The years 1726 and 1727 must have been particularly rich in successes in this branch. In 1731 the following ground colours are spoken of[74]:— yellow, dark-blue, sky-blue, peach-blossom-colour, steel-green, sea-green, grey (light and dark), purple and red. In the year 1733 a "pretty looking

Page 16.

Fig. 13. PLATE.
New cut. Flying dog.
25 cm.

Page 16.

Fig. 14. PLATE.
New cut. Dragon and heron.
25 cm.

yellow-glazing" is mentioned as having been invented by Hoeroldt[75]. In the next year on coloured glazing (such as purple, yellow and others) even on gold variegated flowers and figures were successfully painted. The like of these had never been seen before and were not to be found in any Japanese china[76]. On Table 3, *80* a tureen with cover is shown. It is, together with a shell-like stand, decorated with painting on a yellow ground and belonged to the so-called hunters' service (1725) of August the Strong.

Page 16.

Fig. 15. PLATE.
New cut. Rock and bird.
25 cm.

The copying of oriental decorations in Meissen did not last long. The form and painting became more original and adapted themselves more than before to European taste. Here France in connection with Holland took the lead. In some cases french influence had shown itself in Boettger's time, for instance in gold and silver borders and cartouches (pouches) but things in China-Japanese style were preferred to any others. The business connection of the Meissen factory with the Paris merchant Lemaire probably played a large part in this change of taste. As Lemaire's customers did not, any longer, care for productions in Chinese taste, articles were made in Meissen after models and drawings of Paris artists. One of these was Meissonier[77] who was a goldsmith at first and an architect and designer in the King's collection of curiosities afterwards.

Now the china articles were richly bordered above and below and cartouches were fastened on their principal plain. Single parts were ornamented with a net-like pattern in whose meshes dots and small flowers were placed. All this was mostly executed in gold, while the ground was sometimes covered with an irridescent brownish-red. This ornamentation beautifully designed and stylishly executed in the taste of the french ornamentators, consists of wreaths arranged in spiral-form, of ribbon-work or of flourishes which are occasionally made to imitate a fine lace web. Sometimes coats of arms[78] were painted in the cartouches, although beautifully executed scenes were placed in them for preference. These took the form of lovescenes out of society life and pastorals in the Watteau- and Boucher-style (Table 3, small vase) or landscapes of the netherlands. Happenings out of the lives of city and country folks and hunting and war episodes after Rugendas, Wouwermann and other especially netherlandic artists (Table 5, E *163*) were also represented. During this period of wavering between asiatic and european taste we find both styles mixed, as for instance in Fig. 16 where Japanese flowers are strewn over china painted in Barock-style, or chinamen are painted in the gold-cartouches.

The factory had much trouble with the "bungling", the designation for Meissen china painted outside and much against the will of the Royal Manufactory. Before Hoeroldt had come to Meissen this had happened many times. Then it was not thought necessary to protest against this. As the painting department in Meissen improved this was much felt, as because of it the factory suffered not only pecuniarily but with regard to its good name. Among the many people accused of "bungling" were two painters before employed at the factory: of whom Dietze had been discharged by Hoeroldt for quarrelsomeness, while Schindler had run away of his own accord. Both had learned to prepare and use china colours and made use of their knowledge (the first-mentioned in Meissen itself) to their own profit and to the injury of the factory[79]. To obtain unpainted china was probably not a difficult task to one acquainted with the ins and outs of the works. Although, probably at the end of the years between 1720—30, an order was given for unpainted china not to be sold, damaged china was divided among the workman who nevertheless disposed of it as they pleased. Further the commission asked in 1731 whether the King wished to let the old order of things stand with regard to these damaged goods or if, "to increase the income,

Page 17.

Fig. 16. VASE
with chinese painting and gold cartouches, Q *165*.
44 cm.

they were to be sold"[80]. It seems that the King decided to have certain white pieces of china sold, because among those sold in Dresden and Leipsic a few of same are mentioned[81].

Further a certain Prussian Joh. Fr. Metzsch, then living in Dresden is mentioned as having bought a complete unpainted tea-set of the factory on which he made an attempt to exercise his art of painting in gold and colours much belauded by himself. He had therefore asked always to get white china for painting. As it was feared that he would soon begin painting wholesale and therewith harm the factory his request met with a refusal[82].

J. A. Bottengruber[83] who lived in Breslaw about 1720 and for a short time in Vienna afterwards, painted on Vienna, Chinese and Meissen china patterns in a peculiar vigorous Barock-style also scenes from child-life and from mythology very well. For colouring he favoured mostly violet, iron-red and gold. It is mentioned of the Breslaw artist Preussler that he is supposed to have painted "foliage and ribbon-work in black painting relieved by gold"[84] on Meissen china. A distinguished amateur C. Ferd. von Wolfsburg, also of Breslaw who, as supposed by Pazaurek (see note 83) was a pupil of Bottengruber, was in Berlin in 1736. Here he has according to a report of the saxon ambassador[85] presented the crown-princess with a whole "set of white Meissen china", painted by him "in enamel". This set was greatly admired. The Dresden museum for art and industry possesses a Meissen plate (certainly the work of this artist) which is ornamented with a coat of arms painted in colours and divided in four and a gold border of arabesques. On the back of this plate the following may be read:—"peint par Charles Ferdinand de Wolfsbourg à Breslau l'an 1748".

III. PERIOD:
UNDER THE CHIEF INFLUENCE OF KAENDLER
(1735–56).

GENERAL WORKING.

Through Hoeroldts great and varied skilfullness the factory had in a few years admirably developed. He was unequalled in imitating east asiatic china and "in bordering in gold", but his knowledge of the chemico-technical part of the work should not be depreciated either. He was not, however, able to keep his responsible position overlong. For as tastes altered, different artistic requirements were set and more originality exacted, his ability did not prove itself equal to this task. He was put into the back-ground by Kaendler who artistically was far above him. This made a great change in the character of the ornamentation of the articles made in Meissen. The oriental manner of decorating flat surfaces was more and more left in the back-ground and plastic ornamentations came into vogue.

Although the credit of the factory being brought to a flourishing state is first of all due to the capabilities of Kaendler as an artist, still, it should not be forgotten that the skilful way in which it was managed had much to do with it.

At the coming to the throne of August III 1733, the affairs of the factory were supervised by the Cabinet minister Count Heinrich von Bruehl who zealously fulfilled his duties and had all particulars reported to him by the commissaries (see note 19). His influence in the affairs of the factory still grew when he was appointed Principal Manager and von Hennicke[86] his representative.

Notwithstanding many complaints, slanders and calumnies of the officials, Bruehl knew how to keep things in order and, however not free from nepotism, he managed to improve the affairs of the factory in an artistic as well as a pecuniar sense. Although he was obliged to be strict, he knew how to soften his severity by increasing salaries and granting titles, thus setting many a dissatisfied official to work with renewed energy. It is also certain that his much belauded taste proved of advantage to the factory. The exceedingly large number of china articles which he ordered for his own use were not only of advantage to the buyers, although they brought no profits to the factory, but also had a great influence on the Meissen artists[87].

Schubert, Hoppe and Stoeltzel, and in 1731 Hoeroldt as well, were initiated into the secrets of the arcanum. After the death of the two first mentioned Dr. Petsch was admitted into it. When in 1737 Stoeltzel died as well, the commission sought to set the chemist Schertel in his place. Schertel was a favourite of Bruehl's. Hoeroldt objected to this for various reasons and recommended Dr. Schatter instead. At last a decision was come to to employ both as arcanists[88]. As such they were made aware of all the trade secrets and their duties consisted in mixing the pastes and the glazing, as well as in overseeing the baking. Besides they had to seek to bring innovations and improvements into the works. They were well-paid, enjoyed special priviledges and thought themselves indispensable, because of their knowledge. Often, however, they abused their priviledged position. Mostly they were envious and lived in discord with each other. Occasionally their hatred took such a form as to make the factory suffer heavily under it. So Stoeltzel once spoiled a paste got ready by others for fabrication through anger at its being better than the one made under his direction. The same happened in 1740 with the glaze. Hoeroldt put the blame this time on Schertel[89]. Because much other unpleasantness was the result of this envy and hatred, Bruehl gave the secondary direction of the factory over to the Counsellor of mines von Heynitz in 1740. He was ordered to deliver weekly reports. The arcanists and the master of models had to apply to him when they had any doubts about the work or thought themselves imposed upon by each other[90].

This innovation greatly vexed the arcanists and made them show a kind of passive resistance. Heynitz too seems to have hardly understood how to manage such disagreeable people. According to the report of the Counsellor of chambers von Nimpsch[91], he was possessed of a hasty temper, dismissed and employed workmen at his pleasure and, in many cases, granted undeserved priviledges. Above all Hoeroldt, the arcanist who had been of most use to the factory, rebelled against the new management. Little by little the position of power which he held formerly as sole manager of the factory was withdrawn from him. The disputes at one time became so violent that Bruehl thought it necessary to come to Meissen himself[92]. He patched up an outward peace, but the relations of the man remained unpleasant as before, because they had no wish to work successfully together and to mutually support each other. So at times complaints were heard of the yellowishness of the china, which showed black dots and was generally faulty and cracked. This was all thought to be mainly the fault of the arcanists: but it was also due to the fact, that the great increase in the number of orders made it impossible to attend to the work properly, especially to the baking[93].

The occasionally undertaken expansions of single parts of the works did not give sufficient room for the possibility of supplying goods enough to satisfy the growing demand for Meissen china. In 1744 they built a new plant for baking with a kiln for biscuits baking and two kilns for final baking[94], in 1752 a new stamping mill[95] were erected. An old granary near the castle was put at the disposal of the factory and the storing-place in Dresden and Meissen had been several times enlarged; but all these extensions did not make the complaints of cramped space and insufficient kilns cease.

The factory was at that time required to turn out an exceedingly large quantity of goods. King August II had ordered at the factory (1725—33) 50846 talers' worth of china[96]. The orders of his successor August III were still greater and amounted to 516669 talers in the years 1733—48. To this should be added the extensive orders of Bruehl and other high and mighty persons of the Saxon court, besides the ever-increasing sale to dealers.

It was ordered January 22nd 1740 that white china should only be sold when simply painted unless it were in many places slightly cracked and could not stand the enamelling fire[97]. This order was given because much ill-use had been made of this middling rate unpainted china. It was first to September 1st 1750 sold in Meissen, afterwards it was disposed of in Dresden[98]. The damaged china was as before divided among workmen unpainted; as these in many cases dealt in it, much trouble arose. Kaendler therefore made a proposition of destroying it altogether; this proposition was not accepted[99].

The first-class china was sold in the warehouses in Dresden, Leipsic and Warsaw by the managers and their assistants. One of these must be particularly mentioned as having great merits about the factory: Georg Mich. Helbig. He was born in 1715 in Ahrensfeld (Wolkenstein). In 1735 he found employment as assistant at the Dresden depot, in 1744 he was book keeper and in 1749 he received the title of Counsellor of commerce. From this time he did not content himself by caring about the mercantile part of the business, but interested himself in the manufacturing part as well. He made suggestions for many technical and artistic improvements and his influence was so great as to gain him in 1756 admission to the secrets of the arcanum[100]. His main significance for Meissen falls, however, in the next period.

According to the extension of the works the number of workmen had to be greatly increased. From 1742 to 1754 there was an increase of 178 employes[101]. It was probably not always easy to keep them in subordination, as they were mostly described as frivolous bohemians. Occasionally it was suggested that they should be kept in stricter subordination. The young workmen were to be especially supervised. Marriage was not to be permitted till after they had completed their twenty-fifth year and other restrictions were to be put on them[102].

In 1752 most of the workmen were led to a demonstration against the towns people in the question whether in Meissen only home-brewed beer, or imported sorts as well could be drunk and 400 of them made a demonstration in the streets[103]. In the same year it was discovered that more than 13 workmen had purloined and sold painted and unpainted china[104].

Hardly a year passed without the factory being obliged to dismiss one or another of the workmen, although this was very unwillingly done because it was feared that on dismissal they would betray the trade-

Table 7

Page 36.

Works by Kaendler.

1. Luke the evangelist, *5*.   2. Mark the evangelist, *13*.   3. The Virgin with the Infant Jesus, *158*.
47 cm.   47 cm.   17,5 cm.

4. St. Nepomuc, *208*.   5. Praying nun, *300*.
18,5 cm.   17,5 cm.

Table 8

Pages 34, 35, 36.

Works by Kaendler.

1. Turk, *349.*   2. St. Nepomuc, *337.*   3. Gardner, *338.*   4. Bag-pipe player, *297.*

26 cm.   39 cm.   27 cm.   26 cm.

5. Froehlich and Schmiedel, *290*.*   6. Cuirassier, *187.*

26 cm.   27 cm.

secrets. Attempted bribery, discovered in time, is often recorded, while many times single workmen fled. At any rate they were tempted to use the knowledge gained in Meissen to their own profit elsewhere. All attempts made in this direction were carefully persecuted in Meissen.

So it was soon recognised that the above mentioned Potsdam factory made not porcelain but white, bluish and quite blue glass decorated with gold[105]. Further it became known that the artist Adam Friedrich von Loewenfinck had allowed himself to be enticed away to the Bayreuth factory. In 1746 he helped to found the Hoechster factory, 1750—54 he is to be found as "artifex" in Strassburg and Hagenau[106].

It was reported from Mannheim that in 1741 a "Saxon Elias Vater" pretended to make china[107] and that a certain Bengraf really made some[108].

In Berlin on December 8th 1742 Professor Dr. Pott advertised in the "Berliner Nachrichten" that he was able to make china and was ready to teach the art to others for a pecuniary remuneration. One of the Meissen arcanists was therefore sent to him, but the china was found imperfect[109]. Lastly in 1737 the Commissioner of mines and painter to the Court Magnus von Quitter showed some blue painted china in Cassel. In Meissen it was thought that the two Mehlhorns — already spoken of above — had their hand in this game.

It was however supposed that there was no need to fear any of these. The only real competitor was considered to be the Vienna factory which was overtaken by the Empress Maria Theresa. From the very beginning of its existence many of the men who had fled from Meissen were here employed. Besides the above-mentioned the painters, Joh. Gottfr. Klinger, Hitzig, Fleischer and Richter, also Ludwig Luecke, at that time "Obermodellmeister" seem to have been before employed in Meissen[110].

The second Silesian war caused many obstacles to the progress of the Meissen works. It was decided to stop all work at the factory from December 7th 1745 to January 7th 1746 because of the disturbances of war. The arcanists, bakers and moulders were sent to Dresden for safety, while the painters remained without employment in Meissen. After the battle near Kesselsdorf (15th December 1745) the Prussians had put up a lazaretto in the Albrechtsburg which remained there till May 1746. Besides the enemy despoiled the factory of 8218 talers worth of fuel and lastly Frederick the Great took away 42666 talers worth of china with him as spoils of war[111], while the Prime minister Count von Podewils, the generals Lehwaldt, Stille, Kyaw, Gessler, Rochow and the colonel Aulaix appropriated a breakfast set each.

Notwithstanding all this the factory was able to close accounts profitably in 1745 and 1746. It recovered very quickly and kept up its manufacture successfully until the beginning of the seven years' war, which was fated to affect its history in a more perceptible manner.

THE MODELLING.

I have already mentioned the great fondness of August the Strong for east asiatic china. It not only brought rich treasures to Dresden, but led to the invention of Saxon china. A taste for the effectful (which reigned at the court of the sovereign) first of all roused the thought of how to exhibit such a precious possession in the most effective manner. According to Sponsel[112] a trial was made to arrange the china in the sideboard saloon in the Dutch palace (afterwards Japanese palace) in Dresden. This proved so effective, that the King conceived the idea of decorating the whole palace in like manner with beautiful china; even the park was to be decorated as well. We have good, reliable information on this subject in Keyssler's travels of 1730 and Sponsel's[113] researches. The japanese and chinese porcelains were to fill the lower story, while the productions of the home factory were to be placed in the chambers of the upper story. While the former were represented in great numbers and required only a few purchases to complete the collection, of the latter it can only be said, that almost everything required for actualising the plan was wanting. Whole rooms were to be furnished with china painted each in one of the following colours; seladon, yellow, dark-blue, pale-blue, purple, green and peach-blossom coloured ground. Other rooms were to be decorated with vases of extraordinary dimensions and with numerous life-sized animals. Besides: life-sized apostles, a peal of bells, an altar, a pulpit, an organ and a throne, the principal parts of which were to be made of china were ordered for this palace.

The King seems to have been very eager to bring his plan into execution, he drove the factory to the rapid delivery of his orders. The fabrication of the plates, utensils and small vases did not give much trouble, as the ground colours were, one after the other, manufactured by Hoeroldt, so that it was vigorously proceeded with. This was different with the large pieces. It is said in praise of Kirchner that he already

Page 25.

Fig. 17. VASE with swan-handles, R *145*.
54 cm.

made large animals. To be sure Count Sulkowski who for some time had to negotiate these affairs, spoke very unfavourably of them and complained of their unnatural position and colours as well as of the quality of the material[114].

When August the Strong saw that the fullfilment of his plans progressed but slowly, he realized that he could not do much towards the furthering of them with Kirchner alone. He therefore began to look for a more suitable man. This led to Kaendler's being employed in Meissen.

Johann Joachim Kaendler[115] born 1706 in Fischbach near Arnsdorf was the son of the local clergyman. He received a good education which included the development of a taste for mythology and for the works of arts of the ancients. These tastes were inherent in him and he early showed signs of on artistic talent. As a result he was sent in 1723 to the court sculptor Benjamin Thomae[116] to Dresden to learn the art of sculpturing. Thomae was an able, although not a highly-gifted, artist; with him Kaendler had the opportunity of learning the technique of sculpture and of getting thoroughly to know the trend of the taste of the time. It is particularly mentioned that he did not neglect the art of drawing and diligently studied antique art[117]. Kaendler was asked to take part in the renovation of the Green Vaults and proved his ability as a sculptor several times. The King who here seems to have taken stock of his knowledge sent him to the Meissen factory (1731) to help in the making of the china articles for the Japanese palace.

Here he at first collaborated with Kirchner, after the taking leave of the latter, he took his duties over as well. Kirchner had been "bound Modellmeister" that is he had not only to create new models himself but to direct the moulders and their apprentices in their work. Kirchner's function and title were in 1733 transferred to Kaendler. He was not then really the chief the white corporation, that is of the plastic branch. In 1738 already Kaendler[118] thought it a mismanagement that not he but Hoeroldt had the sculptors, moulders and turners under him; because the latter understood nothing of their work, often gave false directions, did not know how to divide the labour, did not recognise that most of the turning wheels were spoiled etc. Probably the King saw the mistake and corrected it by given over the supervision of the "modellers, moulders, turners and what belongs to this" to Kaendler in 1740. In 1751 this was expressly confirmed[119]. But Hoeroldt remained as before the overseer over him and his people a fact which led to many discordances[120]. Although Kaendler might have been right, he did not at first act properly himself. The useless denunciation he composed with Reinhardt has already been discussed above. Besides he, together with his father-in-law Eggebrecht, intrigued against Hoeroldt[121]. Kaendler only then renounced Eggebrecht when he began to see through his deceit. Then he seems to have been content to bring his opinion of the improvements in the works to the management in different reports. To be sure this could hardly ever be managed without in some way accusing Hoeroldt. The fact that he made so free with the minister Bruehl proved the respect which he had gained by his artistic capabilities.

Page 25.

Fig. 18. VASES in Cober-style and perforated.
1968   *142*
36 cm.   35 cm.

Fig. 19. TUREEN FROM SWAN SERVICE, 1*.
Page 29.
50 cm.

For in that respect he was then the soul of the factory and perceptibly influenced the whole period. His outer successes kept pace with the increased respect as he gained it. In 1733 he was master of models, probably in 1740 leader of the plastic branch, in 1749 Commissioner of the Court. His salary at the beginning amounting to 400 talers, was raised in 1740 to 696 and in 1731 to 1196 talers. Through his work after vacationhours he earned yet more, because in 1753 he had 1323 and in 1754, 1871 talers paid out to him[122], sums which at that time were considered very high.

After Kirchner's leave Kaendler was the only sculptor in Meissen; for only a number of partly very able moulders and finishers worked with him. In December 1733 Kaendler's brother Christian Heinrich (born 1709) took his place among them. He is called a moulder and embosser but can hardly be considered a sculptor, although with time he brought it so far as to take his brother's place during the absence of the latter[123].

On April 18th 1735 Eberlein was appointed to assist Kaendler. From him he received assistance worth mentioning in an artistic sense. Besides at the end of 1739 Ehder and on April 1st 1743 Reinecke, both sculptors, were employed in Meissen[124].

Although these new employes severally delivered original models to the factory — which will be spoken of below — still it was their principal duty to perfect to a certain extent the work roughly began by Kaendler and to aid him otherwise in matters of art. With these few assistants Kaendler succeeded not only in creating a great number of models for the factory but in altering many of the main principles of the art of formation of china.

Up to this time the greatest stress had been laid upon the colouring. In going back to the east asiatic models simple forms were preferred, particularly such of them as abounded in large, plain white spaces, because they were particularly anxious to exhibit their painting in all its splendour. Now this ornamentation of plain surfaces gave place to the Barock-style more popular at home. This required greater attention to he paid to the plastique.

Kaendler was, as before mentioned principally brought over for the sake of modelling the animals, apostles and other large pieces ordered for the Japanese palace. This was a task into which he entered with great zeal. In 1733 he had already modelled 7 birds and one apostle. In 1734, 439 animals were ready for delivery to the Japanese palace, namely 16 of each kind ordered of the 33 quadrupeds and 27 birds, besides 5 quadrupeds and 23 birds which had not been demanded[125]. Although some few of these animals were made by Kirchner, the greater number and the best of them doubtless owe their existence to Kaendler's hand.

In a comparatively short space of time he managed to get used to the work and to create things which deserve great praise for the freshness of their conception and their truth to life. The principal difficulty here, as in other large pieces, lay less in the artistic than in the technical execution. So in 1732 the large pieces of china were already greatly cracked in the biscuit-kiln and broke entirely in the final baking. Not one part of the large apostles had then been successfully made[126].

To satisfy the wishes of the King as far as possible new attempts were continually being made

Page 29.
Fig. 20.
POT FROM SWAN SERVICE,
475.
20 cm.

Page 29.
Fig. 21. PLATE, Sulkowski.
23 cm.

Page 30.

Fig. 22. PLATE, Oldozier.
25 cm.

Page 30.

Fig. 23. PLATE, Oldbrandenstein.
25,5 cm.

to find a paste most fitted for the making, turning, moulding and baking of the large pieces. As is gathered from a report of the discoveries[127] made in 1735, this was thought to be found. At the same time they boasted of being able to make table tops and figures over 1 3/4 m. high; they owned, however, that the latter came out slightly cracked, although made in two pieces.

This problem was not completely solved at that time; indeed it could not have been solved at all as they wished to make of china what that material did not adapt itself to. The baking at high temperature, the fineness and expensiveness of the paste and its delicate glazing makes it unfit for the manufacture of large articles. The attempts to produce the above-mentioned large articles were connected with loss to the factory. They disturbed the ordinary work of the factory and spoiled a great deal of paste through failures in baking. Even at that sacrifice, the pieces considered as good did not come out of the baking without considerable cracks. It was impossible to make such large articles of the ordinary paste. It had to be made more pliable. This was done by the addition of more clay, but this made the china lose one of its chief charms:—the beautiful, white colour. These arguments are proof enough that the problem set in Barock's sense was technically incapable of being solved.

That Kaendler, after having gained a surprising mastery of the material, went too far in many cases is comprehensible. He persisted in his opinion that everything, almost without exception, could be made of china. He did not wish to be limited in his work by the possibilities afforded by the material; this was an opinion which he expressed in writing to Bruehl[129]:—"that he would shortly make such things as had been thought impossible" and further:—"everything whatever desired can be made of china, if it is too large it can be made in two pieces".

Kaendler reached a great deal by his ceaseless attempts to improve matters at the factory. He had been able to alter the whole artistic part of the Meissen works to his mind. He was the one who created a really European style of china; sometimes however his plans came to grief over the largeness of the things he wished to make of porcelain. An instance in point is the large monument of August III to which I return.

When August the Strong was succeeded by his son in 1733 he also eagerly continued the execution of the plan with regard to the Japanese palace, this enthusiasm lasted

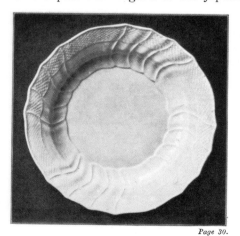

Page 30.

Fig. 24. PLATE, Newozier.
25,5 cm.

but a few years. For soon the orders of the King were considered as secondary to those of his influential ministers and even to the manufacture of such articles as were required for sale. After the large delivery to the Japanese palace described above 1734, I have found such entered only from 1735 to 1737[130].

When Kaendler came to Meissen he found, to quote his own words[131] not "a single properly made handle". In quite an astonishingly short space of time

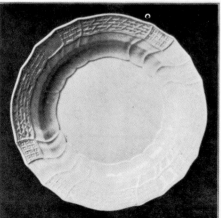

Page 30.

Fig. 25. PLATE, Newbrandenstein.
25,5 cm.

Table 9

Pages 33, 34, 35, 36.

Works by Kaendler.

1. Avvocato, *942.*   2. Janitschar, *420.*   3. Infant Jesus, *430.*   4. Soldier, *559.*   5. Pandur, *407.*

16 cm.   16 cm.   16,6 cm.   15 cm.   22,5 cm.

6. Group of musicians, *250.*   7. Harlequin, *237.*   8. Columbine and Pantalone, *279.*

17 cm.   18,5 cm.   17,5 cm.

9. Group of free-masons, *376.*   10. Lid of a hunting vase, *219.*

22 cm.   20 cm.

Fig. 26. PLATE. Swan pattern.
23,5 cm.

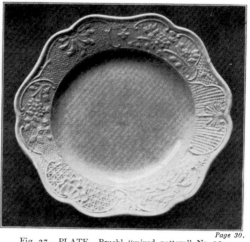

Fig. 27. PLATE. Bruehl "mixed pattern" Nr. 13.
26,5 cm.

he remedied this, as he worked not only with great skill and ease but very dilligently as well. He was untiring in inventing new models, in modelling handles, cover-tops and feet tops of walking sticks, snuff-boxes etc. He once suggests to Bruehl[132] that it should be sought to make as many patterns as possible in tea and coffee-sets, "of which a thousand variations could be had, looking so beautiful and requiring so little exertion to design and to produce". He wished "long ago to show a new knife-handle", which Hoeroldt prevented him from doing, as he preferred having "the old, miserable club-shaped things" made.

He was in his element when he could, to a certain extent, revel in forms, as in the modelling of such vases as an example[133] is shown of in Fig. 17, R *145*. These articles which were made in the middle of the thirties are bulged and pulled in, in their plan they are not round but combined of many larger and small, straight or slightly curved lines. They were "covered" with leaves, flowering branches etc. in a more naturalistic manner than in the former period; to this egged moulding and coats of arms were added, the lids were crowned with plastic bunches of flowers, the handles were made in the shape of women's heads, dolphins, swans or cupids. So great is the weight laid here upon plastic shapes that it was thought possible to dispense with colouring altogether using only gold relief.

As a proof of Kaendler's industriousness and the richness of his imagination, I may mention that he modelled the following breakfast-sets in 1740—41 only: one with "applied flowers", one with plastic blue-painted forget-me-nots, one ornamented with snow-balls, one with "japanese application" and one each article of which was of the shape of a lemon surrounded by leaves and blossoms. The three last-mentioned were intended for Queen Maria Josepha. Besides he had made during the same year cups with "application of vine branches" for the Baron von Wessenburg and complicated application for chocolate-goblets and "godronierte"[134] oval saucers[135] for Mr. Bonnet.

Plastique is the principal thing that Kaendler considered in his work. Occasionally he went so far as to put a slightly relieved ornament over the whole or at least over the border of plates, which article essentially requires to be flat. At times he cut whole forms or single parts out, so that the impression of basket work was made (Fig. 18, *142*) and used this all through (Fig. 18, *1968*) or only on the borders as plastic decorations. On this plastic principle the snow-ball-blossom pattern is used by Kaendler in 1740 (Fig. 117 and 118).

Now and again whole table-services were made in Meissen according to special directions. They came into the market under the name of the orderer and, as far as I have been able to find statements about them, may be here shortly described:—

The seven china services of the Saxon court, with the exception of one described

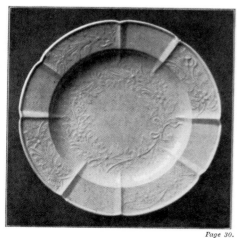

Fig. 28. PLATE. Gotzkowsky.
25,5 cm.

Fig. 29. PLATE. Dulong.
25 cm.

Fig. 30.   PLATE.   Marseille.   *Page 30.*
22 cm.

Fig. 31.   *Page 31.*
HOLY WATER POT, *171.*
26 cm.

under 1, were stored in the Dresden court silver plate treasure chamber, parts of them have been at different times restored and completed. Most of these services are in use to this day.

1. The remains of the so-called hunting service of August the Strong, made about 1725, are still to be found in the Dresden collection of china. It is of simple partly shell-like form and painted in yellow ground with chinese flower-patterns in medaillons (Table 3, *80*), gilt edges.

2. The Saxon-polish service, executed about 1730, is painted with chinese flowers strewn and corn ears, with arabesques in gold and the Saxon-polish arms in a strongly-formed cartouche. The shape of the plate is plain, that of the presenting plate shows ten cuts from which ridges or indentations run to the centre. (Illustrated: The Meissen china, Fig. 173.)

3. The red-dragon service (Table 3), which was delivered in 1736 to the silver-plate treasure chamber and confectionary is painted with two fighting cocks in the middle and with two dragons and two ornaments in iron-red and gold on the edges.

4. The yellow-lion brown bordered service (Fig. 11 and 12), which was made at the same time was delivered to the court confectionary in Warsaw 1738 (it was however not yet complete in 1740). Here the painting takes the form of a lion, more closely resembling a tiger, winding round a bamboo-stem. The service shows a pattern of black-thorn and flowers strewn about in chinese fashion. In 1731 already dinner plates were painted with blue, yellow and red lions.

Although belonging to the next period the following may be here described in this connection.

5. The green Watteau-service was delivered 1765 in 340 pieces to the court kitchen and the court silver-plate chamber[136]. The use of Watteau-grey as ground colour for copper-green was already known in Meissen before 1746. It shows Gotzkowsky-pattern (see page 30). In the centre of the plate is painted a Watteau scene in green with flesh-colours, while on the four border parts which are left plain, many-coloured bunches of flowers are painted. On the saucers, the middle of which was mostly covered, four green Watteau scenes are painted on the sides, while the centre is decorated by a coloured rosegay. The sweet plates show perforated borders with green flowers. (Illustrated: The Meissen china, Fig. 199).

6. The blue and gold service in the style of Louis XVI was made in 1777. The plate edges are covered with small oval rings which are either all perforated at the twelfth or are altogether closed and show a chamois mosaik-pattern outwardly and blue paint inwardly. Between the edge and the cavity a gold circle with a reddish-brown ribbon twisted round it is placed. The centre is painted with coloured flowers, fruits or birds (Fig. 192).

7. Lastly here may be found a small service intended only for 50 persons in Louis XVI style. It had been ordered by Karl Chr. Jos., son of August III and Duke of Courland, at the end of the eighteenth century and given back to the Saxon court in 1853[137]. It shows a golden rod round which a green ribbon is twisted, as well as coloured flowers and gilding. The plates are openworked at the edges in the shape of pipes.

8. In 1725 Hoeroldt by order of the King made a tea-service and chocolate goblets ornamented with the Sardinian

Fig. 32.   CANDLESTICKS.   *Page 32.*
1172^b   *1172**   *1172*
40 cm.   60 cm.   40 cm.

Page 32.
Fig. 33. HOLY
WATER POT, *1016.*
23 cm.

Page 32.
Fig. 34. HOLY WATER
POT, *1017.*
30 cm.

coat of arms. This was probably intended as a present to Victor Amadeus II, King of the Sardinian monarchy. A cup belonging to this service is to be found in the Dresden collection of Klemperers. It is small of simple shape, without handle and is marked ℛ. The saucer shows besides chinese flowers a border of gold arabesques and the Sardinian coat of arms with trophies, supported by two lions in the back-ground. The cup shows many-coloured chinamen and the monogram of Victor Amadeus of Sardinia.

9. The Dresden museum of art and industry (Kunstgewerbe-museum) possesses a turine with a highly arched lid and scroll-shaped handles which was probably made about 1730, it is painted with a chrysanthemum and heron pattern and shows three hop-poles on red ground in an oval plate. This coat of arms points perhaps to the family Hoepfner or Hopfner.

10. A service belonging to about the same time that is painted with mythical animals and plain red edges, bears the coat of arms of Muenchhausen: a Cisterian monk with a red book and a staff on a golden field.

11. In the years 1735—37 the Minister Count (after 1752 Prince of the Empire) Alex. Jos. von Sul-kowsky (February 5th 1738 precipitated in Saxony, died 1762) had a table service made. It was painted in gold and colours slightly relieved, and flowers in chinese style and bore the coats of arms of Sulkowski-Stein. In the boldly formed scrolls and handles, in the luxuriously-shaped figures and the characteristic masks, Kaendler appears in all his greatness as an artist of the Barock-style. Everything is modelled so boldly with such devotion to the work and such an understanding for the qualities of china, that we must pay the artist full tribute. Even when he has, now and again, as in the tureen, had to make use of a plastic shape intended for silver work, he had done the work round it with great skill and taste. Most pieces were supplied with a border of basket work in the style described on page 29[140].

12. The Dresden museum of art and industry possesses a large dish in Sulkowski pattern on which flowers in chinese style and a coat of arms of a married couple, headed by an counts coronet, are painted. The husband's coat of arms shows a blue rafter on golden ground in which a fruit is placed[141]; that of the wife a red rafter and a red tournament collar on white ground. The first is perhaps that of the Count von Ruebener, the second of Westfalen.

13. The wedding present of August III to his daughter Marie Amalie Christine (married to Charles III, Infant of Spain and King of Sicily) consisted of several breakfast sets, drinking-goblets, vases, tureens etc. It was painted with rich gold ornamentation, golden chinese or many coloured japanese figures, landscapes or Watteaux, besides ground painting in red, seladon or yellow and the Sicilian or Saxon-polish and Sicilian coats of arms. On June 29th 1738 it was ready to be sent away[142] from Meissen being packed in red leather cases ornamented with gold outside and lined with glacé silk trimmed with silver lace.

14. In 1738 the russian fieldmarshal general Count von Muennich (born 1683, died 1767) a person of importance in Russia from 1734 to 1741, ordered a table service which shows the Sulkowski pattern and similar painting. His coat of arms applied here consists of a double-eagle in a heart shaped shield and of a square escutcheon which shows the half figure a monk on golden ground and of a swan in a blue field. The escutcheon is surmounted by a counts coronet and chain and cross of the order of St. Andrew. At the side two oval shields resting on trophies may be seen, in them a monogram v. M. under them the motto "Obsequio et candore" are painted[143].

15. In the same year (1738) a table service was made for the ambassador, later Cabinet minister

Page 33.
Fig. 35. STAG, *875.*
25 cm.

Page 33.
Fig. 36. CROW, *953**.
37 cm.

Page 34.

Fig. 37. SIX ORIENTALS.

1294	1287	1286	1301	1293	1299
22,5 cm.	22,5 cm.	22,5 cm.	22,5 cm.	23 cm.	20,5 cm.

Count Wackerbarth-Salmour (died 1761). It was white, painted with variegated flowers and is spoken of as having been made after choice models[144].

16. At about the same time a table service for the Prussian minister Count Heinr. von Podewils (born 1695, died 1760) seems to have been made. It showed a cut out and shell-like border and was later sold as "Podewils-fashion" many times.

17. The manufacture of a table service intended for A. St. von Goetzendorf-Grabowsky, Archbishop of Ermeland (born 1698, died 1770) may be supposed to have been made in 1735—40. It showed, bold simple forms and was painted with flowers which were over well shaded, also with insects and the coat of arms of the possessor surrounded by the blue ribbon and star of the Order of the White Eagle[145].

18. In 1740 they worked at a table service intended for the Kurmainz ambassador Baron von Gross-schlag. All the forms were here perforated (basket-work) over and over, while the chocolate goblets were of shell-like shape as well[146].

19. In 1741 the hunting service for one of the richest princes of the church of his time Clemens August Duke of Bavaria and Elector of Cologne (1723—61). The plates are bent in six small and six large arches. In the centre of the small arches six plastic gilded shells are seen. This service is painted in the same way as that described under 17 only it shows a monogram of the letters C and A with the crown of the Electorate as well as the ribbon and cross of the German Order of Knighthood, instead of the coat of arms in 17. The large tureen shows two shields with crown, sword and key while a Putto scattering flowers, or a boar's head with shell-work crowns its lid. At the foot a tree with a stag and a hunter was placed as an ornament[147]. A goblet, about 42 cm. high, formed part of this service, on its summit a hunting scene "par force", while on its lid a thatched cot with flying game were represented.

Besides in the years 1740—41 following order for table china were mentioned:—

20. Oval and plaited tureens with saucers in three sizes and a "godroniert" slop basin for Mr. Bonnet.

21. An oval covering for a salver for the minister Count Hennicke (Bruehl's successor since 1739)[148].

22. Knife handles to match his service for the Privy counsellor von Rex.

23. For the wife of the Privy counsellor von Loos the large top of a centrepiece was altered and made higher by the addition of neat little feet, the stand belonging to it was plaited all round to make it match the rest of the service.

Page 34.
Fig. 38. GIPSY SORCERESS, 1036.
38 cm.

Page 34.
Fig. 39. MORLACKEN GROUP, 418.
28 cm.

Table 10

Works by Kaendler.

Pages 33, 34, 35, 37, 57.

1 and 2. Children's bust, 2744.   3. Man with lyre, 960.   4. Ravishment of Proserpina, 1448.

25 cm.   20,5 cm.   24 cm.

5. Fox at the pianoforte, 474.   6. Camel in parade, 1434.   7. Count Bruehl's pug-dog, 510.   8. Drummer-pigeon, 827.

16,5 cm.   22 cm.   26 cm.   22 cm.

Fig. 40. SIX CRIERS.

Pages 34 and 44.

| *877* | *1030* | *1025* | *1044* | *2785* | *965* |
| 19 cm. | 20 cm. | 19 cm. | 19 cm. | 19 cm. | 19,5 cm. |

24. The grandest and most stately table service ever manufactured in Meissen was the "Swan service" made for the minister Count Bruehl. This was a piece of work where Kaendler could give full vent to his taste for bold plastique. Lachapelle, Bruehl's confectioner, gave him some workman-like advice, but he was not in any way limited or his imagination fettered; only this service was to excel in brilliancy any before made. So each piece, even when it would have been more convenient to have it flat shows reliefs. Its name of "Swan service" was due to the fact that not only saucières, chocolate-jugs, handles and the tops of lids were formed like a swan but most pieces were ornamented with either two swimming swans, a flying and a standing heron or a relief consisting of reed-grass and wave-like lines. The swans and cupids, the nereids, tritons and dolphins, the masks and scrolls which were here copiously used are treated in so beautiful, light and yet bold a manner as to show perfect ability to copy the forms of nature. For this reason it seems to me that the swan service is the most considerable collection of china articles ever produced by the factory[149]. Fig. 19, 1* shows one of the large tureens the modelling of which Kaendler began in July 1738 while the vinegar and oil vessels (Fig. 20) were begun in December of the same year[150]. The pieces here represented show forms which were renewed by Helmig at the end of the 19th century.

Eberlein has also worked independently at this service, among other things made by him a tureen and a Nereid carrying a fruit dish may be here mentioned.

The models made for such orders were otherwise made use of as well. Some of them became so popular that they kept being made for years as well-selling patterns. The following table service, modelled after Kaendler, are still being made in Meissen:—

1. Sulkowski pattern (Fig. 21, 62). The flat rim edged with a cord is cut into twelve even double-arches. Where one arch meets the other pearl-like cords or rods run radially downwards, thus dividing the plate into twelve parts. These parts are decorated by a sort of coarse basket-work and each four parts meet in a right angle.

Fig. 41. SIX MINERS.

Page 34.

| *1328* | *1309* | *1325* | *1336* | *1340* | *1342* |
| 20 cm. | 20 cm. | 20 cm. | 21 cm. | 21 cm. | 20 cm. |

Fig. 42.   CARPENTER, SADDLER, COOPER.
1369   *1385*   *1379*
22 cm.   23 cm.   22 cm.

Page 34.

Fig. 43.   HUNGARIANS (woman and man).
1281   *1285*
22 cm.   22 cm.

Page 34.

2. Oldozier pattern (Fig. 22, *54*). The basket work covering the edge, as well as the twelve ray like dividing rods and the outer finishing are more daintily treated. The basket-work is concentric and radially arranged. The edge is cut into twelve even arches.

3. Oldbrandenstein pattern[151] (Fig. 23, *58*), originated in 1741. The border is edged with a thick roll and is divided into four parts ornamented with large-meshed basket work; on both sides of each of these four wide divisions a narrow field, divided into twelve small squares each of which is ornamented with a rosette, is placed. Between two such fields four times a narrow undecorated field is inserted. The edge is cut into large and small arches which bend in and outwards.

4. Newozier pattern (Fig. 24, *55*). The plastic ornamentations do not occupy the whole of the outer border, but only three quarters of it. The dividing rods are S shaped and go over the edge towards the centre of the plate where they are bound by a line which is shaped like the outside edge.

5. Newbrandenstein pattern (Fig. 25, *56*). Number 3 is here altered as 2 in 4.

6. Swan pattern (Fig. 26, *93*). The edge is cut into 30 arches and is ornamented with sloping wave-like lines or with basket work also arranged in a sloping manner; the border and the flat part of the plate are slightly spiral and shell-like in form. The latter shows the swans and herons in relief above mentioned.

7. Bruehl's mixed pattern (Fig. 27, *13*), originated 1742. Rococo flourishes, bunches of flowers and shell-like decorations rest upon different kinds of basket-work. The cutting of the edge shows six times two small curves outwards; these are connected with deep flutings.

8. Gotzkowsky pattern[152] (Fig. 28, *17*), originated 1741. The edge is cut into four larger and four smaller arches, from the places where they join ridges are drawn radially across the plate. The larger of the divisions formed by these ridges are decorated with flowering branches in relief. A wreath of flowers tied with a bow of ribbon occupies the centre of the plate.

9. Dulong pattern[153] (Fig. 29, *60*), originated in 1743. The edge is cut into four large arches between each of which three small ones are placed. Notwithstanding this division Rococo flourishes decorated with flowers are drawn over the border and the outer part into the centre. This plate was afterwards altered into Newdulong through the rigdes being drawn in S shape.

10. Marseille pattern (Fig. 30, *61*). The plate shows here between each of six

Fig. 44.   DOVE COT, *1393*.
44 cm.

Page 34.

Fig. 45.   TRUMPETER AND DRUMMER.
2165   *1963*
19 cm.   19 cm.

Page 34.

Fig. 46. DRINKING PIPER,
160.
14,5 cm.

flutings a large and two small arches, while on its border are three wide Rococo scrolls so as to reach the centre of the plate.

Besides following less popular designs in services may be mentioned:—

11. "Pattern 95" has an altogether plain border which shows very styleful flowers and leaves in relief.

12. "Spanish design". The plate shows twelve arches and the border three ornamented shields.

"13. Prussian musical designs" shows no rounded of corners. On the border drawn into the centre are six Rococo cartouches filled with musical and other emblems and with bunches of flowers[154].

14. The ribbed pattern (plain, double and fancy ribbed, Fig. 109) which was probably only used with blue painting is mentioned in the records of the court silver-plate chamber already about 1736.

Page 35.
Fig. 47. CHEVALIER BESTRIDING A GOAT, 107.
44 cm.

The "new cut" as may be seen in both plates on Table 3 was first used by Kaendler in 1745.

The variety of shapes and forms grew year by year in a really astonishing manner. All articles imaginable were made of china. In a stock list of the china to be found in the storehouse in 1739 following articles are mentioned:—key rings, swinging-kettles, chamber-pots, clock-cases, temples of Venus, temples of idols, writing-stands, bells, holy water pots (Fig. 31, 171), beads for rosaries, drinking-shells, "masks", waistcoat buttons, crucibles, counters for the play of "hombre", flag-stones, lanterns, chains, colour-shells, shoe-buckles, eggs, syphons, water-pails and shirt buttons[155].

At the time of Louis XV coquetry and pleasure-seeking reigned supreme in France, then the Rococo-style and flourishes and cambered surfaces came into vogue. "The capriciousness and playfulness characteristic of the period were reflected in the much-zigzagged lines and the luxuriant plant like framework"[156]. As France, in matters of taste, was an example to be copied for most cultured countries (for Meissen as well) the above-mentioned style came into fashion here also. It is interesting how this change came about during the manufacture of the "Swan service". The shape itself, with its many turnings, boldly drawn scrolls, dolphins and tritons is essentially in Barock-style, while the waved, shell-like pattern appearing on many flat surfaces point to the change which was to take place in the art. Out of the records we learn however that Kaendler made[157] a large ladle in French style (equivalent to Rococo) for this service. As such a remark is found about other pieces as well, I believe that the year 1740 may be marked as the one in which the Rococo-style gained a footing in Meissen. That it made itself at home here in a very short space of time is due to the fact, that this style with

Page 35.
Fig. 48. TAILOR BESTRIDING
A GOAT, 171.
22 cm.

Page 36.
Fig. 49. VIRGIN, 903.
45 cm.

Fig. 50. CHRIST AT THE STAKE, *947/1121.*

40 cm.

Page 36.

its bent outlines, with its aversion to symmetry, with its liking for lightness, gracefulness, triviality and daintiness is particularly adapted to being produced in china. The use of straight-lined, strict forms was made very difficult by the qualities of the paste and by glazing which veiled the subtleness of the lines.

The salt cellars (illustrated Table 5, *2680—81*) with gardner's boy and girl as well as the three candlesticks (Fig. 32, *1172*) serve as examples of this style in Meissen. The forming of the rocaille-ornaments, the winged angels' heads and the gracefulness of the small figures with the slight relief in colours of single parts, as well as the painted fragrant bunches of flowers show what characteristic and charming things were produced in Meissen. Holy water pots (Fig. 33 and 34, *1016—17*) with the graceful angels' heads and statures also belong to the number of charmingly dainty productions. They are things produced by Kaendler in 1748[158].

Kaendler had been untiring in inventing the most varied models and forms for executing in china, he was just as energetic in developing the ideas conceived by him with regard to his plastic work. He has hardly left one side of this art untouched and has thereby increased the great and very precious store of forms and models already given by him to Meissen. The greatest amount of credit is here due to him who, taking the principles of monumental plastique, applied them in miniature to china so well. Still some of the praise is due to the assistants working under his supervision and influence. Meyer joined their number in 1748. Occasionally even now ready made drawings and models were sent to be executed in Meissen, so, for instance in 1738 the Countess von Schellsack asked for cows after her drawings[159]. In 1737 the Paris dealer Huet sent 13 models, according to which he ordered chinaware to be made, while in 1749 or 1750 Duke von Luynes sent, for a similar purpose, four wax-models which represented a wind-mill, two peasants' houses and a pastoral group. Probably the last mentioned group is represented on Table 11, *1359,* as it shows a type varying from Kaendler's work and answers the description in every respect, only a goat has been added.

It has already been said that Kaendler, at the beginning of his work in Meissen had to model animals which

Fig. 52. HOLY FAMILY, *1045.*

17 cm.

Page 37.

were to be as large as possible for the Japanese palace. He did this work very skilfully, first working from drawings and then from nature, so that he very soon surpassed Kirchner in truth to life and conception.

Fig. 51. HUBERTUS GROUP, *303.*

49 cm.

Page 37.

Table 11

Pages 14, 32, 33, 34, 35, 37, 44, 57.

2—5, 7—9 and 11 by Kaendler, 1 and 6 by Reinicke.

1. Chinaman, *436*.   2. Spring, *2736ᵃ*.   3. The lover disdained, *464*.   4. Summer, *2736ᵇ*.

12 cm.   13 cm.   17 cm.   13 cm.

5. Autumn, *2716*.   6. Bird-catcher (woman), *554*.   7. Moor with spanish white horse, *1067*.   8. Bird-catcher, *357*.

14 cm.   20 cm.   41 cm.   21,5 cm.

9. Vessel for spice, *476*.   10. Shepherds' group, *1359*.   11. Vessel for spice, *150*.

20,5 cm.   22 cm.   21 cm.

Table 12

Pages 35, 37, 39, 44, 65.

8 perhaps by Reinicke, the rest by Kaendler.

1. Terpsichore, *595*.   2. Group of Poles, *502*.   3. Poetry, *347*.   4. Katharine II, C *92*.
26 cm.   18 cm.   27 cm.   25,3 cm.

5. Elisabeth of Russia, *1059*. 6. Saxony and Bavaria, *828*. 7. Loving couple, *778*.
23,5 cm.   19,5 cm.   12 cm.

8. Peasant on horseback, *1175*.
21 cm.

Fig. 53. TWO SATURNS. RAVISHMENT OF PROSERPINA.
1565   *3057*   *1836*
23 cm.   27 cm.   19 cm.

Page 37.

Page 37.
Fig. 54. CENTAUR WITH CUPIDS, *1680.*
21 cm.

Kaendler still continued working at this animal plastique, even after the idea of furnishing the Japanese palace had been given up; he only made use of smaller dimensions as they better adapted themselves to porcelain. The illustrations on Table 1, *1127* and *62ᵃ* and on Table 4 with the exception of the wag-tail made by Kirchner (*58**) and the ure ox probably the work of Reinicke (*2687*) show such creations. The parrot (*20**) for instance has been modelled from life by him for Countess Mosczinka at her house in 1741[161]. The statuette of a Bologna-terrier in the act of scratching itself (*333*)[162] was probably made at the same time, while the pointer (*1124*) which together with another was made for the Bishop of Olmuetz dates from 1746. In the same year the little boar (*742*) originated, in the next year a wild boar's chase (*739*) — "for his Royal Highness"[163] —, and a bear hunt were produced. The pug illustrated on Table 10, *510* was modelled from life for the Minister Bruehl[164] in Hubertusburg, it was almost entirely made by Kaendler and only completed and finished by Ehdern. The turtle-pigeon (Table 10, *827*) was made by Kaendler in 1745, the white spanish steed with the Moor (Table 11, *1067*), "the camel on parade" (Table 10, *1434*) about 1750; the flying stag (Fig. 35, *875*)[165] in 1747 and the crow (Fig. 36, *953**) in 1739.

The figures of the "Comedia dell' arte", an Italian characteristic comedy, which were very popular at that time had already been made in stone-ware by Boettger. Kaendler working with the help of his assistants (especially Reinicke) treated these figures very effectully, in the forties. Some examples of them may be seen in the dancing (Table 9, *237*) or in the deeply bowing harlequin (Table 6, *632*) — the latter with his face covered with a half mask —, in the dignified lawyer (Avvocato — Table 9, *942*) and the group of Pantalone and Columbina (Table 9, *279*)[166].

Another branch greatly favoured by Kaendler is that of national types. Here as well he has managed to make his representations characteristic and true to life. He probably began with

Page 37.
Fig. 55. FIRE-VASE, *321.*
66 cm.

Page 37.
Fig. 56. CAN-SHAPED VASE, EARTH, *309.*
66 cm.

Fig. 57. TWO CAN-SHAPED VASES, WATER AND AIR.

320
64 cm.

327
65 cm.

Page 37.

modelling the chinese (Table 11, *436*). These figures, being closely related to pagodas, probably belong to Kaendler's creations at an early period; later they appear more like Europeans dressed in chinese clothes. Afterwards other nations took their place among the representations, of which the Turk (Table 8, *349*)[167] richly dressed in under and upper garment, the well-armed Pandur (Table 9, *407*), the Janitschar (Table 9, *420*) and six oriental figures in gorgeous dress (Fig. 37, *1286—87, 1293—94, 1299, 1301*)[168], a gipsy sorceress, particularly boldly conceived (Fig. 38, *1036*) were modelled between 1748—63; while the Morlacken group (Fig. 39, *418*) originated in 1743.

More often still he has created types of craftsmen in the making of which he seems to have gone by some existing engravings. So the pedlar, coppersmith, gardner, male and female-hawker (Fig. 40, *1030, 1025, 1044, 2785* and *965*) are found to resemble Bouchardon's "Cris de Paris" which were engraved by Michel le Clerc 1737—42[169]. A number of miners which must have originated at the festival of miners at the Saxon court on the Plauen ground, may here be mentioned (Fig. 41, *1328, 1309, 1325, 1336, 1340, 1342*). One of these (Fig. *1336*) is supposed to represent August the Strong. The organ grinder (illustrated on Table 10, *960*) was made in 1747, while the two shepherds' figures (Table 13, *1331—32*) originated in 1750. Reinicke probably assisted in the modelling of another series of craftsmen (Fig. 42, *1369, 1385, 1379*), the Hungarians — woman and man — (Fig. 43, *1281* and *1285*), the dove cot (Fig. 44, *1393*) but most of all in the trumpeter and the drummer (Fig. 45, *2165* and *1963*).

Most of the novelties must have originated in Kaendler's mind, especially those pieces in which utensils are combined with figures, for instance the

Page 37.

Fig. 58. VASE, WATER, *961*.
80 cm.

Page 37.

Fig. 59. VASE, AIR, *1021*.
84 cm.

Fig. 60. AUGUST III, *194.*
44 cm.
Page 38.

Fig. 62. AUGUST III, *448.*
54 cm.
Page 38.

gardners boy and girl with salt-cellars (Table 5, *2680 —81*), the gardner with a flower basket resting his foot on a pumpkin (Table 8, *338*), the Potpourri candle-stick (Table 13, *1038*) and the bird-catcher shown in Table 11, *357*.

He has made the bag-pipe-player (Table 8, *297*)[170] as well as another drinking out of a wine glass (Fig. 46, *160*) after a drawing in 1748. Of the large number of soldier-types only a foot cuirassier presenting (arms modelled by Kaendler[171] in 1741 (Table 8, *187*) and a roman soldier (Table 9, *559*) are here portrayed.

The so-called "crinoline figures" and groups which represented scenes from the lives of the nobility were very popular, as they gave painters and sculptors full scope for displaying their art. Here mostly the morals of the time are excellently, grace-fully and often humorously treated. Especially is this true of the various love-affairs of court society and of some of the happenings interesting it. If there be any truth in all the little stories told about them is open to question. In the records only seldom a hint of these is found[172].

The figures under the name of Romans (man and woman) (Table 6, *2733* and *2735*) represent Louis XV and Pompadour in the stage-costumes of Galathea and Acis and have been modelled after a painting by Cochin. On the same table (*550*) a group is pictured which is often spoken of as portraying August III and Maria Josepha. The man really bears a resem-blance to the King, while the woman is not at all like the Queen (see Maria Josepha, Fig. 63). In the Meissen records this group is described[173] in all particulars as having orig-inated in 1744, no reference to the persons represented being made. In the groups hereafter mentioned no people are named either, although decidedly the idea for them was given by certain people and events. Such are the lover disdained (Table 11, *464*)[174], the loving couples (Table 6, *344*, Table 9, *250*[175] and Table 12, *778*), the group of freemasons[176] (Table 9, *376*) and the kissing the hand of the Poles[177] (Table 12, *502*). To the number of these the following groups may be added the "Bruehl tailor" dressed as a knight bestriding a goat (Fig. 47, *107*) 1737, a group of the two court jesters Froehlich and Schmiedel (Table 8, *290**)[178], Froehlich with a lady in a sleigh (*251*)[179], the two last productions dating from 1741 and fox at the pianoforte (Table 10, *474*) from 1743[180]. A smaller group of a tailor on a he-goat was made by Kaendler in 1740 (Fig. 48, *171*).

Kaendler was successful in working as a church artist as well.

August the Strong had, as above mentioned ordered apostles over life size for the Japanese palace. As a result

Fig. 61. AUGUST III, *310.*
95 cm.
Page 38.

Fig. 63. MARIA JOSEPHA, *1251*.   *Page 39.*
41 cm.

Fig. 64. THOMAS AND PETER.   *Pages 40 and 41.*

9   *3*
49 cm.   50 cm.

Kirchner made an image of St. Peter which although possessing faults was fit to be sent to Dresden in February 1732. Kaendler now sought to model a St. Paul two meters high as a "pendant". As this figure "was not of the right proportions and therefore did not remain straight in the baking" he made another. But he seems to have come to grief over technical difficulties here as well, and, as the orders for the Japanese palace were discontinued with time, it was preferred to make the apostles smaller in size. He seems to have completed a series of apostles in 1736, at any rate St. Peter and St. Paul in richly gilt vestements and ornaments were sent to Rome. He began working at a second series in 1737. The greater number of apostles he modelled in the years 1740 and 1741[181] and executed the Evangelists in like size as well. Two of them, Luke and Mark, are shown on Table 7, *5* and *13*.

In 1738 and 1740 he created two images of the Virgin Mary with the Infant Jesus (Fig. 49, *903*[182]

Fig. 65. BUST OF KING RUDOLPH I, *13*.   *Page 40.*
38 cm.

and Table 7, *158*). At about the same time the "praying nun" (Table 7, *300*) originated. The holy Nepomuc whom Kirchner had already represented in 1731 has also been modelled by Kaendler several times (Table 7, *208*). The copy illustrated on Table 8, *337* dates from 1744[183]. For the Count von Thun he has created the little Infant Jesus (Table 9, *430*)[184].

In 1738 a model for a many-figured group representing the death of St. Francis Xavier was ready The formation of these figures in paste was seriously begun[185] only in 1740. The group "Christ at the stake" (Fig. 50, *947/1121*)[186] was made in 1741, while the large groups of the Crucifixion (*913—914*) and

Fig. 66. POPE'S BUST, *33*.   *Page 40.*
36 cm.

COLOR PLATES

Table 1

Pages 13, 14, 16, 33.

1 by Kirchner, 2—6 by Kaendler.

1. Parrot, *343.*   2. Oak-jay, *1127.*   3. Magpie, *62ᵃ.*   4. Mustard pot, *607.*   5. Oil-jug, *608.*
86 cm. to basis   38 cm.   52,5 cm.   21 cm.   21 cm.

6. Tea-pot, A *44.*   7. Plate with buckle ring.
10,3 cm.   23 cm. diam.

Table 3

Pages 11, 16, 17, 26, 31.

1. Vase with new applied flowers, Watteau painting, *8.*   2. Vase with branch-pattern, *32.*
14 cm.   32 cm.
3. Butter dish about 1750.   4. Plate with new cut, "little table" design.
11,5 cm.   25 cm. diam.
5. Plate with new cut, brown dragon pattern.   6. Tureen with shell-like stand, *80.*
25 cm. diam.   30 cm. without Saucer.

Table 5

Pages 13, 17, 32, 35, 05.

1 and 2. Vases with handles at the top, E *163.*
36 cm.

3. Capture of tritons, C *35.*
31 cm.

4—6. Lids of hunting vases by Kaendler, *2706, 217, 220.*
12,5 cm., 16 cm., 21 cm.

7 and 8. Salt cellars, *2680—81.*
13 cm.

Table 6

Works by Kaendler.

Pages 33, 35, 64, 65.

1. Harlequin, *632.*   2. St. Palafox, D*14.*   3. Loving couple with harlequin, *344.*   4. Pompadour, *2733.*
15,5 cm.   32 cm.   16 cm.   20,5 cm.

5. Louis XIV, *2735.*   6 and 7. Monkeys' concert, *8, 6.*   8. Crinoline group, *550.*
23 cm.   14,5 cm., 14 cm.   21,5 cm.

Table 14

Pages 42, 46, 64.

1—3 and 6—8 by Kaendler, 4 and 5 by Eberlein, 9 and 10 by Meyer.

1 and 2. Shepherdess and shepherd, *1306, 1314.*   3. Cupid on a dolphin, *1738.*   4. Hebe. *469.*   5. Graces, *536.*
24 cm.   11 cm.   21 cm.   20 cm.

6. Danceuse, *2357.*   7 and 8. Child-comedians, *11ᵇ and ᵃ*.   9 and 10. Gentleman and lady with dogs, *1476, 1446.*
20 cm.   11,5 cm., 11 cm.   17,5 cm., 18 cm.

Table 22

Pages 65, 76, 77.

1. Vase by Schoenheit, H *16*.   2. Plate with painting after Boucher.   3. Vase by Kaendler, D *91*.
24 cm..   25 cm. diam.   27,5 cm.

4. Lessons in love by Juechtzer, K *44*.
46 cm.

Table 24

1. Zephyr and Flora by Juechtzer, I 10.   2. Vase with Watteau painting, G 59.
29,5 cm.   30 cm.

3. Vase with painting pâte-sur-pâte, H 20.   4. Plate with perforated edge, 8.
31 cm.   23 cm. diam.

5 and 6. Baskets by Schoenheit, F 41 and 46.
19 cm., 18 cm.

Table 25

1. Tureen, Ozier.   2. Serving dish with Watteau painting, P *174*˚.
        31 cm.   48 cm. long.
3. Coffee service, blue fish-scale pattern (Coffee pot Z *62ª*).
            Coffee pot 25 cm.

Table 33

Pages 104, 105, 107, 108, 112.

1. Giraffes by Pilz, X *162.*   2. Mandrill by Pilz, X *143.*

33 cm.   21 cm.

3. Lady with a gray-hound by R. Hentschel, Z *187.*   4. Group of Dutchmen by Lange, Z *193.*

25 cm.   29 cm.

5. and 6. Plates with landscapes by R. Hentschel, T *22,6.*   7. Polar bear by Jarl, T *182.*

15 cm. diam.   11 cm.

Table 35

Page 108.

1—3. Children's figures by K. Hentschel, W *124, 118, 117.*
12,5 cm., 17 cm., 11 cm.

4, 6 and 7. Figures by Koenig, A *259, 258, 257.* 5. Blind man's buff by Eichler, W *115.*
25 cm., 20 cm., 22 cm.   27 cm.

Table 37

Pages 104, 105, 108.

1. Guinea-fowls by Walther, Z*155*. 2. Skaters by Koenig, Z*196*.
   38 cm.   21 cm.
3. Oriental musician by Hoesel, V*129*. 4. Falcons by Fritz, X*185*. 5. Rooster by Hoesel, V*130*.
   21 cm.   31 cm.   18 cm.
6. Toucan by Walther, Z*188*.
   30 cm.

Page 40.

Fig. 67. DOG AND HUNTER, *503*.
31 cm.

Page 40.

Fig. 69. APOLLO AND POLYHYMNIA.
369,27   *369,7*
44 cm.   40 cm.

the group with St. Hubertus originated in 1741—44 (Fig. 51, *303*). The first is supposed to have been ordered for Pope Clement XIII, the second for August III. The holy family in Bethlehem is also a group which must be ascribed to Kaendler (Fig. 52, *1045*).

I have before this drawn attention to the fact that in Kaendler's education his knowledge of and taste for the antique had been fostered. It is not therefore surprising that he should have found mythological and allegoric themes which he was anxious to bring into his work. As examples I may mention Meleager and Atalante which he modelled for the Minister Bruehl in 1740 for a cake dish, a Saturn with a scroll intended for inscription (Fig. 53, *3057*. The figures illustrated *1565* and *1836* were made in 1750), the Terpsichore which he created for Friedrich the Great in 1744 (Table 12, *595*), Poetry (Table 12, *347*), the ravishment of Proserpina (Table 10, *1448*), a Centaur with cupids (Fig. 54, *1680*), Diana with Cupid (*1161*), cupids as the four seasons (Table 11, *2736ᵃ* and *ᵇ* and *2716*) were all made in 1740. Kaendler was quite in his element when creating, together with his fellow-craftsmen those robust little cupids in all imaginable impersonations poses and costumes. They breathe such original freshness and life, and are so boldly and humourously conceived that they conquered the world in a trice[187].

The richly ornamented vase symbolizing Fire[188] (Fig. 55, *321*) may be proved to be the work of Kaendler. The four elements have been impersonated by him in the thirties in tankard-like vases and in 1741 and 1747 in vases differently shaped. Of the first those representing Earth, Water and Air (Fig. 56 and 57, *309*, *320* and *327*), of the last Water (Fig. 58, *961*) and Air (Fig. 59, *1021*) may be here shown. Besides the four seasons (for instance Winter made in 1755 [*2380*]), science and arts, the five senses, glory and conquest must be added. He was hardly able to satisfy his own energy and sought again and again to view the work he loved so much from different stand-points so as to enable him to create new and newer forms.

Meissen's store of forms and models which originated under Kaendler's influence is so exceedingly great that a complete enumeration can not here be even thought of. The pieces mentioned and illustrated by me are only to be considered as examples. I therefore refer to a document published[189] by me in which the china articles in the possession of the Minister Bruehl on October 1ˢᵗ 1753 are seperately

Page 40.

Fig. 68. VASE FOR FRANCE, *98*.
85 cm.

Pages 42 and 43.

Fig. 70. DANCER, SUMMER, VENUS, VENUS, GARDNER'S GIRL, JOSEPH.

| *492* | *178* | *318* | *998* | *754* | *305* |
| 18 cm. | 19 cm. | 20,5 cm. | 18 cm. | 17 cm. | 17,5 cm. |

enumerated. It can be well imagined that, occupying the position he did in the factory, he had everything that pleased his fancy made for himself and taking into consideration his fondness for china and the luxury by which he liked to be surrounded, it can well be imagined that the list above mentioned will not exclude much of what was best.

In the work spoken of many times reference has been made to such articles as had been made by special order. What I have been able to ascertain on this subject, besides that already spoken of will be here discussed.

The three portraits of August III had been ordered by the Saxon court. The figure representing the King in the robes of the Roman emperors (Fig. 60, *194*) was modelled by Kaendler in 1736. The boldly conceived figure is bent in S shape and rests on the right leg. It is effectully wrapped in a large white mantle which is fastened on the left shoulder; a roman helm is laid near the left foot[190].

Only the head of the statue (Fig. 61, *310*) made in 1740—41 which represents the King in the dress

Page 42.

Fig. 71. POLISH CLOCK-CASE, *452*.
71 cm.

of a polish magnate was modelled by Kaendler, the figure itself was made by Eberlein, the orders by Ehder. According to Sponsel[191] it was copied from a picture of Silvestre, only the head which is quite different from that in the picture was copied by Kaendler from life.

For the third time Kaendler in July 1745 made a statue of this King, dressed in an emperor's robes, bestriding a galloping steed (Fig. 62, *448*). It was true to life and modelled by an artist's hand. Here as well Eberlein assisted Kaendler. It was ready and placed on the King's table on August 3rd of the same year[192] and pleased everybody so well that, after a few years, a wish arose to have it executed on a large scale and put up on the "Judenhof" (Jews' court) in Dresden, in a similar way to the monument of August II in the Hauptstrasse. Bruehl gave this order to Kaendler (in 1751) who began to execute it joyfully and energetically; as in it he had a piece of work quite in keeping with his ideas. First of all he requested a Modellier shed to be built; his request was granted in June. Then Kaendler made a model of the whole statue, in reduced size, which was perfect in conception and execution. It was baked in china in Meissen in 1753[193]. The figure on horseback itself is like the one of 1745, but, probably out of consideration for technical difficulties, in the large figure a support was made under the horses belly; this support is masked by the figure of Envy. For this figure of the King on horseback a socle rich in figures and allegories was made.

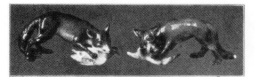

Page 42.

Fig. 72. FOX WITH ROOSTER AND HEN.
623   *626*
5 cm.   5 cm.

Table 13

Pages 34, 35, 57, 64, 65.

Works by Kaendler.

1. Ortolana, D 33.   2. Pulcinella, D 30.   3. Avvocato, D 37.   4. Coviello, D 43.   5. Shepherdess, 1332.
19 cm.   19 cm.   17 cm.   17,5 cm.   28 cm.

6. Shepherds group with carrier pigeon, A 29.   7. Shepherd, 1331.   8. Spring, 35.   9. Potpourri candlestick, 1038.
22 cm.   28 cm.   17 cm.   28 cm.

10. Summer, 37.
16 cm.

Page 42.
Fig. 73. ADAM AND EVE, 665.
37 cm.

Page 42.
Fig. 74. TURK WITH SUGAR
BASIN, 771.
18 cm.

In November 1754, Kaendler reported that he hoped to be able to begin forming the "large statue" in porcelain paste in two or three months time, and asked that it should be seen to that paste should not be wanting for the work. But notwithstanding this request, Bruehl was obliged to order 120 bales of paste to be placed at Kaendler's disposal in 1755. In the mean time he continued working at the statue which together with the socle, was about 10 m. high. This statue was viewed with great interest by the King and Queen, the Princes Xavier and Charles with their suites on May 3rd 1755 when they were passing from the Leipsic fair to Dresden. During the same year many parts of the large statue had been executed in china and several rooms for storing them were put at Kaendler's disposal. As the number of china parts as well as of the forms became greater and greater, Kaendler was obliged from Michelmas 1756 to use one of the stories of his own house for storing the former.

This work in china would have been the grandest ever created by artists in porcelain in Europe; Kaendler worked at it, with six foreign sculptors and three carpenters, for five whole years, but it was never completed. When the disturbances of war disturbed the work of the factory, all further attempts of making the statue were given up. The plaster model was kept in the model house until it fell to pieces with time. The King's head in plaster is still to be found in the Dresden collection of china, but of the porcelain parts nothing more was found, although to this time it is rumoured in the factory that such parts, among them, a huge horse's leg, have been seen. This may serve as a proof that Kaendler had not only formed parts of the socle in china, but had begun making the figure on horseback itself as well.

Page 43.
Fig. 76. PIPEHEAD.
FROEHLICH.
4,5 cm.

Sponsel who treats this monument particularly[194] says that the statue was not completed owing to the disturbances of war, the bad relations between Kaendler and Helbig and finally the death of King August III; this would outwardly supply the reasons. That this undertaking was not further carried on after the end of the war and the fall of Helbig was probably due to want of money, as well as to the fact that no one except Kaendler thought the construction technically possible; so that it was left altogether, although it had cost a large sum of money and although many parts of it were already made in porcelain. So it is said in 1761 of the statue that "the perfecting of it spoken of by the arcanists as possible — is still subject to many doubts". It is not however improbable that Kaendler would have surmounted technical difficulties which the other craftsmen thought it impossible to overcome.

Kaendler had, besides the King, modelled Queen Maria Josepha, the daughter of Joseph I and Amalie. In the group portrayed under Fig. 63, 1251 she may be seen sitting on a beautiful arm chair in Rococo-style ornamented with a crown. The pretty slender page standing next to her and the Moor carrying her train, serve as an excellent foil to her short stature[195].

The group (Table 12, 828) of two figures (a man and a woman) dressed in ermine with the Elector's hat and grasping hands were made for the King's marriage. It was to serve to commemorate the double wedding through which a union between the Saxon and Bavarian royal families was made[196].

It was probably in 1742 that Kaendler created the group illustrated on Table 12, 1059. It represents Queen Elisabeth of Russia dressed in male apparel on horseback. She is dressed

Page 43.
Fig. 75. WHOOP, 278.
31,5 cm.

Page 43.
Fig. 77. PIPEHEAD,
TURKISH LADY.
8,5 cm.

Page 43.

Fig. 78. PEASANT'S HUT, *2230.*

17 cm.

in the uniform of one of her regiments and has a moorish runner by her side. The rearing horse is supported by its long tail and the trunk of a tree which is covered with flowers and leaves.

In 1737 the King had ordered an altar with apostles at its side for his mother-in-law Queen Amalia. This altar was to be executed after an engraving delivered by Bruehl. One of the apostles attached to it is portrayed in Fig. 64, *3.* It is expressly said that he has modelled after the drawings given to him[197]. The apostle Thomas (*9*) was made by Eberlein. To the altar the following articles belonged:—"6 large candlesticks, between them a large crucifix, 1 'credenz'-plate and 2 jugs for wine and water respectively, 3 ciboriums, 1 holy water pot, 1 basin and 1 watering-can, 1 bell with handle and 1 'credenz'-plate as well as a chalice lined with gold"[198]. For the same Queen Kaendler and afterwards Reinicke in 1744—46 made a series of busts of the Habsburg Emperors. These busts which were about 33 cm. high and left entirely unpainted, must have later come to be sold as they are met with in different places[199]. Fig. 65 represents King Rudolph II.

Kaendler with the help of Eberlein made in 1743 several busts of popes[200]. They had been ordered by Cardinal Albani were 42 cm. high and were executed with extraordinarily skill. One of them, probably that of Pius V is shown in Fig. 66.

For the Princess Maria Anna (see note 196) he modelled her favourite dog which is led by a string by the hunter Wentzel (Fig. 67, *503*). The artist must have put particular weight on making this group true to life[201]. In the same year he made chimney piece ornaments for the Russian Empress, which I am not able to describe.

The very large vases with signatures, coats of arms and busts of Louis XV and August III were probably ordered by the Saxon court as a present to the french court. Some of them are made with snow-ball-blossoms, others without them, they show strong Barock outlines and Rococo details and copious ornamentation of figures, scrolls and flower wreaths which should represent the flourishing state of the french kings house (Fig. 68, *98*)[202]. Kaendler created them in 1742 with Eberlein's help.

In 1745—46 Kaendler assisted by Eberlein and Ehder copied, for the Minister Bruehl, the Neptune spring which had been set in the garden of the palace (then belonging to Bruehl) in Dresden Friedrichstadt by the architect Zacharias Longuelune and the sculptor Lorenzo Mattielli. The following figures find a place on it:—"Neptune, Amphitrite, a Triton, a nymph, a Triton child and two old men to represent the two rivers the Tiber and the Nile. Besides two sea-horses and various shells and rocks". (M. A.)

As a present for his daughter Maria Josepha who had been married to the dauphin of France (Louis) since 1747, the King ordered in 1748—50 a mirror frame 3 m. high. It was very richly decorated with figures, flower-wreaths and foliage and had a properly sized table belonging to it. The figures of Apollo and Polyhymnia belonging to it (Fig. 69, *369,7*) will give an idea of the world of forms in which Kaendler then moved; it is the graceful manner of the full blown Rococo-style which meets us here. It was considered a matter of such importance that this grand and fragile piece of work should reach its destination in good order that Kaendler together with Helbig was deputed to deliver it. They were therefore as the records report gone on a journey to Paris from August 5th to October 6th 1750.

Such an amazingly great number of forms and models could not have been made by one artists hand, however industrious and gifted the artist. So Kaendler made use of the help of a few artistically able assistants for going on with the work outlined by him and for finishing the pieces made in porcelain paste; their work was afterwards corrected by himself. So

Page 43.

Fig. 79. POTPOURRI VASE, *864.*

21 cm.

Page 44.

Fig. 80. NEPOMUC, *521.*

22,5 cm.

Page 44.

Fig. 81. BUST OF A SAINT, *3*.
30 cm.

Page 44.

Fig. 82. BUST OF A SAINT, *14*.
31 cm.

it is for instance reported that the three glories belonging to the group of St. Francis Xavier were corrected by him in paste. He corrected the expression of the faces and the outlines of the hands where it was necessary[203]. Through this, and through the fact that his work so well adapted itself to china paste, he was able to teach people to work according to his ideas, and that made it possible for his work to show such brilliant results. Besides helping Kaendler his assistants independently made some articles which are so original that they might well be considered. After the investigations made by Prof. Hoesel in old forms and in Meissen archives it is possible to get an idea of their individual abilities.

This will be the first attempt made to bring to light the individual work of each of these assistants. Completeness can not here be expected, for the old forms in Meissen have not been thoroughly enough examined while the archives are incomplete. But some former doubts may be settled, some mistakes may be now corrected, while many a piece that, because of its strange appearance, was believed not to have been made in the Meissen factory, can be now ascribed to it again.

Johann Friedrich Eberlein was the first to be employed (at a salary of 12 talers) by the Meissen factory as assistant to Kaendler in April 18th 1735. He was born in Dresden 1696 and died in Meissen June 20th 1749. His first work at the factory was to complete and make in porcelain paste animals begun by Kaendler. These animals consisted of two large swans, an owl with a pigeon, a goat, some lambs, a stork, a turkey and a sheep. Then statuettes and different utensils were added as well. I have already spoken of the assistance Kaendler received in making the large statue of the King in polish raiment, the Bruehl service, the apostles, the bust of the pope and the Neptune spring.

Of Eberlein's independent work I particularly wish to mention the following:—

In 1737 he worked together with Kaendler at a large oval shell-like swinging kettle with two Japanese figures and a handle consisting of a bird. It was intended for Count Bruehl. The work of the two men can not here be separated. In 1739 he himself seems to have made another swinging kettle for the swan-service[204]. Then he made apostles of the same size as Kaendler; the apostle Thomas (Fig. 64, *9*) may serve as an example of this. Besides he made most of the lids for the hunting vases — among these is one on which a hunter with a hawk, two hares and a dog is represented. In 1740 he made a "tailor's wife on a she goat" (Table 15, *155*), a St. Joseph, a Virgin Mary with the Infant Jesus in her arms and — for the Minister Bruehl — a "Venus and Adonis with Cupid".

In 1741 he modelled for the Baron von Stecken "a moor sitting and holding a 'credenz'-plate, a moor in turkish costume with a flower basket, a moor standing next to a sugar basin

Page 44.

Fig. 83. HARLEQUIN, HARLEQUIN, BELTRAME, CLOWN, DOCTOR.

| *454* | *538* | *1355* | *592* | *544* |
| 14,5 cm. | 13,5 cm. | 13 cm. | 13 cm. | 15 cm. |

Page 44.

Fig. 84.   FIVE CHINESE.

439   421   435   444   437
15 cm.   17 cm.   15 cm.   16 cm.   16 cm.

and a mooress as pendant" to it, a Mercury (Table 15, *198*)[205], Peace with the olive branches (Table 15, *266*), a woman's figure with two children the group representing "Love" (Table 15, *272*), another one holding an anchor and a hawk in her hands representing

"Hope" (Table 15, *273*), Apollo and Daphne, Neptune with a sea-shell, Juno with a peacock and for the spanish ambassador a "St. Joseph with the Infant Jesus" (Fig. 70, *305*). In 1·742 Eberlein was mostly occupied with the four large vases impersonating the elements. The vases were intended for France. In 1743 he worked together with Kaendler at a clock-case over 1 m. high for August III. It represents the "kingdom of Poland, on it an eagle holding Your Majesty's portrait:—as well as two children with the King's insignia a Flora scattering flowers and Pallas with an owl. On one side Peace crowning the polish coat of arms in sitting, on the other side, however, Mars takes his stand. The summit is taken by Fortuna with her sail standing on a winged globe. This clock-case stands on four sphinxes which rest on a pedestal richly ornamented in french style" (Fig. 71, *452*). Further he (Eberlein) alone modelled several national types belonging to the Bruehl confectionery-ornament, such are:—a Persian and a Turk with a camel, also a harlequin with a birds' nest and a cat (*456*) and a clown with rabbit and dog (*461*). In 1744 he made a polish lady (Table 15, *509*) and a large clock-case as "pendant" to the one described above which represents the "Electorate of Saxony". Then he has completed many of Reinicke's productions (in the same way as Kaendler had done with his), so a Turk with a guitar and a Pantaleone. In 1743 he made a Hebe (Table 14, *467*), in 1745 a hunter with an iron-trap and a dog (*628*), foxes with hens, roosters and hares (Fig. 72, *623* and *626*), the story of Adam and Eve (Fig. 73, *665*), the three Graces (Table 14, *536*). All these besides groups of the four seasons, the five senses and of four continents for a Grand Duchess of Russia. In 1746 he modelled a Dutch peasant, a Dutch girl crotchetting and the following articles for Minister Bruehl: an Indian woman ³/₄ yds. high with two baskets, a gardner's girl (Fig. 70, *754*)[206], a woman hunter, a Turk with a sugar basin (Fig. 74, *771*) and one with a sea-shell; in 1747 figures of Roman soldiers, Neptune, Mercury, Faith,

children impersonating the seasons (spring, summer and winter), mustard and vinegar pots with figures and for Bruehl a potpourri vase with an impersonification of Love at the foot (Table 15, *884*).

Further I must mention the pieces represented on Table 15 which were also made by him and which a date can not he put to. These figures are:—Atalante and Meleager (*180*), Acis and Galathea (*472*), Nemesis (*624*), Bacchus

Page 44.

Fig. 85.   BUST OF ST. ROSALIA, *26*.
32 cm.

Page 44.

Fig. 86.   BUST OF ST. SEBASTIAN, *20*.
31 cm.

Page 44.
Fig. 87. TURK WITH
GUITAR, 539.
17 cm.

Page 44.
Fig. 88. TYROLIAN
WOMAN, 579.
16,5 cm.

bestriding a panther (1862), Bacchante (533) and (in Fig. 70) dancer (492), Summer (178) and two Venus (318 and 998).

Although Eberlein managed to make himself at home in Kaendler's ideas and gave the greatest satisfaction in carrying out to the end what had been conceived by the latter, still his own work are of an original type distinctly differing from Kaendler's productions. The most characteristic part is the slanting position of the eyes which all his figures show to a certain extent; besides one finds a face narrowly shaped with a nose drawn downwards and a particularly sharp chin. Kaendler based his work on the principles of monumental plastique and is often very particular about detail; while Eberlein has done more than all the sculptors in Meissen for the material, basing his work on the possibilities afforded by it. He is more stylish, is often satisfied with an allusion and makes larger parts of garment in wide surfaces.

A certain Joh. Friedr. Eberlein is entered in the Meissen list of employés of 1765 as embosser receiving a wage of 10 talers monthly, he was probably a son of the Eberlein spoken of above. In 1774 he was dismissed owing to his bad behaviour.

At the end of 1739 Johann Gottlieb Ehder (born in Leipsic 1717) came to the Meissen factory where he was employed till his death on October 16th 1750. Ehder must have been a useful and reliable assistant.

Page 44.
Fig. 89. CROCODILE WITH CHILD, 826.
30 cm. long.

He had given the last touches to many large and small articles at which several others had already worked. The reparation of forms which had become spoiled was also entrusted to him. He had to finish some forms of utensils which had been roughly turned by Juergens in plaster. As he had little creative force and was not gifted with imagination he did much less independent work than others.

It is for instance reported in 1741 that he made a pedestal for figures ornamented with 4 shields, a goblet, a snuff-box shaped like a sea-shell one with a flame-like ledge and one with french ornamentations. The foot of a large fruit basket with "french ornamentations" was also his

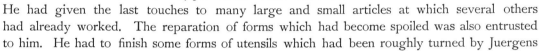

Page 44.
Fig. 91. PEASANT,
1241.
19 cm.

work. Ehder was probably the first who with Kaendler introduced the Rococo-style into Meissen. As a proof of his ability to execute artistic orders, I might mention that he was commissioned in 1745—46 to make the model of a silver epergne for the King.

Of his independent figure-models I shall mention the following:—1740 a parrot, 1741 a silk-tail, two whoops (Fig. 75, 278) and a pastoral group of six figures, in 1742 pipeheads with portraits of Schmiedel and Froehlich (Fig. 76), one with that of a turkish lady (Fig. 77), in 1743 partridges, a sheep, titmice, two chamois bucks, a pug-dog in the shape of a pipehead, Bacchus, a woman with four faces, face of Satyr and of a Japanese, a ship's steward; besides these a peasant's hut with an oven and a kennel (Fig. 78, 2230) for the Bruehl confectionary, a peasant's shed, a barn with pigeons sitting on it and a church. In 1744—45 he made a mirror frame, 1,5 m. height, and a watering-can to match the Danish service for the King of Denmark; the first-mentioned was copiously ornamented in Rococo-style. In 1745 he modelled a hunter with a horn standing next to a dead stag and in 1747 a potpourri vase the foot of which represents a mountain behind which a dog lies in ambush for partridges (Fig. 79, 864).

On April 1st 1743 Peter Reinicke entered Meissen as a sculptor. He was born in Dantzic in 1715 and died on May 2nd 1768. In 1749 it was attempted to entice him and the finisher Luecke away from Meissen to another factory, but he proved too conscientious to

Page 44.
Fig. 92. PEASANT
WOMAN, 1242.
19 cm.

Fig. 90. SATURN, 837.
17,5 cm.
Page 44.

Fig. 93. FIVE DUTCH PEASANTS.

Page 44.

1598	*1614*	*1612*	*1606*	*1607*
8 cm.	7,5 cm.	8,5 cm.	8,5 cm.	7,5 cm.

consent to this. In 1750 he asked for his wages to be increased:— he had begun working for 12 talers monthly and had once had a rise of 4 talers. He was now to receive a salary of 21 talers as he had been warmly recommended by Kaendler. Reinicke seems to have been mostly employed in assisting Eberlein, for while Kaendler and Eberlein overtook the large pieces Ehder had to help with the small ones. Feet of vessels, handles for lids, pipeheads and utensils are often mentioned as having been made by him. With time he managed to satisfy Kaendler so well that he spoke of him as being steady, industrious and skilful, and he was allowed to take a part in modelling figures. So, Reinicke helped with the figures of the Italian comedy, with the criers, with the figure of St. Nepomuc (Fig. 80, *521*)[208], with some of the busts of saints (Fig. 81—82, *3* and *14*) in 1743, with the large crucifixion group and the busts of the Kings. Among others he modelled Albert II, Maximilian, Ferdinand and Matthias I; Kaendler gave them the required "correction". Many of Reinicke's figures show so much originality that they may be entirely attributed to him; for instance in Fig. 83 the harlequin (*454*), the harlequin (*538*), the Beltrame (*1355*), the clown (*592*) and the doctor (*544*). These figures were ordered for the Duke of Weissenfels and executed 1743—44. Of the criers the baker's man[209] (Fig. 40, *877*), the water-carrier and the grinder are expressly mentioned as having been made by him.

In 1743 already he made five small chinese figures (Fig. 84, *439, 421, 435, 444, 437*)[210] for the Bruehl confectionary, as well as the bust of St. Rosalia (Fig. 85, *26*) which was intended for Prince Albani; he also finished the St. Sebastian begun by Kaendler (Fig. 86, *20*). In 1744 followed a turk with a guitar under his arm (Fig. 87, *539*), two eagles (about 5 cm. high) with heads against each other and open-worked crown, the eagles standing on a pedestal (*534, 534**), a peasant woman with a basket and a bird-cage, a bird sitting on her hand (Table 11, *554*), a tyrolian woman with a jewel box (Fig. 88, *579*), a hunter with a hare in his game bag and a dog at his side (*691*). In 1745 two figures Mary and John about 14 cm. high were modelled after drawings (*653* and *651*). Then he began working at the figures of the apostles 21 cm. high and at the groups "Asia" and "America" which correspond with those of Eberlein, being only reduced in size. In 1746 he made a turkish lady dancing, small hares and ure-oxes, in 1747 a crocodile with a child in its jaws (Fig. 89, *826*), an angry and a flying ure-ox, as well as a Saturn (Fig. 90, *837*). The dancing peasants (man and woman) (Fig. 91—92, *1241* and *1242*) and perhaps the peasant on horseback (Table 12, *1175*) as well as the Dutch peasants (Fig. 93, *1598, 1614, 1612, 1606* and *1607*) were probably modelled in the years 1748—63 when single articles are not any more mentioned.

Reinicke was a useful and industrious sculptor who very quickly appropriated Kaendler's style and whom Meissen has to thank for a great number of good models. With regard to adaptiveness to the material Kaendler held about the middling stake between Eberlein and Reinicke. Eberlein best knew how to show off the wide and large surfaces of china, Reinicke managed this worst. He is more trivial, more natural and the folds in the raiment of his figures are more creased than in those of both the others. As an artist he is not to be compared to Kaendler or even Eberlein.

To take Eberlein's place in June 1748, Friedrich Elias Meyer (born 1724 in Erfurt) came to Meissen. He worked by the piece and in this way earned the comparatively large sum of about 38 talers monthly. Before he had been employed at the Court of Weimar where he received 200 talers yearly besides sums which were

Page 46.

Fig. 94. WATER-CARRIER, *1786.*

18 cm.

Page 46.

Fig. 95. LOVING GROUP, *1439.*

29 cm.

Table 15

Pages 41, 42.

5 by Kaendler, the rest by Eberlein.

1. Polish lady, *509.*   2. Nemesis, *624.*   3. Bacchus, *1862.*   4. Bacchante, *533.*   5. Pole, *496.*   6. Hope, *273.*
  15 cm.   20 cm.   27 cm.   21 cm.   15 cm.   20 cm.

7. Peace, *266.*   8. Potpourri vase, *884.*   9. Mercury, *198.*   10. Love, *272.*   11. Atalante and Meleager, *180.*
  19,5 cm.   30 cm.   20 cm.   19 cm.   20 cm.

12. Tailor's wife, *155.*   13. Acis and Galathea, *472.*
  18 cm.   20,5 cm.

paid for extra work. As at the end of 1754 he was able to earn nothing because of an illness, he requested to be paid a yearly salary as well i. e. besides the payment received for working by the piece. As the management did not agree to this, he only remained a couple of years and tendered his resignation in the middle of 1761, giving as a reason the small amount of his earnings at the factory. Helbig delivered this resignation with the remark that the real

Fig. 96. WINTER, FIRE, WATER, AMERICA.

1697 14,5 cm.   1681 16,5 cm.   1688 14 cm.   1690* 16 cm.

cause was the unfriendly relations of Meyer with Kaendler. That was certainly true. This might however only have been the result of difference of opinion with regard to their artistic work. Helbig accused[211] Kaendler of having, out of spite, had Meyer's forms not properly treated so that the heads became disproportionate to the figures. This statement was later rejected as untrue. It was Meyer's idea to make tall, slight figures with very small heads. This originality did not perhaps please Kaendler and might have caused him to make violent reproaches to Meyer. This was not only his right, but his duty as master of models. Meyer, very naturally, was angry over this. It is therefore possible that in order to clear himself of the reproaches which had been made him, he invented the fable mentioned above and made Helbig believe it. The latter, being Kaendler's enemy, was only too pleased to lay it before the commission. Meyer's resignation was accepted, because it is noted in January 1762 that he had taken on a situation in Berlin, but would remain some time in Meissen for the sake of enticing a few more men away from the factory. He was employed at Gotzkowsky's china factory at a salary of 1500 talers. In 1763 he was engaged as master of models by Frederick the Great, this place he filled up to 1785[212].

The notes usually kept in Meissen of the makers of single models are missing for the time that Meyer was working in Meissen and for three years afterwards, i. e. 1748—64. They were probably lost or destroyed by Helbig during the disturbances of war. We are therefore obliged to content ourselves with regard to the work to be ascribed to this artist, with a list compounded later in which certain models are notified as "Meyer's style". This gives us, however, so many points to go by that we may, with certainty, constitute his particular style. Meyers originality is not to be doubted. His very small heads on tall slight bodies have already been noticed above. Besides one might speak of a family likeness between his figures most of which show piquant, slightly vulgar features. These peculiarities not only made an impression, but seem to have formed a school. Kaendler himself was slightly influenced by him, however much he might have found fault with the peculiar proportions of his figures.

Leda and the swan (Table 16, 639) is a model which, according to the list of forms, originated about 1744. As it, however, shows many of the Meyer's proportions, I believe that it must have been later "corrected" by Meyer. Probably two of the figures belonging to the "criers of Paris", were modelled by him — those are the woman-cooper (Table 17,

Fig. 97. COFFEE POT, Oldozier, with insect painting. 24 cm.

Fig. 98. PLATE, Oldozier, with German flower painting. 25,5 cm.

Fig. 99. SALVER, painted with German flowers and figures, *429.*
38 cm.

Page 49.

1669) and the water-carrier (Fig. 94, *1786*). As Meyer's independent productions, I believe I may mention the following with certainty:—a cavalier with a bull-dog and a lady caressing a spaniel (Table 14, *1476* and *1446*), a loving couple with a man playing a guitar (Fig. 95, *1439*). Then the pieces belonging to series illustrated on Fig. 96:—Winter (*1697*), Fire (*1681*), Water (*1688*), America (*1690**). Meyer has again impersonated the continents this time as children, two by two, Table 17, *1259* shows America and Europe. Of his further allegories "Spring" (Table 17, *1277*) represented by three children, and "Poetry" (Table 17, *2471*) in the person of two children, may be shown. The last model Meyer has made over again in Berlin. Table 16 shows "Precaution" (*1452*) and "Justice" (*1450*) among them are "Strength", "Generosity" and "Honour". Besides "Prodigality" (*1537*) and "Abundance" (*1447*). Kalliope (*1887*), Apollo (*1837*) and Klio (*1872*) represented on the same table belong to a series of Muses. Mythological persons are further found in the marriage of Bacchus and Venus (*2425*) and Aktaeon (Table 17, *1661*). Lastly the following of his productions may be mentioned:—On Table 17 a dancing shepherd and shepherdess (*1782* and *1784*), Chinese (man and woman) (*1523* and *1519*), a woman with a bird's nest (*1432*), and on Table 16 a woman with a jug (*1868*), a Temperentia or Hebe, a figure with a triangle (*1624*), August III on horseback and a hunter blowing his horn (*1647*).

THE PAINTING.

Although Hoeroldt had been by degrees obliged to give up the management of the whole factory, he still had the surveillance of the painters entrusted as before to him. He kept order among them — this was not always an easy task —, gave them work, corrected it in some cases and saw to their pay. He himself has, however, painted very little. It seems that he was not any longer quite capable of performing his duties. The reports which sought to explain irregularities in the state of the factory mostly attacked the management of the painting-branch very violently. Certainly much might have been exaggerated out of spite and enmity, still the conformity of unfavourable opinion throughout, does not speak in the favour of Hoeroldt. The two managers[213] demanded in 1739 better superintendence of the painting, because some of the colours especially blue, green and yellow cracked off, and the "painting had no drawing". They expressed an opinion that there was only one painter able to paint groups and figures and ornament them[214]. The commission as well as Kaendler expressed themselves several times in a similar manner. The latter put forward the complaint—among others—, that no "inventions were made" in painting and that what was now seen, in cups for instance, was painted after the old humdrum course[215]. In 1751 he said straight out[216] that Hoeroldt was not equal to the work

Page 50.
Fig. 100. INKSTAND with chinese pattern.
Blue under glazing, B *38**.
Inkstand 9,5 cm.

Page 50.
Fig. 101. BASIN with chrysanthemum pattern. Blue under glazing, *37.*
32 cm.

Fig. 102. PLATE with thistle pattern. Blue under glaze.
Page 50.
24 cm.

Fig. 103. DISH with willow pattern. Blue under glaze, F *135.*
Page 50.
24 cm.

in the painting department, the director of which should be able to create independently, i. e. "to be able to do more than draw a Japanese figure and to paint what he had learnt". "Of the 190 painters employed in Meissen hardly ten were fit to work at painting". "Hoeroldt did not know how to distribute the work:—he gave for instance - landscapes and animals to a painter of flowers, fruits and insects, while a Watteau painter got flowers, fruits, insects, portraits, histories and war-scenes to paint". As many colours such as "ponceau" (scarlet)[217] were missing the Meissen flowers were not valued in France. The masters of drawing were not able to make good original drawings which were now in great favour. "Among foreigners especially the French complain that almost everything is copied from french engravings and nothing original is produced".

Already in 1739 Kaendler proposed that there should be two different managers in the studios, one for blue and another for coloured painting. This proposition was not agreed to, but the painters Heintze[218], Aug. Dietze, Erbsmehl, Hoyer and others were engaged to work under Hoeroldt. The position of some of them was to a certain extent independent, as they were made overseers of single divisions. In 1745 Wagner, Buerckner, Hentzschel, Eggebrecht and Colmberg as well as Heintze filled the above mentioned posts. They did not work by the piece any more, but received fixed salaries[219].

In 1739 a certain Wagner was engaged as a miniature painter. He is praised as "skilful in making portraits and other paintings". Further the following are mentioned as miniature or portrait painters: Richter, from Freiberg, who delivered a very good piece of chinaware for trial in 1740, then Toepfer who asked to be pensioned off in 1742 and lastly Johann Martin Heinrici. The last was probably the most important of these. He was born in 1711, came to Meissen in 1741, fled from there to Hoechst or Frankenthal 1757; but was pardoned and again employed in 1761. He was created Court painter in 1763 and laborant of colours in 1764 — as such he died in 1786. The records speak of him not only as of the best portrait painter, but as of an able teacher as well. His great ability as a portrait painter is proved by two large Meissen china plates on which he has painted the busts of Maria Josepha and August III. These plates are in the possession of their royal Highnesses Prince Johann Georg and Princess Mathilde and bear the mark J. M. Heinrici 1754 1756 respectively[220]. Another painter who like Heinrici made many attempts, especially with gold ornamentation, was Joh. Friedr. Herold, probably a cousin of the Counsellor of mines, who had already come to Meissen in 1725[221]. A painter called Wanes had from 1740–52 been constantly

Fig. 104. PLATE with onion pattern.
Blue under glaze.
Page 50.
24 cm.

Fig. 105. PLATE with onion pattern. Blue under glaze.
Page 50.
24 cm.

Fig. 106. SALVER with onion pattern. Blue under glaze, *563*.
27 cm.
Page 51.

Fig. 107. PLATE with new onion pattern. Blue under glaze.
23,7 cm.
Page 51.

engaged in painting little children on snuff-boxes and vessels, was dismissed as useless and refractory. Shortly before the seven-years' war the Meissen factory possessed in Gloss one of its best miniature painters, his work was however two expensive to enable the management to engage him for long[222].

In the thirties the apprentices had been taught drawing which had been from several parts considered as strictly necessary, but this gradually lapsed, so that in the fifties they were not taught at all. After Kaendler had complained about this, it was arranged in 1740 that he should himself teach the moulders apprentices and Erbsmehl the painter's apprentices drawing for an hour every day. In October 1743 C. H. Jak. Fehling a special drawing master was employed who received help from young Aug. Hoffmann; for Fehling was quite old and probably not capable of breathing new artistic life into Meissen. The commission, however, praised both teachers in 1745 and expressed the hope that with time they would be successful in finding newer and more modern patterns. For up to that time they had only let their pupils copy after successive engravings bought for that purpose. These were engravings of Watteau and the large botanic works of Weimann as well as other drawings of the sort, besides those of Albani who is so much praised for his artistic treatment of all species of birds according to their shape and colouring. These were at that time shortly expected from England. Hoffmann died 1751, Fehling in 1753. After them the two overseers of the studios Buerckner and Hentzschel were charged with the teaching of drawing[223].

In order to find out the individual abilities of each painter it was decided on June 23rd 1752 to let each painter, painter in blue and apprentice employed in Meissen, paint a trial-plate with his name and the date at the back[224].

Fig. 108. SALVER with german flowers. Blue under glaze, *O 50*.
30,5 cm.
Page 51.

Although much fault may be found with the painting of that time, still it should not be too much depreciated. It is certain that it has done its part towards the development of the factory to a flourishing state. To be sure it did not reign above all other factories as exclusively as before but had to give up it place to plastique. It was, however, understood how to improve the effect of a form by slightly colouring reliefs or painting modest ornamentations, sometimes the proper effect was only thereby produced. The ornamentation of figures and groups and the treatment of flesh parts are mostly of admirable delicacy and daintiness.

As in modelling so in painting at first east asiatic patterns were preferred. But European taste began to put itself forward. This at first gave use to a mixed style. Birds and animals were made less flat and were

Table 16

Pages 45, 46.

Works by Meyer.

1. Kalliope, *1887*.   2. Leda, *639*.   3. Wedding of Bacchus and Venus, *2425*.   4. Hebe or Temperentia, *1868*.
10 cm.   11,5 cm.   25 cm.   11,5 cm.

5. Triangle player, *1624*.   6. Precaution, *1452*.   7. August III, *1796*.   8. Justice, *1450*.
10 cm.   22 cm.   27 cm.   21,5 cm.

9. Prodigality, *1537*.   10. Klio, *1872*.   11. Bugle horn player, *1647*.   12. Apollo, *1837*.   13. Abundance, *1447*.
19 cm.   10 cm.   13,5 cm.   10 cm.   22 cm.

Table 17

Pages 45, 46.

Works by Meyer.

1 and 2. Dancing shepherdess and shepherd, *1784, 1782*.   3. The poetry, *2471*.   4. Woman with bird's nest, *1432*.
Each 18 cm.   12 cm.   20 cm.

5 and 6. Chinese lady and Chinaman, *1519, 1523*.   7. Coopers wife, *1669*.   8. The spring, *1277*.
32,5 cm., 31 cm.   20 cm.   27 cm.

9. Aktaeon, *1661*.   10. America and Europe, *1259*.
18 cm.   24,5 cm.

formed with greater truth to nature. The dispersed flowers also became very popular. These are flowers lightly strewn over the surface of the china ware and are either in oriental or "natural" (German) style. Instead of the flowers sometimes beetles, insects or butterflies were used. It has been sought to give these a more plastic effect by applying to them an exaggerated shadow (Fig. 97). The effectful Barock ledges and golden scrolls were made as well until Rococo flourishes in different colours took their place. In the cartouches (scrolls) above mentioned landscapes, hunting-camps and battle scenes were depicted, afterwards pastorals after Watteau were painted in them, while the large surfaces were decorated with "German flowers" (Fig. 98 and 99, *429*).

The time following the year 1740 naturally brought the Rococo-style into vogue in Meissen. The colours became more airy and paler, pastorals and strewn flowers in more naturalistic style appeared more often, while many ornaments showed the flourishes characteristic of Rococo-style. Here above all form and colour combined excellently and effectfully together. Now and again china was painted in one colour only. In this so-called Camaïeu-painting green and scarlet were preferred.

It has already been remarked that the painters closely followed the french engravings. So it is reported that in 1741 Heinicke, Bruehl's librarian delivered at various times 230 copper engravings to the factory and that the Paris agent Le Leu received 327 talers as payment for copper-engravings delivered[225].

Instead of the enamel colours generally used in the previous periods, now such colours were used as required less addition of flux. The colours and the mixtures of them became more numerous. So for instance in the middle of the forties pink[226] and pompadour-red[227] were added to the old yellowish-red and brick-red. Scarlet colouring gave much trouble as in it its different shades played an important part. Often it was reddish- or blueish-violet. All these were colours over glazing that is colours that were baked in a lower temperature. Besides blue only two colours brown and after 1736 another colour, probably pea yellow[228] required sharp fire baking. These were either applied upon the baked glazing or mixed with it before baking. The only real under-glaze colour for painting was cobalt blue.

THE PAINTING IN BLUE.

As the Meissen china originated as an imitation of the chinese goods, at the beginning it was sought to imitate the blue painted Nanking-porcelain as well. But although the cobalt ore necessary for this was to be found in the Saxon "Erzgebirge" (ore mountains), still it was a long time before its proper use was discovered. The unsuccessful attempts to paint in blue were probably due to the fact that the Meissen china was "two degrees harder" then the east asiatic ware. The difficulty — which was not at that time recognised — was that the leading of the flame had to be different from that used in baking china. In 1720 the chief-master Koehler presented trial pieces which came near a complete solution of the problem. His blue colour was in "itself were pretty and could be made at a small cost". It was not however, by any means faultless for it, as Hoeroldt reported, ran in the painting or in the baking so that it was impossible to make a clear drawing. Koehler, out of ill-will, did not fully explain the combination of the blue colour to his successor Stoeltzel in 1725, however, when lying on his death-bed he briefly gave Hoeroldt some instructions. Notwithstanding this the secret was lost and it took a long time to re-discover it. After many vain attempts Hoeroldt succeeded in making blue paint although in a tiresome and very expensive way. But in the kiln it became greyish, "blackish and lead-stained". Stoeltzel put the blame on Hoeroldt, saying that the painters had applied the paint unevenly and carelessly. Hoeroldt proved

Page 51.
Fig. 109. PLATE, ribbed, with immortelle pattern.
Blue under glaze.
22 cm.

Page 51.
Fig. 110. TUREEN COVER with cupid pattern.
Blue under glaze.
24 cm.

Fig. 111. PLATE with festoon pattern. Blue under glaze.
24 cm.
Page 51.

Page 51.
Fig. 112. PLATE with flower-wreath.
Blue under glaze.
24 cm.

in 1731, however, that the fault lay in the incompatibility of the colouring, paste and glazing. In 1732 it was boasted that a glazing was invented which showed the blue colour to advantage and made it out-flow less. In 1733 further progress was made and light and dark blue were spoken of. In 1734 and 1735 they arrived at greater technical perfection, so that they were able to work cheaper and make the "unsightly stains" disappear[229]. In 1739 a glazing was discovered under which the blue colour appeared prettier than before. From that time they probably worked more steadily, as the complaints, all but one, stopped altogether[230].

The china painted in blue under glazing was extremely popular from the very beginning as it was not only effectful, but could be cheaply made as a wholesale article.

As a result of the great demand for it already at an early time a number of painters were especially occupied with blue painting under glazing. In 1731, for instance, not fewer than seven, of the 40 painters employed in Meissen, were engaged in painting in blue, while three painted in blue and colours.

In 1745 therefore the painters were altogether divided into two categories. Carl Frederick Eggebrecht was made manager of the painters in blue[231]. Besides him who must have been one of the ablest painters, I should like to bring into prominence Joh. Dav. Kretzschmar (born in Wurzen 1697) as being of particular importance. He was employed as a painter in blue in Meissen from 1726 until 1752 and is praised as a master of his art many times[232].

The patterns in blue painting were for a long time akin to those on the east-asiatic models (Fig. 100, B *38**). The most popular were the rock and bird and the butterfly designs as well as the pattern with the little table, the chrysanthemum pattern (Fig. 101, *37*), the thistle pattern (Fig. 102) and the willow pattern (Fig. 103, F *135*). The so-called onion pattern however excelled all the rest in popularity. This pattern has really nothing in common with onions. The fruits decorating the borders must be denoted as japanese peaches and pomegranates. Some of the latter are slightly open and show the seeds. Besides, peonies and peculiar sharp-pronged leaves may be seen. In the case of plates the centre was connected with the border by an edging consisting of very stylish flowers and circles. The centre of the plate was ornamented with a large aster and a branch twisted round a bamboo stem and copiously decorated with leaves and blossoms. Not only plates and dishes but other utensils as well are painted with this pattern. This design probably became so very popular because its outlines adapted themselves to being so beautifully drawn.

The Dresden museum of art and industry possesses a chinese porcelain dish which probably originated in the first quarter of the 17th century. It shows this pattern in blue under glazing. I should suggest the proposition that Kretzschmar[233] mentioned above as an artist copied this on a similar plate in Meissen in 1745. Fig. 104 shows this pattern probably painted at this time. It is a little simpler than the chinese model, and less shaded, shortly not exactly copied. So the acanthus-like leaves which appear three times on the border are narrower and more pointed and bent. With time this pattern has been much altered and not to its advantage. The fruits on the border which were before directed only inwardly were now made to point outwardly as well, the drawing was simplified and flattened as it showed less light and shade (Fig. 105). The stylisation of the forms which

Page 51.
Fig. 113. PLATE with foliage edge pattern.
Blue under glaze.
24 cm.

was partly not well understood went still further in the pattern used this day (Fig. 106, *563*) in which, at the lower end of the bamboo-stem, the sign of the swords is seen. Lastly Fig. 107 shows us an attempt made by Sturm in the end of the nineteenth century to alter the design by other divisions and other fruits and blossoms.

In blue painting as well as in painting in many colours often German flowers (Fig. 108, *O50*) are used in the forties. Of the ribbed pattern it has already been said (see page 31) that it mostly appears in combination with blue painting. Fig. 109 shows an example of this with the much used immortelle pattern. When this modest design originated it is difficult to tell, but it was very often copied by Thueringen and Copenhagen factories. I think that it is already to be found in the catalogue for 1765 (see page 62). Here as well may be seen, the lid of a tureen illustrated Fig. 110 which is of oval shape and ornamented with playing children à la Raphael. In this connection three plates out of the end of the century may be here pictured, they show the festoon pattern (Fig. 111), the flower-wreath design (Fig. 112) and the foliage border (Fig. 113), they are simple pleasing patterns which did not cost much to produce.

IV. PERIOD:

INFLUENCE OF THE SEVEN-YEARS' WAR (1756—63).

riedrich II won the campaign of the first year, hardly three months after his invasion into Saxony (29th August 1756). He now looked upon Saxony as a conquered country which was obliged to provide him with a great part of the money necessary for carrying on the war, and took up winter quarters in Dresden.

When his troops entered here they seized the 500 talers which they found in the cash office of the stores and having chosen china for their King had it packed in 30 cases. The three depôts in Dresden, Leipsic and Meissen were sealed, the china itself offered for sale. On November 29th Colonel von Horn had the working premises of the factory sealed as well so that all work had to be completely stopped. The commandant of Dresden, in the meantime, after being urgently requested to allow the work to be carried on, gave his permission. The three stores of china with all their stock, including the chinaware standing in the garrets and other places, valued at 300000 talers were yielded to the Saxon Akzisrat and the prussian Privy counsellor Carl Heinrich Schimmelmann[234] for 120000 talers cash.

The Dresden agent the Counsellor of commerce Helbig, — who was to play an important part in this matter — later asserted that it was he who persuaded Schimmelmann to do this transaction, at any rate it was of advantage to the factory. For if Schimmelmann had not done this Wegely, with a company of Breslaw Jews would have taken his place in this affair. This Wegely had been since 1751 the possessor of a china factory in Berlin, so he had not only the interest of a dealer at heart in trying to make the purchase, but would have used this opportunity for destroying, as far as possible, the Meissen factory which was his most dangerous competitor. Had he bought the china he would have taken the machinery and any workmen willing to go with him to Berlin.

After the Meissen works had, through Schimmelmann's purchase escaped this danger, a second one began to threaten them. This was not fated to cause any great loss either. A few days after the completion of the deal, Wegely appeared in Meissen and presented an order of his King that everything that he wished should be shown him in the factory. He, however, as Nimpsch writes, "did not derive the slightest satisfaction from this, as most of the kilns had been destroyed, the machines were not in working order and not a single workman was to be seen on the premises". He was not very successful in his attempts to entice the employés away from the factory either. Only "4 painter's apprentices, the loss of whom did not harm the works" followed him to Berlin.

As Schimmelmann did not draw the expected advantages from the sale of china he made Helbig a proposition to buy back the chinaware from him otherwise he should be forced to sell it to Wegely who had already offered 150000 talers for it. In order to save the factory from this danger, Helbig decided to make the purchase. He reported

Fig. 114. VASE (BC.).
75 cm.

Page 56.

this to the Queen, then living in Dresden and talked over the plan with the Cabinet minister Count von Rex and the Commissary von Nimpsch. Everywhere his plan was accepted. As Helbig did not possess the money required for this deal, he put himself in connection with Privy counsellor Count von Boltza and the Superior counsellor for account Thielemann. After this they signed a purchase deed with Schimmelmann on December 11th according to which all the chinaware was to be given over to them for a sum of 170000 talers. Schimmelmann had received permission from the Prussians to have made, in Meissen, some pieces wanting to complete his service. He carried over this condition in the purchase deed. As a result of this Helbig, whose name does not figure in the contract, but who should nevertheless be considered as the originator of the plan, acted so as to obtain his permission for the factory to go on working. The prussian Minister von Borck who came to Meissen in January 1757 spoke of this in a hasty manner and said that this order of things went against the contract. At a suggestion of Helbig's Schimmelmann from 1st March 1757 rented the factory from the Prussians for

Fig. 115. APOLLO AND DAPHNE, 2900.
42 cm.

Page 56.

2000 talers to be paid monthly in advance. These (the Prussians) promised not to disturb the working of the factory and to pay for any china the King might wish to obtain. Schimmelmann sublet it on the same conditions to Boltza, Thielemann and Helbig.

From this time the factory again began working as regularly as was possible under the difficult conditions. Instead of the three arcanists who had been sent out of the country to Frankfurt a. M. in order to keep the trade secrets, the master of machines Teichert had to mix pastes and glazings and oversee the baking etc. As the expenses were lessened by lowering of the wages by a third (instead of 7500—4500 talers were paid out) and the goods sold comparatively well notwithstanding the disturbances of war, the future of the factory seemed secure[235].

The one to whom this happy issue of affairs was primarily due was certainly Helbig. The credit due to him for this can not be disputed. But it seems in my opinion unjustifiable to speak of his sacrifices and unselfishness, as the case has been often, only because his plan met with success. Certainly Helbig used his capital and credit for the factory's weal, but he knew better than any one that the Meissen chinaware bought back by him was worth double the amount paid for it. When he and his two partners made the contract with Schimmelmann they only lent their names to the business, the man who really hired the factory being King August III himself. In an order issued on December 8th 1759 it is expressly said that although Helbig was not to be considered to have hired his Majesty's factory, he was to have the management of it, as he had saved it from

Fig. 116. PAN AND SYRINX, 2921.
49,5 cm.

Page 57.

Fig. 117 SNOW-BALL VASE, 320.
64 cm.

Pages 25 and 57.

Fig. 118. TWO SNOW-BALL VASES.
Pages 25 and 57.

2760   2767

20 cm.   48 cm.

Page 57.

Fig. 119.   WINTER, 2378.

32,5 cm.

ruin or from transportation to Berlin, until the moneys he had advanced should he refunded to him. The commission was to support Helbig's authority[236].

It seems to me that the whole undertaking was nothing more than a bold speculation on Helbig's part, a speculation by which he could gain much and lose very little. He knew very well that any money he would have lost by the transaction would have been refunded him by the King. As a favourite of the Minister Bruehl he might have felt particularly secure[237].

From the beginning of the "hiring" of the factory Helbig had managed it alone. On July 7th 1760 Nimpsch was appointed co-director. Now both directors mostly together sent their reports to the King or to Bruehl. From these it may be gathered that Friedrich the Great was greatly interested in the Meissen factory. He often visited it in company with Prince Heinrich and the Margrave Carl von Schwedt. It was considered as a sign of special grace that he never requested to see "some places concerning the arcanum". On November 8th 1760 he remained for over an hour in the store room, inspected one of the studios, looked at the chinaware ordered by him and expressed his full satisfaction. He only spoke indignantly of the newspaper articles which accused him of brutality towards the factory and which he believed to have been written under the influence of Meissen. When the high bailiff of the country Lorenz asked for "protection of the factory", the King replied:—"I do you no harm, you know me well enough, only stop your newspaper articles". During this inspection of the factory it struck him that the rent paid was too low; he ordered a letter to be written to Schimmelmann to Hamburg about it. As no reply was received from him some one else was looked for to take over the factory. The above-mentioned Lorenz therefore closed a contract with the war commission in his name, with the approval of August III. From January 1st 1761 the monthly rent was raised to 5000 talers and it was decided that the chinaware ordered by Frederick II, a value of 30000 talers, should be delivered free of charge. In place of this the rent for November and December 1761 was not to be paid.

But the raising of rents did not stop at this stage. In the next year already the Prussians demanded 7000 talers monthly and 17400 talers worth of chinaware, in 1763 the sums were raised to 10000 and 35000 talers respectively. When at last at the beginning of 1763 the prospects of peace increased, after much negotiation a decision was come to that the prussians should give up the rent for February and pay 10000 talers.

At this time Helbig wrote a letter to August III in which he requested to be excused from rendering accounts till January 1760 and asked that 12000 talers yearly besides 5% interest should be paid out of the factory moneys until all debts should be entirely paid off. His requests were acceded to on March 4th 1763[238].

With the declaration of peace on February 15th 1763 the heavy conditions for the Meissen factory fell away. That it had been able to exist at all during this critical time is a wonderful fact. For besides the direct burden of 260000 talers rent and 80—100000 talers worth of china, it had to bear the burden of many unfavourable

Page 57.

Fig. 120. CUPIDS.

2505   2503   2515   2517

13,5 cm.   13,5 cm.   13,5 cm.   14,5 cm.

Table 18

Works by Punct.

1 and 2. Shepherd's boy and shepherd's girl, *2936, 2934.*   3. Commerce, *2946.*

16 cm., 15,5 cm.   17 cm.

4 and 5. Shepherd and shepherdess, *2940, 2933.*   6 and 7. Shepherdess and Shepherd, *2928, 2929.*

24 cm., 21,5 cm.   20,5 cm., 21 cm.

8. The water, *3011.*   9. The air, *3010.*   10. The taste, *2980.*

19 cm.   19,5 cm.   19 cm.

Table 19

Pages 68, 75.

Works by Acier.

1 and 2. Device children, F *5* and *9*.　　3. The broken eggs, F *65*.　4. The broken bridge, F *63*.

12,5 cm., 13,5 cm.　　　　　　25 cm.　　　　　　25 cm.

5. Mine, D *17*.　6 and 7. Galant figures, F *34*.　8. Girl at a child's cradle, E *76*.

18 cm.　　　15 cm., 13 cm.　　　　19 cm.

9. Astronomy, C *46*.　10. Fire, D *80*.　11. War, C *40*.

14,5 cm.　　　23 cm.　　　14,5 cm.

Fig. 121. JAPANESE.

2671   2672

16 cm.   15,5 cm.

Page 57.

Page 57.

Fig. 122. JAPANESE.

2676   2677

18 cm.   17 cm.

circumstances. As a result of the disturbances of war food products became very dear, a fact that caused dissatisfaction among the employés. In January 1761 the painters, because their wages had not been raised at their request, decided to strike, although only for a short time. At that time the management was pretty powerless against the agents who sought to win Meissen workmen for other undertakings. For this purpose the Secretary Jacobi for some time domiciliated in Meissen.

The painting of Meissen china outside the factory, especially in Dresden, had reached fairly large dimensions. It was not possible to stop the sale of white china notwithstanding all prohibitions. Some officers had obtained whole services of unpainted china, because it was difficult to summon up courage to refuse their request during war time. As loss was sustained by the factory through this, a printed order was issued on August 27th 1761 by which this bungling was threatened with strict punishment[239].

It is not surprising that the sale of china decreased during this time. The uncertain communication and the outstaying of bills due to lapse led many an old business connection to being dissolved. To this it must be added that the factory often had not sufficient time for making china for the market as the orders of Friedrich the Great took so much time to execute and had the preference for all others. Although much chinaware was delivered to him free of charge, he has paid considerable sums of money to the factory. The lively interest he took in the china works is proved, not so much by his many orders, as by the fact that he had found time to enter into all the details notwithstanding the troubles of war.

Instead of the 16 large vases at first demanded, 32 small ones were delivered. This was probably due to the absence of the arcanists. In the King's further orders breakfast sets and snuff-boxes took a prominent place. Single pieces are not so often mentioned. I found, among others, a director of a monkey band, 10 pagodas, 4 "monarchies", large and small "continents", 6 muses, Mercury, Fame, Europe, Silena with an ass, Hercules with a globe, "musical, theatrical and Ovid groups", the judgement of Paris, as well as 8 mythological representations which were probably intended as table decorations. A large case for a musical clock was to be made according to a drawing of a Berlin artist. Kaendler promised to carry this out, asking to be allowed to make some alterations — for instance instead of the Japanese figure he wished a beautiful Apollo to crown it and his nine muses to be attached all round the case[240].

But most time and money were spent in producing the six table services which had been ordered by

Page 57.

Fig. 123. JAPANESE.

2473   2548   2472   2678   2642

13,5 cm.   17 cm.   11,5 cm.   16 cm.   11,5 cm.

Page 57.
Fig. 124. GARDNER'S WIFE AND
GARDNER.

2368   2369
10,5 cm.   13,5 cm.

Page 57.
Fig. 125. PARFORCE-RIDER, 2692.
14 cm.

the King one after another. At the beginning he was content with the creations of the factory, but soon he began to express especial wishes. For instance he wished the oval tureen of the second service ordered to be inscribed with the motto:— "Dubium est sapientiae initium"[241]. It is said of the third service that the painting of the "façons" and artistic decoration had been made according to the "invention" of his Majesty himself in imitation of Bruehl's service. The painting here consists of a border of green and black scales. For the next service the same shape was called for and particular directions given as to the painting. Here also a border consisting of scales was to be painted, while an "Indian flower" was to accupy the centre. Besides gold only a light red "such as His Majesty the King of Poland particularly liked" was to be used. Friedrich demanded first to be shown a plate of this service for approval. The services he cared for most were probably the ones ordered last, i. e. the "festoon" and the "Japanese" service. Of these we have reliable information from Kaendler who had discussed them with the King in all particulars. The plates and dishes of the festoon service were partly to have a border of open work and were to be ornamented with "antique hanging 'Vestuns' (probably festoons) which are fastened to cupids' heads and are in flat relief for which His Majesty

Page 57.
Fig. 126. STAG, 2690.
12 cm.

Page 57.
Fig. 127. STAG, 2704.
9,4 cm.

has given me (Kaendler) drawings executed by himself". "The form of a beautiful antique vase on which two genii are to appear" was asked for as a centre piece. Everything had to be painted with flowers, those drawn by the King being considered first; those were:—"tuberoses, orange-blossoms, pavos (?), tazettes and anemones". For the japanese service a rare plate was given to Kaendler to copy. The forms were to be slightly antique, the centre piece was to show japanese figures, but the painting was to represent "indian" animals after the King's drawings — "camels, ostriches, parrots, crows, apes, tigers and panthers"[243].

Besides the King, Prince Henry of Prussia, Margrave Carl von Schwedt, General von Ziethen and many others managed to obtain china from the factory. The first mentioned must have had a service specially made for him; as in the sixties "Prince Henry sort" of china is mentioned[244].

Among the artists who were employed in Meissen during this time, Kaendler still stood foremost. It was he who executed Friedrich's orders to the satisfaction of the monarch. The management of the factory reproached him for having entered into the King's ideas too readily, thus encouraging him to give further orders. In June 1761, according to his own statement, the King offered him to serve in Prussia, but met with a refusal. Through this preference and perhaps for other reasons as well, the relations between Helbig and Kaendler became strained. This caused the former to accuse the latter of being greedy of gain, of wishing to keep all merits to himself alone and of treating the sculptors under him badly. It is a fact that the moulder Lueck (see note 283) fled to Frankenthal in 1757 and the sculptor Meyer left for Berlin in 1761. It is however open to question whether those men fled from Kaendler's ill-treatment or from the bad conditions caused in Meissen by the disturbances of war which drove people away. At any rate at this time Kaendler was still an authority.

The shape of the vase (BC.) illustrated on Fig. 114 which was painted in 1910 after a sketch of Achtenhagen, was made by Kaendler for Frederick the Great. It was afterwards repeated in various sizes and altered with regard to the side-figures. For the same King he made as above mentioned the Judgement of Paris, a larger group, which is stocked in Meissen under 2906—16 and 8 mythological loving couples. Of these the first group Apollo and Daphne (Fig. 115, 2900) shows most purely the Kaendler type, while in the others[245] Meyer's help

Page 57.
Fig. 128. ASS, 2155.
8,5 cm.

Page 57.
Fig. 129. COW, 2641.
6 cm.

is to be noticed. The peculiarities of the latter especially his elongated limbs are most clearly seen in the group of Pan and Syrinx (Fig. 116, *2921*).

The three vases (Fig. 117, *320* and Fig. 118, *2760* and *2767*) may serve as examples of Kaendler's manner of decorating at that time. He already made the large tankard-shaped vases in 1742. Now they were covered over and over with snow-

Fig. 130. PARIS CRIERS.
Page 57.

24 15 cm.   *17* 14 cm.   *5* 14 cm.   *8* 15 cm.   *7* 14 cm.

ball-blossoms. The two other vases must have originated in their shape in 1760. In 1755 Kaendler modelled the group representing "Winter" (Fig. 119, *2378*). The other three seasons had been finished by him shortly before. Here Hebe with a goblet and a mask is represented among clouds, by this the "winter pleasures of the great lord" should be shown, opposite to her is Saturn the god of time. Of Kaendler's further works, I mention both children's busts (Table 10, *2744*), children representing the four seasons (Table 11, *2736ᵃ* and *ᵇ* and *2716*), a series of groups of lovers (Table 13, *35* summer and *37* spring), further the creation of charming little cupids in most varied guise and, probably, the other Cupids slightly larger on Fig. 120, *2505*, *2503*, *2515* and *2517*. It is possible that Reinicke has helped him with these. As the results of their collaboration, I might mention two grotesque harlequins (*3023** and *3025*), the single figures (Fig. 121—122, *2671—72* and *2676—77*) and groups of Japanese (Fig. 123, *2473*, *2548*, *2472*, *2678* and *2642*), the strongly moved figures of gardners (woman and man) (Fig. 124, *2368—69*), as well as the little group of a man on a galloping steed (Fig. 125, *2692*). At this time Kaendler made other animals of as small proportions as this horse, of which the stags (Fig. 126, *2690* and Fig. 127, *2704*), the ass (Fig. 128, *2155*) and the cow (Fig. 129, *2641*) may serve as examples.

In all probability the exceedingly graceful French criers were also made by Kaendler with Reinicke's assistance. They were modelled ofter coloured drawings which are signed C. G. H.[246] partly described in french and dated 1753. They were at first ascribed to Acier and brought with them much praise for their supposed creator, but it is not true that Acier made them. When he came to Meissen they had already been made. They consist of 40 figures of which the following are illustrated Fig. 130:—the man with the magic lantern and the organ (*24*), the seller of oranges holding a kettle in her left hand (*17*), a player of the Flaschonette beating a drum (*5*), a peasant woman with two flower baskets (*8*), a peasant selling grapes by the pound (*7*)[247].

Of Kaendler's assistants whose merits have been spoken of in their time, Reinicke and Meyer were employed in Meissen to 1768 and 1761 respectively. Carl Christoph Punct was newly employed, probably to take the place of the latter — at any rate he was engaged during the seven years' war. During the comparatively short time he worked in Meissen he proved himself very industrious and able. He must have been considered a good worker from the very beginning, as in the list of employés for 1763 he is put down as Court Sculptor and in the next year it is reported that he received 33 talers and 8 groschen monthly. This was a very large sum for those times, taking into consideration that Reinicke who had been employed in Meissen for 21 years was paid only 21 talers. He died in August 1765 of consumption[248].

The figures made by him are not to be compared to the graceful, overslender shapes created by Meyers. Some of them even show a certain stiffness. The high, straight overhanging foreheads are very characteristic of him. His models have mostly been able to keep their original form, as, not having been very popular, they were but seldom used and did not require reparation.

Page 58.
Fig. 131. CULTURE OF THE VINE AND AGRICULTURE, *2902*.
13 cm.

Page 58.
Fig. 132. HOLY WATER BASIN, *2003*.
31 cm.

There is, for instance, a spanish dancer (236) which was probably made by Reinicke and Kaendler in the middle forties, besides a spanish danceuse (234) a model which probably originated in the same way, but having been repaired by Punct became similar to the productions of the latter.

Table 18 consists of his independent work. He seens to have principally made shepherd's figures mostly in pairs. Such a pair of figures, with the shepherd playing the violin is pictured under 2928—29, another pair is 2933 and 2940, a third pair in children's figures is 2934 and 2936. Then he has, as was usual in his time, preferred allegories and representations. So there are two series of different sized groups of children, to one of which "Commerce" (2946) belongs, while the other is here represented by "Culture of the vine and Agriculture" (Fig. 131, 2902). Besides he has impersonated each of the elements in the figures of three children of which "Air" and "Water" are here represented (3010—11) and lastly a group of two figures called "Taste" which is one of a series of the five senses. The holy water basin (Fig. 132, 2003) can also probably be ascribed to Punct.

With regard to painting no innovations seem to have been made during this time. Under the supervision of Hoeroldt who, with age, had lost all creative power, the work went on in the old rut, this naturally caused many complaints. Besides as a result of the unfavourable conditions caused by the war, the factory had lost many of its ablest men. Karl Wilhelm Boehme who excelled in figure and landscape painting and Joh. Balthasar Borrmann who was considered one of the best painters of landscape and perspective fled to Berlin in 1761. The first mentioned, who was a brother-in-law of Dietrich (to be spoken of later) was employed in the Gotzkowsky factory and later in the Royal china factory and both did very good service. Boehme was made leader of the painters together with the artist Clauce; this office was filled by him till 1789. Another of Meissen's men, the mosaic-painter Karl Jak. Chr. Klipfel, worked himself up in the Berlin factory to the position of inspector 1763—86 and co-director 1786—1802[249].

It is therefore not surprising that Meissen was outdone by other factories, especially with regard to painting. It was but natural that in seeking for means to save it from further decay, this branch should have been first attended to.

V. ACADEMIC PERIOD (1763–74).

GENERAL MANAGEMENT.

The seven years' war caused not only incalculable pecuniary loss to the Meissen factory, but very greatly increased the number of competitors. This happened in the following manner: many men were dissatisfied with the conditions of life due to the disturbances of war, fled from Meissen and were only too gladly employed by other factories, where they made use of the knowledge acquired by them in Meissen. The greatest loss was sustained through the Vienna and Berlin factories. The former undertook to export a large quantity of china-ware to Turkey (this had before been done by Meissen), the latter was in 1763 overtaken by Friedrich II from its former owner Gotzkowsky. As a result of this not only the sale but the transit of Meissen china through Prussia was forbidden. Nevertheless the factory would soon have been able to regain what it had lost, had it been able to hold its own in the matter of artistic productions. This was however not the case. The painting was greatly neglected at that time and the sculptors did not take the change of tastes into consideration. But no proper means were taken to remedy this state of things. On March 23rd the direction was given into the hands of the Counsellor of commerce Helbig[251]. He was the very person who was mostly responsible for the faults. Alterations in the working of the factory can not be said to have originated at that time.

After the death of August III on October 5th 1763, the Elector Friedrich Christian who reigned but too shortly succeeded to the throne. This highly-gifted King, notwithstanding his delicate health, went energetically to work to restore order to the country. In this he was successfully supported by his spouse Maria Antonia. He entrusted her first with the whole state of finances and finally November 28th 1763 with the general management of the factory. Through this Helbig's power was broken. He was still for a short time a member of the commission consisting of the Privy chamber counsellor von Heynitz and Chamber counsellor von Fletscher

as well as himself and retained the management of the ware-houses. But von Nimpsch[252] who had to that time only been "Kommissar" was created a Privy counsellor and Director of the factory.

After the death of Friedrich Christian on December 17th 1763 his brother Xavier became regent during the minority of the Kurprinz (till 1768). Xavier, following in the steps of his brother, encouraged commerce, industry and art. Naturally he took the liveliest interest in the development of the Meissen factory and it was his desire to bring it to its former flourishing state again. Having recognized the decay of painting and art in Meissen, he founded an art School with the Court Artist and professor of the Dresden Academy of Arts

Page 62.
Fig. 133. PEDESTAL WITH
BASKET FOR PLATMENAGE, A59*.
29,5 cm.

Page 64.
Fig. 134. GLORIFICATION OF SAXONY, A80.
36 cm.

Page 64.
Fig. 135. RICH OLD WOMAN
WITH YOUNG LOVER, A *46.*
15 cm.

Christ. Wilh. Ernst Dietrich as principal. Hoeroldt and Kaendler had to subordinate themselves to him in questions concerning art. Besides it was one of his duties to bring one or more skilful sculptors to Meissen[253].

Although Dietrich tried his best to justify the trust put in him, he has been able to do but little. Through his school he put the work of the painters on a more artistic basis, it is also due to him that they practised drawing after plaster models of antique statues and painting after the good italian and netherlandic painters which had been lent from the possessions of the Elector. He, for instance, in July 1764 begged to be given two copper-engravings out of the Electoral library for use in the Meissen art-school "because they were quite unacquainted with antique here". He has not, however, been able to influence the artists in a favourable manner, quite the contrary. The painting on china lost all freshness and originality and an art, mostly imitated and without soul or sentiment began to reign in Meissen. This was not at all adapted to porcelain.

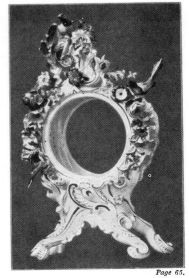

Page 65.
Fig. 136.   CLOCK-CASE, B *16.*
35 cm.

Page 65.
Fig. 137.   THE MUCH-WORRIED
HUSBAND, B 22.
18 cm.

It was soon realized that the installation of Dietrich in Meissen had been a mistake and on August 3rd 1770 the commission asked that he should be recalled, "as it had never been intended to have him constantly engaged at the factory"[256].

In order to increase the income of the factory in August 1764 sale by auction of the Meissen china was begun in different towns. In the same year Counsellor of the embassy Ernst took his leave from the commission. Dr. Poerner who had been created Counsellor of mines in 1770 was the ablest of the arcanists. Besides him Walther may be mentioned, he however at first caused loss to the factory by advising to use Seilitz clay instead of Schnorr's clay, because it was then not understood how to use it properly. In 1769 a number of employés was dismissed to lessen expenses[257].

Page 65.
Fig. 138.   AIR, C *99.*
13 cm.

As it was in the meantime recognised that the greatest danger was threatened by the superiority of the goods turned out in other factories, it was decided to seek the cause of their flourishing state and to learn from them. For this purpose Fletscher who had been created co-director went to Paris in 1766. He wished above all to learn the trend of french taste and to buy some models. He took two painters with him who were to obtain employment in Sèvres and learn the manufacture and use of the "effectful and beautiful royal blue" and to introduce it into the Meissen factory[258]. The painter Otto was sent to Holland to find out the

Page 65.
Fig. 139.   TUREENS.

D 10   D 9
26,5 cm.   20 cm.

Table 20

Pages 68, 75.

Works by Acier.

1. Gardners' group, F 94.   2 and 3. Galant figures, F 50, 51.   4. "Swedish court group", F 98.
21,5 cm.   14,5 cm., 14 cm.   24 cm.

5. Group of vine gatherers, F 92.   6. Loving group, B 75.   7. Girl at a churn, F 52.   8. Lessons in love, F 74.
16 cm.   22 cm.   17,5 cm.   30 cm.

9. Boy with target, F 54.
17 cm.

Fig. 140. THE LOVER DISCOVERED, D 64.
12,5 cm.
Page 65.

Page 65.
Fig. 141. CLOCK-CASE, D 16.
35,5 cm.

reason of the perceptible decrease in the sale of Meissen china there. For the investigation of new forms and tricks of technique, the modeller Mueller was sent to Vienna, Muenchen and Augsburg, while the painter and the modeller Hummitsch and Elsasser betook themselves to Paris on the same mission[259]. The two last took it upon themselves to obtain the consent of an able sculptor to come to Meissen. At first they believed to have found a fitting person in Delaistre. He however went back upon his word; but they succeeded in winning another Paris sculptor for Meissen. He was Michel Victor Acier (born at Versailles 1736). Both agents said that he had more experience, skill and possessed greater knowledge in miniature art than Delaistre. As the administration willingly agreed to their propositions Acier was installed in Meissen in the end of 1764.

Then the arcanists at home were requested to think of improvements and innovations. When they were called upon to report in 1766, Teichert wrote that he had found "a beautiful biscuit paste", Walther that he had combined a "pale, yellowish-brown glazing", Busch that he had produced in 1765 "the french or dark blue which had be to applied to the already baked china. The use of it was, to use his own words:—that, because it was applied to sharp baked china, the articles were not liable to crack or lose their shape, as in such cases where the colour was laid or put on under glaze"[260]. Then he had invented "a better white glazing and had ordered two kilns to be altered so that the chinaware came less cracked out of them". Only the arcanist Schertel resignedly declared that "since his release from the fortress of Koenigstein he had found out no improvement in the glazing, colouring, burning or in the paste itself, neither had he discovered anything new". A short time before this he had been accused by Hoeroldt of treason and imprisoned at Koenigstein. As his innocence was soon proved he was given back his freedom. In order to prevent such quarrels among the arcanists in future, Xavier decided to have them work, as far as possible, separately from each other. Shortly after in October 1765 Hoeroldt was pensioned off after having been employed at the factory for 45 years. He died in Meissen in 1775.

In 1765 it was decided, in order to find work for the wives and daughters of the workmen, to employ women as well, as a result 15 were engaged in painting in blue and 2 in lace making.

Kaendler's brother Christian Heinrich had in the mean time risen to the post of conductor of chambers. It was his duty as "chief of the turners and modellers" to give out and carry out all orders and to survey the plaster models. Although the last mentioned task seems to have been performed by him to the great satisfaction of the management, still the continual increase in the number of forms which had already in 1749 required more rooms was the cause of much inconvenience. Therefore it was decided in 1763 to have the models numbered and ordered the moulder Petri to do this[261]. He probably went to work by numbering the models one after the other, first the large and then the small

Fig. 142. MYTHOLOGICAL GROUPS.
Page 65.

D 28   D 57   D 58   D 44
19 cm.   30 cm.   31 cm.   19 cm.

forms, in order of their position. Both sorts had been placed separately as each had been modelled. Naturally many exceptions are to be found as the order had not always been strictly kept. When on June 19ᵗʰ 1764 number 3051 was reached, numbering with letters and figures was begun, the first models thus numbered bore the figures A *1—100*. The models numbered *1—3051* are such as were made before 19ᵗʰ July 1764. Certainly the china made at that time can not have numbers as, with the exception of the very last no numbering seems to have been done till 1763. For the forms which were made in the V Period we find A *1—100*, B *1—100* etc. till E *60*, for those made in the VI Period E *61—M 100*, for those in the VII N *1—T 183* (the articles numbered T *101* etc. were afterwards put aside, because they were models made from pressed glass and unfit for being made in chinaware). These numbers were made use of as elsewhere for VIII U *1—Y 57* etc. to Z *100*, then A *101* to *200* etc. These numbers give us an approximative idea as to the time when the different models originated, still we must consider that there may be some exceptions. Thus series which together required several years to make were either numbered all together or separated in the numeration. Then some series were numbered separately as the large apostles (*1—15*), the french criers (*1—40*), the comedy children (*1—12* in pairs marked *a* and *b*), the little gardners (in pairs *1—23*), the disguised cupids in various characters, also in pairs:— large series (*1—27*), small series (*1—25*), the "gallant band" (Desfort sorte) (*1—16*), the monkey band (*1—20*), shepherd's figures (in pairs *1—10*), the russian order (*1—40 —* 36 pieces are now kept in stock), screens (*1—244*), birds small series (*1—19*), as well as the following busts:— Apollo and the 9 muses (*1—10*), greek men of letters (*1—12*), the gods (*1—13*).

THE MODELLING.

The old models which had made the factory famous were, in many cases, still used. For instance those with applied chinese flowers and vine leaves seem to have still been popular, as well as the designs for table-services invented in the thirties and forties. Very seldom is any alteration in these noted. Thus Kaendler altered the shape of a dish belonging to the Ozier design in such a way as only to keep the outside curves. Besides he altered the old model of the small "Platmenage" "gave the figures the required beauty and arranged it so that the shell at the top could be screwed off". (This probably refers to illustration Fig. 133, A *59**.) In the new models the Rococo-style was used, it was only more luxuriant than before. But the study of the antique fostered by Dietrich made itself felt and greatly influenced the new style. Already at the beginning of the period this is distinctly noticeable and at the end of it the style was entirely altered into Louis XVI. The new lace-figures (Fig. 159) were an innovation that beautifully suited the new style. The lace on them was made by women, employed at the factory, who received a wage by two thirds lower than that paid to the men.

In order to increase the sale as much as possible, it was sought to produce such articles as the factory had never turned out, or such as had been before made in but rare occasions. Thus the printed catalogue[262] for 1765 contains among others the following china articles: — thimbles, flowers, penholders, scissor-cases, spools, needle-boxes, trinkets, waist-coat buttons, ear-rings of several shapes, watch-cases, cases for toothpicks, needle-boxes in the shape of asparagus, of babies in swathing clothes etc., ball-shaped boxes for soap and sponges, pomatum pots etc.

The management had for some time already disagreed with Kaendler's artistic views on china-production. He had been accustomed to working according to the qualities of the material, and was not quite able to go with the tide and adopt the new style resembling the antique. Besides

Page 65.

Fig. 143. VASE, D *18*.
58 cm.

Page 65.

Fig. 144. ST. PETER, D *72*.
55 cm.

Kaendler during the long time he had been employed in Meissen, must have altered in all respects. He was quite unable to go over to the style of Louis XVI as was required of him, although not even he remained altogether un-influenced by the new direction set for the style of chinaware. This difference of opinion in matters artistic led to rude contradiction between Kaendler and the manage-ment. This embittered Kaendler to such an extent, as to allow him to let his ill-humour make itself felt among the people working under him. In various reports, complaints of Kaendler may be read, it is said, that most sculp-tors remained but a short time in Meissen owing to his hard and rough treatment of them. For this reason it was sought to assure Acier's position with regard to

Fig. 145. TRIUMPHAL PROCESSION OF AMPHITRITE, 2.
48 cm.

Page 65.

Kaendler from the very beginning. Although the latter, during the ten years he co-operated with Acier, was still director of the modellers, Acier was made independent of him and received the title of "master of models" as well as Kaendler. Indeed when in 1767 Prince Xavier wished the models for the Electoral silverplate altered according to drawings of Meissen sculptors, it was expressly ordered that this should be done under the direction of Acier[264]. Kaendler who had before done such work to great satisfaction, had become un-fashionable with time. Notwithstanding this, he at this time still created a series of considerable works, which to day are esteemed much better than anything Acier has ever done. As he was unable to go with the tide in following the new taste, he had to stand back before his younger contemporaries.

Kaendler began as a sculptor in Barock-style and has, with his bold, excellent, pithy and effectful modelling, laid the foundation stone of European porcelain plastique. In the forties he changed his style from Barock to Rococo and it is astonishing how he now put less stress on the fineness and boldness of the lines, but managed, in the new style, to combine lightness with daintiness and grace and often with a pleasing humour as well. Indeed in the last years he attempted, in his own manner to adapt himself to the new direction with its tendency to the antique.

As a result of the investigation of the Meissen archives the conclusion has been fall-ing down as that the elegant little figures in Rococo-style, which did so much to bring the factory to a flourishing state, were the work of Acier. This opinion was held by me as well till 1900 — but it has been since proved that these statuettes were the work of Kaendler and his pupils, especially Reinicke. It has already been above intimated that the french

Fig. 146. MERCURY, 30.
31 cm.

Page 65.

Fig. 147. SATURN, *31*.
32 cm. (to hand).

Page 65.

criers were not the work of Acier, but had probably already been modelled by Kaendler and Reinicke during the seven years' war.

During this period Kaendler's work still embraced a great deal. Under peculiar circumstances he began working at the group depicted Fig. 134, A *80* on the name day of Prince Xavier. This group is a glorification of the Electoral house of Saxony, where it is represented surrounded by allegories of Time, of Happiness, Glory, Sculpture and Art[265]. As the Prince had expressed the wish to be present at the commencement of the modelling of chinaware, he came to Meissen, with several members of the Saxon Royal Family, where Kaendler showed him what he had wished to see. This pleased everybody so much that the Elector's spouse ordered the tablet which was held by "Time" to be engraved with the following words: — "the 3rd December 1765, the name day of his Royal Highness the Regent has been celebrated at the Meissen China Factory"[266]. It can be proved that the shepherds' group with the letter-carrying pigeon (Table 13, A *29*) originated in 1764. The greater part of the monkey band must have been made by Kaendler in the former period. This is certainly true of the director of this band which had already been delivered to Berlin to Frederick the Great. But some of the monkeys, for instance the fiddler or the bag-pipe player (Table 6, *6* and *8*) seem to have been made by him in 1765. In the same year he created a large number of groups and figures. Thus a parrot (Table 4, A *43*) for the Regent[267], a rich old woman with her young lover (Fig. 135, A *46*)[268], the "French doctor group" consisting of a loving couple: — a young girl and Cupid dressed as an Abbé, the "cherry group" where several people gather fruit from a cherry tree (*2229*), a number of small mythological busts[269], and the child-comedians for Herr von Kayserling, to which the Columbine and Pantaleone on Table 14, *11*[a] and [b] probably belong[270].

Page 66.

Fig. 148. THE PARCAE, *33*.
37 cm.

Page 66.

Fig. 149. APOLLO AND MINERVA, *32*.
38 cm.

Table 21

Pages 66, 75, 76.

Works by Schoenheit.

1. Girl with goat, H 81.   2 and 3. Bird-catchers (woman and man), D 78, 79.   4. Boy with goat, H 82.
14 cm.   18,5 cm., 18 cm.   14 cm.

5. Venus, Cupid and Nymph, G 83.   6. The good father, H 98.   7. Venus, Cupid and Mercury, G 84.
20,5 cm.   21 cm.   21 cm.

8. Loving group, E 14.   9. "Love and reward", I 65.   10. Loving group, E 13.
18 cm.   28 cm.   18 cm.

Page 66.
Fig. 150. CANDELABRE, A33.
34 cm.

Page 66.
Fig. 151. GARDNERS GROUP,
B60.
37,5 cm.

In 1766 Kaendler made to order a clock-case copiously ornamented with Rococo-flourishes and flowers, for the Chevalier de Saxe. It was very carefully copied from a model cast in metal and gilt by fire (Fig. 136, B16). At the same time he made a group of three figures, the meaning of which was borrowed from one of Aesop's fables, for England (Fig. 137, B22)[271]. In 1769 Kaendler made a Bologna dog, probably the one on Table 4, 2841, and renovated the capture of the Tritons (Table 5, C35) for the Prince Regent. Whether the last group was originally made or only renovated by Kaendler can not be said with certainty, some of it is not quite in Kaendler's style. In 1770 a series of the "Elements" were modelled of which Fig. 138, C99 represents air[272]; as well as both tureens intended for Venice (Venetia), one of these was in the shape of a hen and seven chickens (Fig. 139, D9), the other in that of a rooster (Fig. 139, D10), the group of the "lover discovered" (Fig. 140, D64)[273] and lastly the portrait of the Empress Katharine II of Russia on horseback in male apparel which he made as "pendant" to the Empress Elisabeth in the same guise. Both are here represented on Table 12, the one under C92, the other under 1059[274].

Kaendler's first work in 1771 was a copiously ornamented clock-case similar to the one made in 1766 (Fig. 141, D16), then a series of figures of the Italian Comedy which had so often been treated by him.

Page 66.
Fig. 152. GIRL WITH BIRD'S NEST, A78.
22 cm.

Table 13 shows at the top some of the statuettes which originated at that time — Ortolana (D33), Pulcinella (D30), the avvocato (D37) and the Coviello (D43). Besides the four representations on Fig. 142:—a group of a satyr and a human being (D28), a satyr pouring wine into his mouth while galloping on a he-goat (D44) and two groups of a satyr and a nymph, each with a small boy satyr at their side (D57 and 58). The three last groups had been ordered from Venice. Kaendler at this time modelled two large pieces for Rome:—Table 6, D14 represents the Mother of God appearing to the Holy Bishop of Palafox

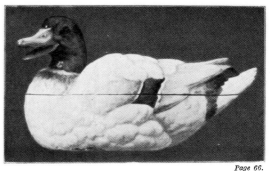

Fig. 153. TUREEN, G78.
Page 66.
17 cm.

and Mendoza (born 1600, died 1659)[275] and a tall vase (Fig. 143, D18). The shape of the last points to the fact that Kaendler was already very well acquainted with the Louis XVI style[276]. The same may be said of the vase illustrated on Table 22, D91.

In 1772 he made the St. Peter represented on Fig. 144, D72, the socle is ornamented with antique ornamentation and a laurel-wreath. It was part of a large order received from the Saxon Court which consisted of the saint Peter mentioned above and the saints Anthony, Laurence, Joseph and Francis, besides a mountain of Calvary.

Page 66.
Fig. 154. HUNTER ON HORSEBACK, A63.
9 cm.

In 1772—74 a large order was executed for the Russian Empress Katharina II. It consisted of no fewer than 40 allegorical and mythological groups, some of which glorified the Empress[277]. Fig. 145, 2 represents the triumphal procession of Amphitrite who is driving through the clouds on a shell-like chariot drawn by dolphins and surrounded by sea-gods; while three small geniuses are flying round her. Kaendler did the drawing of this group in November 1772, began the model in December and completed it in January 1773[278]. In February of the following year he began to make a model of a Mercury sitting in a chariot drawn by ravens and accompanied by a genius (Fig. 146, 30)[279]. In March a Saturn driving in a chariot drawn by dragons[280] (Fig. 147, 31). Both last groups are here meant to represent

Page 66.
Fig. 155.
BOY WITH BIRD,
A79.
23 cm.

Fig. 156. POTPOURRI VASE, A 88.
23 cm.

the constellations of like name. The group of the three Parcae with Saturn and a genius[281] (Fig. 148, 33) dates from June. In April he made Apollo triumphing over a Python whom (Apollo) Minerva and genius accompany[282] (Fig. 149, 32).

The production of all these groups, only a few of which have been here mentioned as examples, was a very long and difficult task and it must be taken as a certainly that Kaendler was quite unable to make them all without assistance. Of his former assistants, Punct worked with him till 1765 (Fig. 150, A 33 represents Punct's last piece of work) and Reinicke till 1768. Fig. 151, B 60 shows a group in which the gardners' children hail from Kaendler's earlier time, while the main pedestal and the four single side ones were made by Reinicke in 1767 and show the new style. Besides these two assistants Kaendler employed the embosser Christ. Gottlob Luecke[283], Hauptmann and Schoenheit. Only the last mentioned seems to have been an able modeller, while both others soon had to return to their ordinary occupation. Only a very few pieces of china can be proved to be the independent work of their hands. A figure of a girl with a bird's nest (Fig. 152, A 78) was made by Luecke in December 1765, after a plaster cast. He also in 1781, that is in the next period, made a tureen in the shape of a duck (Fig. 153, G 78) while a vase with two handles and antique decorations is mentioned as the work of Hauptmann.

Fig. 157. GARDNER'S WIFE, B 65.
49 cm.

Fig. 158. THE GERMAN BACCHUS, D 13.
21 cm.

Johann Carl Schoenheit has in this period often had to repair old models, but his chief work consisted in finishing Kaendler's work. When Acier came to Meissen he employed Schoenheit more and more, while Juechtzer took his place as Kaendler's assistant. Thus Schoenheit helped to work at renovating the capture of the Tritons, at the figures of Italian comedy, at the Satyr-groups and lastly at the russian order. I mention further that he in 1765 renovated, among other work, seven figures of the "gallant band" for which the merchant Desfort sent coloured drawings from France. (In the catalogue for 1765 musical figures Desf. s. are mentioned.) They can not as was formerly supposed he ascribed to Acier, but were created in Meissen before his time. The following of Schoenheit's independent works may be here mentioned as dating from 1765:—a small hunter on horseback (Fig. 154, A 63), a boy holding a bird in both hands (this group Fig. 155, A 79 was made after a plaster cast) — from 1766, a potpourri vase carried by three cupids and showing two heads in relief (Fig. 156, A 88) — from 1767 a female gardner with a flower basket and a wreath (Fig. 157, B 65) — from 1770 the German Bacchus (Fig. 158, D 13) — from 1772 "Sentiment" as a lace-figure[284] (Fig. 159, E 4), a group in which fowls are metamorphised into gods of love[285] (Fig. 160, E 9), two loving couples, one with a peasant and the other with a soldier (Table 21, E 13—14) and two bird-catchers (man and woman) (Table 21, D 78—79).

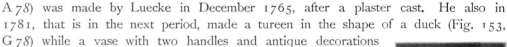

Fig. 159. SENTIMENT, E 4.
14 cm.

For a short time Jean Troy from Luneville was employed in the factory. Having been recommended by several Paris merchants he came to Meissen on September 1st 1768. After having worked on trial for four months, he was employed as a sculptor at a salary of 400 talers. He was however dismissed on May 23rd

Fig. 160. LOVE GROUP, E 9.
18 cm.

Fig. 161. "THE RENDEZ-VOUS BETRAYED", C 17.
27 cm.

Fig. 162. WATER, D 81.
23 cm.

Page 67.

Fig. 163. LOVE GROUP, B 100.
22 cm.

Page 68.

1770 owing to his frivolousness and unfitness for the work[286]. The group represented on Fig. 161, C 17, the "rendez-vous betrayed" is a result of his work in Meissen. Peculiarly formed ruins and unskilful combination are characteristic of him.

In April 1766 the embosser Chr. Gottl. Berger who had been employed at the Meissen factory for six years before, was recalled, although he was known as "given to drink and possessing wild habits of life". While away from Meissen he had been employed for five years in the Sèvres factory as a "sculptor in china working from nature". He seems to have done more for Meissen technically than artistically. Credit for some innovations — such as burning in the enamel-oven with wood instead of charcoal — is due to him[287].

Acier who as above mentioned came to Meissen in 1764 took a leading part among the sculptors. Indeed his artistic ability was esteemed higher than Kaendler's. After having spent but a few months in Meissen, he seems to have regretted having left Paris. The factory managed to keep him in Meissen at a large sacrifice. His wages had to be raised from 455 to 800 talers and he was promised a pension of 400 talers if he stayed in Saxony for 15 years; this sum was to be halved if he left for France[288].

Michel Victor Acier was born in Versailles in 1736. At the end of 1764 he was engaged as "master of models" in Meissen and was pensioned off in 1781. He died on February 16th 1799 in Dresden where he had moved to after having been pensioned off. The documental proofs of his work in Meissen, which have only a short time ago become known, show that a great change must be made of his valuation as an artist. The high respect which his ability was held in Meissen and the preference shown him before Kaendler do not seem at all justified. It can however be explained by the fact that he better than Kaendler knew how to adapt himself Dietrich's "classic" style. A traditional overestimation of Acier was probably the reason why everything that was well made in this period has been ascribed to him. The french criers and the "gallant band" are an instance in point. The credit for them is really due to Kaendler who, notwithstanding his old age had lost neither his rich fancy nor his creative power and created such models as, in our eyes far surpass anything ever made by Acier. As proof of this, I should like to compare Kaendler's boldly modelled triumphal procession of Amphitrite (Fig. 145) of 1772 with the weak group (Fig. 162, D 81) allegorising "Water" after a coloured drawing

Fig. 165. LOVE GROUP, D 93.
46 cm.

Page 68.

sent him from Paris in the same year by a "veuve Lair" "invented" by Acier and produced by Schoenheit. Acier showed neither the rich fancy so characteristic of Kaendler nor his excellent treatment of the material. He mostly, as in the case mentioned above, worked either after drawings sent him from France or after shaded drawing by Schoenau (see page 80). His own inventions all smack of sentiment and home life, this was however quite in accordance with the spirit of the time. His figures are short and stout, his heads comparatively large,

Fig. 164. COMMERCE, C 42.
13,5 cm.

Page 68.

but fairly expressionless. His manner of composition is not particularly fitting for china groups. He does not have them showing to effect in front, as was customary before but attempts to make all-round figures.

Of Acier's productions belonging to this time I notice the following:—Table 20, B*75* shows a sentimental group, in which a mother holds her sleeping child in her lap; it was probably made by himself in 1767. In the other cases Acier only began and probably corrected the models, while the execution may be ascribed

Page 68.
Fig. 166. CHILD AND DOG, E*77*.
19 cm.

to Schoenheit who soon worked quite in accordance with his ideas. The group (Fig. 163, B *100*) of a cavalier kneeling befor a peasant while a young girl is standing in the back-ground was made in 1768. In 1769 he created 13 groups of allegorical meaning each of which consisted of two children, War (Table 19, C*40*), Astronomy (Table 19, C*46*) and Commerce (Fig. 164, C*42*) may serve as examples. Of the productions of the year 1770 I mention various groups of children representing "Gardening and Culture of the Vine", a cook sitting on two sea-shells, groups of the gods Mars, Minerva, Ceres. The group (Table 19, D*17*) representing the getting out of the pit was made in 1777, "Fire" (Table 19, D *80*) in 1772 and the group consisting of six standing or sitting figures on a high rock under a tree (Fig. 165, D*93*)[289]. Of the year 1773 I shall mention a fairly large gardner group of seven figures and of 1774 a group in which a figure is standing next to a pillar crowned with a vase and a casque and has a crane over it, a sleeping lady leaning her arm against a table, and lastly a girl at a child's cradle (Table 19, E*76*). With the help of Juechtzer who will be spoken of afterwards, Acier in 1774 made the group (Fig. 166, E*77*) of a child lying down and playing with a dog. Acier's further work will be spoken of in the next period.

THE PAINTING.

The classic style introduced by Dietrich influenced the painting as well as the sculpture of this period. In 1766 "à la Greque" is spoken of in 1766, table china is ornamented with an Etruscan border and in 1768 plates are painted with "design 'à la Greque' and flowers". Pearl edges, hoops, ribbons, laurel and oak wreaths, flowering branches and festoons came more and more into vogue, and German flowers (daisies, reseda and a border of Leontodon flower) began to preponderate. Then patterns were used in which peacocks' feathers, strawberries and cherries as well as angels with their attributes, fowls and sheep appeared. Many miniature portraits on goblets, cups and plates originated at this time as well thus, among others, that of the Empress Elizabeth of Russia and Maria Amalia Augusta spouse of the Elector of Saxony. The paintings in camaïeu (in one colour) seem to have been very popular. Scarlet was used for this most of all; little roses, other flowers, landscapes, birds, animals, fowl, hunting scenes and cupids; old chinese patterns as well:—such as the "little tables", corn-ears, rocks and flowers were then painted in scarlet. Pink and blue were also used for one colour painting, Mosaik borders had been used before but were now more frequently made in green, blue and scarlet. The catalogue of 1765, mentioned above, gives us a good idea of what was then particularly popular. The chinaware painted in blue under glaze or that painted on a brown or light yellow ground had a large sale. Everything appeared plain or ribbed. As new patterns in blue under glazing the following are mentioned:—designs with four shields and an inner border, with flowers and fruit or garlands or insects; with hanging garlands at the border and playing children "à la Raphael" in the centre.

In coloured painting the following patterns seem to have been new:—with scarlet hoops twisted round with many-coloured flower-wreaths, with scarlet hoops and flowers and garlands, a figure "en treillage" with painting of peasants after Erfurt. In Turkish cups the following designs are mentioned as new:—coloured flowers and red thread, red garlands, strewn flowers in scarlet and green, flower baskets in scarlet and green four scarlet shields, green and scarlet festoons, with twisted garlands, with green-leaves above and red flowers and gold beneath.

Snuff-boxes seem to have been exceedingly popular. No fewer than 34 kinds of them are enumerated. They were painted with flowers, fruits, landscapes, views of buildings, figures, scenes borrowed from mythology or history, or with battles on horseback à la Wouwermann.

In 1763 painting was divided into the four following groups:—miniature, figure, flower and blue painting. In 1771 three workers in coloured glazing were put in charge of this particular brand of painting Wagner, Brecheisen, Heynemann and Birckner are mentioned as particularly skilful painters.

Johann Jakob Wagner had been manager of a department of painting since 1745. In 1765 he painted upon a credenz-plate (waiter) representation of Apollo and Daphne which is particularly praised. Joseph Brecheisen had been called from Vienna because Dietrich thought him indispensable. He is supposed to have stayed for some time in Berlin where he made lovely snuff-boxes. In 1766 he was created Court Artist and ordered to take in Dietrich's absence his place as manager of the painting division. Heynemann also in 1774 received the title of Court Artist, because of the skill he showed in his art. Gottlob Siegmund Birckner, manager of departement, had to supervise the drawing lessons after Fehling's death in 1754 and in place of the late Hentzschel had to see to the division of work among the painters[290].

VI. PERIOD:

MARCOLINI (1774–1813).

GENERAL MANAGEMENT.

In making the Real privy counsellor Count Camillo Marcolini "manager and director" of the china factory on August 20th 1774, the Elector Friedrich August III thought that he was entrusting its fate into firm hands. The former director Privy counsellor von Nimpsch had died in December 1773[291] at the age of 76 years. Although Marcolini very eagerly went to work and was indefatigable in finding out any mismanagement and in proposing improvements, he did not prove fit to overcome the many difficulties and adverse circumstances connected with the management of the factory. He was only able temporarily to stay the decay which had begun to make itself felt in the former period, but was incapable of entirely warding it off.

The rival factories kept on improving their productions and competition was becoming dangerous for Meissen. Besides this the sale of Saxon china was in many countries forbidden or combined with difficulties. Austria, Prussia, Denmark, Sweden and Portugal forbad the importation of it, Russia demanded 40, France, England and Spain 50—60% duty. All connection with Turkey was severed owing to the disturbances there, while Holland possessed a new china factory in Loosdrecht. Thus the factory lost almost all sale for the more valuable porcelain. But, with regard to the ordinary chinaware, it was not much better off either. For the small Thueringia factories had flooded the market with cheap china utensils. As some of them found out that the customers in Russia and Poland preferred articles marked with the Electoral swords they sometimes used this trade mark or one similar to it[292].

Further much injury was done to Meissen by the stone-ware which was at first in great quantities brought from England to Germany and was afterwards imitated by most german fayence factories.

The market was then overcrowded with keramic productions. Meissen had itself fostered this by encouraging auction sales of china[293]. It is therefore not surprising that the sale in the depôts as well as on the Leipsic fair decreased, while orders became fewer year by year. In addition to this the expenses had become considerably greater. Thus it was complained that the wages had become higher, that the apprentices were too well paid and that some work was considered as "over-time" and paid for accordingly without there being any necessity for it.

Page 13.
Fig. 167. CLOCK-CASE WITH CUPID, F 36
31 cm.

Page 75.
Fig. 168. FREDERICK THE GREAT, F 96.
45 cm.

Table 23

Pages 76, 77.

Works by Juechtzer.

1 and 2. Children groups, H 36 and 39.   3. Hero and Leander, I 11.   4. Venus and Cupid, G 72.
12,5 cm., 11,5 cm.   30 cm.   19 cm.

5. Minerva, I 45.   6. Venus, H 57.   7. Bacchus, G 57.   8. The peace, G 31.
20 cm.   18 cm.   19,5 cm.   30 cm.

Page 75.
Fig. 169. GELLERT-MONUMENT, F 90.
30,5 cm.

The investigation of this state of things led Marcolini in 1775 to the conclusion that if the factory went on working in this way, it would yearly show a deficit of 50000 talers. To mend matters he made the three following propositions:—1. That 150 employés should be dismissed or 2. that a monthly contribution of the sum of 4—5000 talers should be made to the factory, or 3. that the wages, pensions and payment for piece work should be lowered.

On January 13th 1776 it was decided to accept the third proposition. The salaries of the employés and the

Page 76.
Fig. 171. PARIS AND APOLLO.
H 42   H 46
27 cm.   26,5 cm.

earnings of the workers by the piece were therefore considerably lowered[294]. Further, by a printed order of October 3rd 1775 the sale of china marked with the Electoral swords or similar marks was forbidden in Saxony. On April 7th 1779 the order was renewed and in that sense enlarged that the sale of china without a mark was also prohibited[295]. In November 1772 the depôt in Warsaw had to be closed for a short time. Marcolini opened new ones in Cassel and Spa[296].

Through these and some other sharp cutting alterations the state of the factory slightly improved so that it was possible to increase the salaries again in October 1777. This was a very urgent measure as the employés were beginning to show dissatisfaction[297].

Count Marcolini had an able assistant in the person of Poerner, Counsellor of mines, who after having been called commissioner in 1777 managed in that quality the works alone for several years[298]. The Counsellor of the legation Clauder seems to have been of little importance, having received the post of second Commissioner in October 1783, he tendered his resignation in May 1789. Ludwig von Wedel seemed more fit for the position. He was made a captain and received Clauder's place on March 16th 1793. Up to that time he had been first lieutenant in the Grenadier Body guard. His principal duty was the overseeing of the factory's people[299]. Poerner died on April 13th 1796 and the

Pages 75, 76 and 77.
Fig. 170. CUPIDS, LOVE GROUPS AND MYTHOLOGICAL GROUPS.
G 30   18   G 29   149   19   160
19 cm.   29,5 cm.   19 cm.   31 cm.   36,5 cm.   30 cm.

Page 76.
Fig.173. SOCRATES, K 5.
18,5 cm.

Page 76.
Fig. 174. GROUP OF THE VINE-DRESSERS, I 2.
30 cm.

Fig. 172. LEDA, BACCHUS, HERCULES, HEBE.

I 18	I 20	I 42	I 16
19 cm.	19 cm.	19 cm.	19 cm.

Pages 76 and 77.

chief-controller Steinauer who had been made the third Commissioner was the man really to succeed Poerner.

Marcolini does not seem to have been particularly lucky in the choice of his helpers. At any rate he was obliged to renew his complaints about want of money in May 1788. The 13524 talers owing from Helbig's heirs[300] were paid by the government office, a part of the 2nd and 3rd class painters were put for some time on half pay, but this was not much use. In 1790 he was so pressed for money that he begged for a contribution of 30000 talers and a loan of 9000 talers. At the same time Poerner received permission to arrange a lottery in which half the premiums were to be paid in money and half in chinaware. Afterwards two other lotteries followed[301]. Notwithstanding all these devices it was impossible to think of keeping the factory going for any length of time. Therefore on July 4th 1799 Marcolini, whose spirit was greatly perturbed at all the failures of his attempts to do his duty by the factory, asked to be allowed to take his leave on July 4th 1799. The Elector, by speaking in flattering terms of his work persuaded him not to leave his post. As a result of this Marcolini who had been created chief-master of equerry went on complaining in the old way.

The affairs of the factory took a turn for the better from 1804 to the middle of 1806. During this time savings to the extent of 40000 talers were made. But as disturbances of war again threatened the factory, this money was soon again swallowed up. On May 28th 1807 Marcolini reported that the sale of chinaware had almost altogether stopped, new orders had not been received and bills had not been paid. Besides the roads were so uncertain that it was a risky matter to send porcelain away. He again asked for pecuniary assistance which he received. 5000 talers monthly were paid him till 1813 which makes a sum of 325000 talers. In 1810 the conditions were so unfavourable that all work had to be discontinued at the factory. This would not do as the workmen threatened to mutiny. The works were therefore reopened, the price of the goods set still lower than had already been done in 1790 and the sale of unpainted porcelain — which was in such great favour — permitted. The last mentioned permission was a desperate measure taken by the management, as it was certain to result in ultimate loss. But any means for getting money seemed to be justified by the low ebb of the finances.

On September 1st 1813 military authorities had some rooms of the factory arranged for the accomodation of soldiers. They also informed the management that the Albrechtsburg would be turned into a fortress. Matters seem however not to have gone so far. On January 1st 1814 Marcolini took his leave, the died soon after on July 10th in Prague.

Kuehn who later filled the position of manager of the factory expressed the opinion that the finances of the factory were in so sore a plight, because it had not made a full and proper use of its business connection with Russia. I do not myself quite share this opinion. The export of Meissen china to Russia had certainly been great, but not so exclusive as Kuehn supposes. Russia mostly obtained its supply of chinaware from the Warsaw depôt. After the first division of Poland in 1772 this depôt had to be closed, though only for a short time, but was again opened in 1796. It had been closed by order of the Prussians who then ruled there. They had conceded the sale of prussian china, to an undertaker with the exclusion of all

Fig. 175. BROTH BASIN, F42.
18 cm.

Page 76.

other china. In order not to be obliged to carry stock valued at 80000 talers back to Saxony, the agent Nahke brought it to two Russian towns Dubno and Wilna and sold it there in two or three years. After the King of Saxony in 1807 had been made Governor of Warsaw; Marcolini in 1809 proposed that a warehouse should be built there, as from Warsaw "they could more easily deal with Russia". In 1813, besides large orders from Constantinople and England as important an order from Russia is mentioned[304]. These very few facts I have been able to gather from Marcolini's very detailed reports. Certainly many mercantile faults have been made, but it is my firm belief, that the decay of the factory was more due to the deterioration of its goods, than to adverse circumstances. The Louis XVI style took the place of the old Rococo which so exceedingly well adapted itself to china. As the style smacked of the antique straight lines were used, narrower forms were preferred and greater symmetry had to be observed. Narrow pearl rods, wreaths with ribbons twisted round them, or intertwining rings were used to decorate socles, the Maeander or the Palmette ornaments used in some parts were painted or plastically decorated with torches thyrsos-rods, sickles etc. Other parts were painted with narrow-hangings, peculiarly creased and folded ribbon bows, or with oval medalions wreathed with laurel. In the medalions heads were portrayed and letters formed of flowers were painted.

In the Empire style which came into vogue in the last decade of the 18th century the same patterns were used, only they were more boldly formed. They were often executed more thoughtfully, but lost much of their elegance and gracefulness. The artists kept returning to the classic style, made sphinxes, pyramids, swans, crowns and other things alluding to the triumphal march of Napoleon and glorifying it. Sometimes the figure of the conqueror took part in the representations. This caused a cold and dry style which showed little lightness or grace. It was not original and showed all the faults of the style it sought to imitate in an exaggerated manner. The freshness and strength of the latter we here vainly seek, while the richness of imagination and gracefulness of style of Kaendler's art entirely disappeared.

THE MODELLING.

One of Marcolini's duties was to make peace between Kaendler, Acier and the "leader of the white brigade". The last-mentioned position was now filled by the former embosser Joh. Dav. Elsasser. On September 15th 1774 Marcolini arranged the competence of each of them in the following manner[305]: — Elsasser had to enter each order in a book, kept for the purpose, and to inform Kaendler of it. The latter had the right of choosing half of all the work to be executed for himself, leaving the rest to be done by Acier. When the model was ready it was given by Elsasser to the moulders and embossers while Kaendler or Acier, as the case might be, each saw to the execution of his own models.

This order of things lasted but a short time as Kaendler died on May 18th 1775. To be sure he seems to have worked at his own models and at instructing the apprentices to the last. In the beginning of 1775 he still began making an Italian gondolier holding an oar in his hand, while Juechtzer had to finish this statuette. Probably foreseeing his speedy death he gave sculpture lessons to three young men (Juechtzer,

Fig. 176. THE THREE GRACES, H71.
41 cm.

Page 76.

Page 77.
Fig. 177. APOLLO, G 89.
25,5 cm.

Page 77.
Fig. 178. FAUN, H 41.
24 cm.

Starcke and Luecke) on Wednesdays and Saturdays from 11 to 12 and wanted them to sit close near him to study his working. He did this, to use his own expression, "so as not to take his art and knowledge with him to the grave". By Kaendler's demise the factory sustained an immeasurably great loss. It lost the man who had for 44 years striven, by the exercise of his art and his untiring energy, to bring it to a high artistic level. In opening to it all the rich stores of his imagination and in putting his artistic knowledge at its disposal, he has been able to do more for the factory (as far as art is concerned) than any man before or since.

As great trust was put in Acier and great faith in his ability, it was not thought necessary to find a man to succeed Kaendler. After having been employed 15 years in Meissen, the former according to the contract made with him had to be pensioned off with 400 talers on January 1st 1781. As the reasons for his resignation he informed the management that his eyes had greatly suffered and that "he had not had the opportunity of showing his full creative power because his sphere of action had been too limited". He moved to Dresden where he died on February 16th 1799[306].

Page 77.
Fig. 179. CHILDREN FOR
SACRIFICE.
134   128
15 cm.   15 cm.

One of the largest pieces of work executed by Acier with Schoenheit's assistance was a centerpiece consisting of three groups and two temples belonging to. In them the idea of glorifying the reign of the Elector Friedrich August III was to be expressed. The first group seems to have consisted of a pyramid ornamented with the portraits of August II, August III and Friedrich Christian, and the personifications of Virtue, Knowledge, Peace and Mercy as well as the nine muses. In the second group the china- and textile industries of the country as well as the making of lace (including blond lace) were represented, while a large Saxonia, accompanied by Abundance and Fertility, stood over them. The third group consisted of 12 figures and showed an idealization of Commerce, Agriculture and Mining (F 57). To the last the two above mentioned temples belong, one in Doric-style with a figure of Victory inscribing the Elector's glorious deeds on a tablet (F 58 and 65), the other in Corinthian-style with a figure of Virtue holding a golden ring in one hand and a sun — representing in this instance "Truth" — in the other (F 59 and 66)[307].

Then Acier in 1779 produced a group of 12 figures which is supposed to represent the glory of Prince Henry of Prussia. It contains a Minerva holding a medalion with the Prince's portrait, a Mars with drawn sword, three of the Prince's generals (among them Moellendorf), personifications of the Elbe, of Dresden etc. The motive for this group was given by the war for the succession of Bavaria in which Prince Henry of Prussia led the Prussians together with the Saxons. The declaration of peace in Teschen in the spring of 1779 was to result in a far grander order for Meissen. It was thought necessary to make Count Repnin — who had in so skilful a way intermediated between Saxony, Prussia and Austria — a valuable present. Acier was

Page 77.
Fig. 180. CHILDREN FOR SACRIFICE.
138   156   121
15 cm.   15 cm.   14,5 cm.

entrusted with the modelling of groups intended as a present for this russian Count. These consisted of seven groups glorifying the Russian Empire and Count Repnin[309], their socles were ornamented with a collection of nicely polished Saxon pebbles set in gold or bronze and a dessert service of 60 plates, with all the large and small dishes, fruit-baskets, basins and ice-pails for bottles and glasses belonging to it. On the richly gilt plates:—views of Dresden, Pillnitz, Teschen, Petersburg, Moskaw etc. were very delicately painted.

Page 77.
Fig. 181. THE HAPPINESS
OF SLEEP, I 13.
36 cm.

In March 1781 all these china articles were ready for several days' exhibition in Dresden. They had to be produced in great haste as it was to appear like an incidental gift. It is quite plain that all the figures could not be newly modelled but several old ones were used as well. The Minerva and the Mars in the principal group were, according to description, quite identical with those of the Prince Henry group.

The clock-case (illustrated on Fig. 167, F 36) is possibly still the work of Kaendler, but the cupid with the bow and arrow standing next to it is Acier's work. In 1778 the latter modelled Frederick the Great on horseback — a hussar is handing him a letter. The socle of this statue is of oval shape and is ornamented with emblems (Fig. 168, F 96). The horse was made by Schoenheit.

The Meissen factory has produced three different Gellert-monuments. The first of these is in

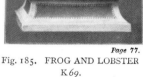

the form of a pyramid ornamented with Gellert's portrait in relief and crowned with "Fame" and a genius, on its socle a weeping female figure and a flying genius may be seen, it was probably made by Kaendler[310]. The second and third monument is the production of Acier. The first of these is an urn standing on a broken pillar — which is ornamented with Gellert's portrait in relief — and surrounded by the Three Graces represented by children (1777, F 72). The last consists of a sarcophagus on which Erudition and Religion holding Gellert's portrait in the clouds are seated (1778, Fig. 169, F 90)[311].

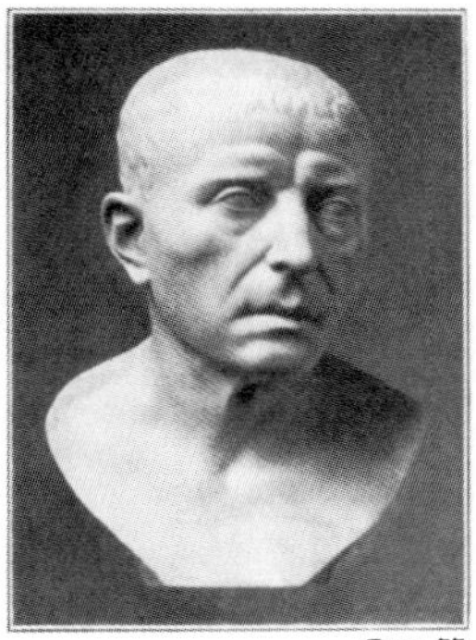

Of Acier's work I further mention the so called "device children" — little charming Cupids shooting hearts, encouraging lovers, calming them etc. — which are always accompanied by an explanation such as:—"Je mets le calme", "Je les accouple". They were made in 1775 after Schoenau's drawings (Table 19, F 5 and 9). The Cupids on Fig. 170, G 29 and 30 as well as Table 20, F 54 and 52 belong to other series. In the Teaching of Love (Table 20, F 74) a large group representing a similar idea is found. Then he has often treated the so-called "gallant-figures" in which the ladies dresses often show lace work. To these figures Table 19, F 34 and Table 20, F 50 and 51 belong as well as the so-called Swedish court group (Table 20, F 98), a girl at a child's cradle (Table 19, E 76), while the following are symbolical groups:—a brocken bridge, the brocken eggs (Table 19, F 63 and 65) as temptation and its results, as well as the vine dressers' and the gardners' groups (Table 20, F 92 and 94).

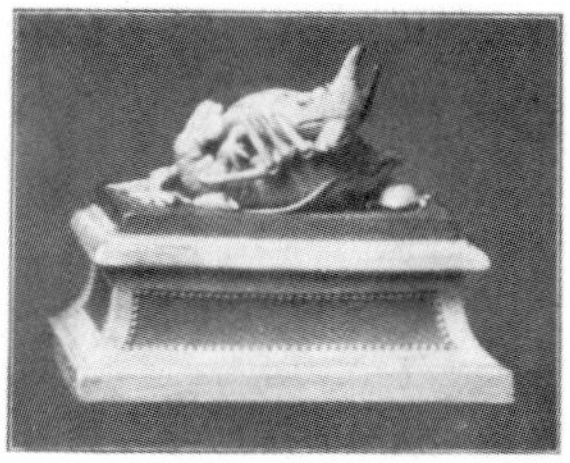

It has been intimated above that Acier made use of the assistance of Schoenau who soon worked quite according to his ideas. Where the records do not particularly point to one or the other as the originator (and here sometimes contradictions are met with), it is difficult to divide the work of the two. Of the following I believe to be able to state that they are principally Schoenheit's work. On Table 21 a girl

Fig. 182. PRIESTESSES OF VESTA. Page 77.
M 13 33,5 cm. H 84 30,5 cm. L 97 34 cm.

Fig. 183. BUST OF CICERO, L 40. 25 cm. Page 77.

Fig. 185. FROG AND LOBSTER K 69. 17 cm. Page 77.

Fig. 184. APOLLO, DIANA, JUPITER, VESTA, BACCHUS, CERES. Page 77.
H 5 12,5 cm. H 8 12 cm. H 9 12,5 cm. H 6 12,3 cm. H 11 12,3 cm. H 12 12,7 cm.

Page 77.

Fig. 186. APOLLO, VASE, VENUS, FAUN, GRINDER.

H 80   E 54   G 85   I 52   G 68

37 cm.   37 cm.   34 cm.   17 cm.   24 cm.

and a boy with a goat (H 81 and 82), Venus, Cupid and a Nymph (G 83), Venus, Cupid and Mercury (G 84), the good father (H 98), Love and Reward (I 65). The imitation of the classic style is distinctly shown by Fig. 171 Paris (H 42), Apollo (H 46), Fig. 172 Leda (I 18), Hercules when young (I 42) and Hebe (I 16). (The Bacchus represented on the same illustration was probably made by Matthaï.) He modelled the bust of Socrates (Fig. 173, K 5) exactly after a plaster model. The sentimental family scenes by Acier are represented by "the decisive choice" (Fig. 170, I 49) and "the noble decision" (Fig. 170, I 60), while the group of the vine-dressers (Fig. 174, I 2) is allegorical. The last group mentioned as well as the broth basin (Fig. 175, F 42) he made after Schoenau's drawings. Besides I may mention as his work the vase H 16 on Table 22 and the two baskets F 41 and 46 on Table 24.

Schoenheit (born in 1730) came as an apprentice to the factory in 1745, worked in it till October 1st 1794, was then pensioned off and died on May 27th 1805.

Of Chr. Gottfried Juechtzer it has above been said that he had to finish Kaendler's work in place of Schoenheit. He was born on June 12th 1752 in Meissen, being a son of one of the painters employed at the china works. Came to the factory as an apprentice in 1769. After Kaendler's death, he seems to have worked independently and to have proved so able as sculptor that after Acier's leave Juechtzer was inofficially appointed to take his place. He did not obtain the position of manager. This post was taken by Joh. Dav. Elsasser who had in the meanwhile been made commissioner of the court and who managed all affairs with the help of his son Joachim Friedrich. After both of these had got leave of absence[312] on June 18th 1790, Juechtzer was to supervise the work, while Joh. Gottlieb Schiffner sen. had to divide it among the workers. But only in 1794 Juechtzer was made "master of models", Schiffner "leader of the white brigade" and Joh. Fr. Lueck "created manager of the moulders and embossers". From June 1796 Juechtzer was allowed to spend the summer months in Dresden, in order to make models in the Mengs Collection of plaster casts. Many times he exhibited his work on the Dresden art exhibition, thus in 1785 the "three graces in biscuit china" (Fig. 176, H 71), 1786 several porcelain groups and in 1800 the Runner of the Capitol and the Dice player of Florence. He died on March 7th 1812.

Table 23 contains the following of Juechtzer's productions:—the two groups of playing children (H 36 and H 39) (these received Rococo-socles under Leuteritz), then a larger group representing "Peace" (G 31), the rest are all groups on mythological subjects:—Venus and Cupid (G 72), Hero and Leander (I 11), Minerva (I 45)[313],

Page 77.

Fig. 187. VENUS WITH CUPID,
H 60
24 cm.

Page 77.
Fig. 188. A GLADIATOR
ANOINTING HIMSELF, G*100.*
36 cm.

Venus (H *57*) and
Bacchus (G *57*), Table 22
"The school of Love"
(K *44*). As illustrations of
the text the following are
seen:—Apollo leaning
against a pillar (Fig. 177,
G *89*), a Faun as a Cymbal-
player (Fig. 178, H *41*),
three "children for
sacrifice" (Fig. 179—180,
I *34*, *38* and *56*) [314] (I *28*
and *21* were made by
Schoenheit), Apollo and
Daphne (Fig. 170, I *9*),
Diana and Endymion
(Fig. 170, I *8*), the "Hap-
piness of Sleep" (Fig. 181,
I *13*) and two of the
three Priestesses of Vesta
(Fig. 182, L *97* and M *13*) [315].

Page 78
Fig. 189. THE COMMERCE OF CUPIDS, L *14*.
30 cm.

The bust of Cicero (Fig. 183, L *40*) was probably made by Juechtzer as well.

The busts on Fig. 184 were made by Juechtzer and Schoenheit after drawings by Schoenau. I suppose
that the former made Apollo (H *5*), Jupiter (H *9*) and Bacchus (H *11*), while the latter must have modelled

Diana (H *8*), Vesta (H *6*) and Ceres (H *12*).
One of these two sculptors must have made
the frog and the lobster on a pedestal,
which are illustrated on Fig. 185 (K *69*).

Johann Gottlieb Matthaï was born in
Meissen in 1753. He was employed as an
apprentice in painting from April to August
1773 and afterwards became an embosser.
On May 11th 1776 he fled to Kopenhagen
with several others [316], but returned to Meissen
in the same year. Already in 1777 he must
have received permission to take up his
residence in Dresden so as to be able to
work for Meissen from the antique models
there and the factory has to thank this artist
for the more or less correct copies of the
classic models. In 1781 he seems to have
modelled a bust of Marcolini. Fig. 186 shows
the Vase (E *54*) à la antique modelled by
him, as well as four figures in the same
style Apollo (H *80*), Venus (G *85*), a Faun
(I *52*), a grinder (G *68*) and, in Fig. 182,
the priestess of Vesta in the centre (H *84*).
The Fig. 187—188 represent a Venus with
Cupid (H *60*) and a gladiator anointing
himself (G *100*). The Bacchus represented
on Fig. 172 (I *20*) is also probably his work.
On January 1st 1795 he took leave of his
work in the Meissen factory in order to

Page 78.
Fig. 190. WEDGWOOD WORKS.
Castor and Pollux, Maria Theresia, spouse of King Anthony's, Sacrifice scene, Frederick II, G *14*,
26 : 21 cm.   18 : 14,5 cm   18 : 14,5 cm.   20 : 24,5 cm.   15,5 cm.
Grandduke of Russia (?), H *93*, The love market, H *95*.
19 cm.   13 : 15 cm.

Fig. 191. WEDGWOOD WORKS.

Pages 78 and 79.

Friedrich Wilhelm III, Prince Maximilian with his spouse and sister, Emperor Alexander, King Friedrich August 1,
10 cm.   14,5 cm.   10 cm.   10,5 cm.
Three antique scenes, Emperor Leopold of Austria, Dancers.
12, 9,5 and 11 cm.   9,5 cm.   10: 25,5 cm.

accept the post of Inspector of the Mengs plaster cast collection.

Of all the other sculptors[317] Schoene and Weger were the most prominent. Joh. Dan. Schoene was engaged in Meissen in 1783. According to Juechtzer's certificate "he made such progress owing to his untiring application as to be able to form all the models that came his way". Thus it was he who principally finished the models set by Juechtzer. "The Commerce of Cupids" (Fig. 189, L *14*) a group completed in 1797 was made by him according to Juechtzer's ideas and under his guidance.

The latter had treated the same subject ofter a picture from Herculanum in the eighties. The group was called the "market of love" and was afterwards altered to a model in relief (Fig. 190), Juechtzer made also the group representing "the temperaments of love"[318]. The following are mentioned as Schoene's new works:—the Muses (L *26* and *27*), various goddesses, Ceres twice (L *41* and M *61*), Flora (M *56*) and Minerva (M *58*), a portrait of the Elector and a scene of sacrifice in relief (Fig. 191).

Andreas Franz Weger came to Meissen in 1802 at the age of 35 years. He seems to have produced a particularly large number of portraits. In 1804 Napoleon and the Emperor Alexander of Russia (Fig. 191), in 1805 Prince Anthony were portrayed by him. Further a small Flora (M *64*) is mentioned as his independent work.

At this time chinaware was often left unglazed. In imitation of Sèvres the Meissen factory was very anxious to make figures in biscuit-china. As these were left entirely white or only gilt in some parts, they excellently supplied the demand for colourless productions made by the customers of that time. Besides them the delicately treated white reliefs on a blue ground (Wedgwood-ware) which originated in England and soon gained popularity the whole world over were particularly often imitated. In 1792 it was said of the sculptor Prasser and a little later of Douay that they had done excellent work in imitating the dainty Wedgwood-ware. Fig. 190 and 191 represent a number of such productions. Fig. 190 shows in the middle a medalion of oval shape slightly elongated with Castor and Pollux. It was made in 1816 after a group modelled by Juechtzer in 1789; as well as two medalions also oval but oblique, which have already been spoken of above. The portraits, I of 1789, represent King Anthony and his spouse, II of 1785 (H *93*) a russian grandduke (?) and III Frederick II (G *14*). The three first mentioned are the work of Juechtzer, the last of Matthaï or Schoenheit. The portraits of Friedrich Wilhelm III, Prince Maximilian with his first spouse and

Pages 27 and 79.
Fig. 192   COURT SERVICE with mosaic border
24,5 cm

his sister Marie Anna, the Emperor Alexander (by Weger), Friedrich August the Righteous and the Emperor Leopold are reproduced on Fig. 191. The following productions find a place in the middle:—two mythological representation and Venus Kallipygos which were possibly modelled after Wedgwood china, while below them "dancing figures" by Juechtzer or Schoene are represented.

THE PAINTING.

In painting as well as in plastique the style very rapidly changed from Rococo to Antique. Here also we often come across rods with ribbons twisted round them, pearl-edges, creased ribbon bows etc. Utensils were ornamented with various patterns in open work relieved in pale colours in order to make them appear lighter. Fig. 192 shows a plate of the Court service described on page 26, it has a mosaic border and is painted with fruit. Fig. 193 is the illustration of a plate the border of which is made of open work in an arched and slightly raised pattern, while the centre is painted with birds and insects. Fig. 194 (L 60) shows an oval basket with straight poles which are joined by slight and graceful leaves, the idea for it originated in the mind of the plaster etcher Daebritz. Many portraits[319] in oval framing were now painted. The painting of silhouettes must be added as well. Then the pictures of Angelika Kaufmann, van der Werft, Canaletto, Berghem (Fig. 195) and other artists were copied on china. Views of Saxon and English towns and castles as well as of glaciers and italian ruins were painted on it, while scenes from Gellert's fables, from the Sufferings of Werther, from Romeo and Juliet are often mentioned as having been represented on china in this period. Further horse races, russo-turkish and american battles (Fig. 196) were represented. On a little dish the reception of Frederick the Great in Elysium was painted, while a scene of his death-bed was placed on a goblet. Count Marcolini ordered in 1795 that the Maria Magdalena of Correggio should be copied for him on a dish, while his family was to be represented on a table top[320].

We now often find black and sepia used. One could for instance see goblets painted with black and blue flowers, with black indian flowers, with black flowers and golden leaves or with black indian garlands.

Complaints had been severally made of the failure to produce blue and green paints and as the arcanists were not thought much of, the management applied to the assessors of the board of mines in Freiberg Klinghammer and Wentzel. The first in 1777 succeeded in improving the green colours. The improvement went so far as to prevent the paint from cracking off. The way the paint cracked off had before often been complained of. Wentzel during the years 1778—90 was variously employed in Meissen for months at a time[321]. He particularly merits great praise for having improved the colouring under glazing and for having given its appearance on baked chinaware greater beauty. He is also credited with having been able to produce the "beautiful royal blue" in Meissen in 1782[322] in a satisfactory fashion. That was the ground colour which had done a great deal towards making the Sèvres factory famous.

At this period a manner of decoration was used which is to be entirely rejected. China was so painted as to represent porphyry, pearl-grey marble or lapis-lazuli. Either the whole of an article or different parts of it were painted in this manner, while some showed the grain and colour of the wood of the pine, the plum or the pear tree or of mahogany. Pipeheads were made à la Meerschaum or so as to appear "coloured" by long smoking.

Page 79.

Fig. 193. PLATE with perforated border
and bird painting.
24,5 cm.

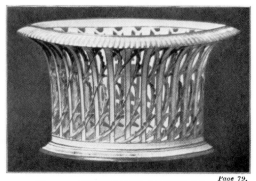

Page 79.

Fig. 194. PERFORATED BASKET, L 60.
17 cm.

Page 79.

Fig. 195. PLATE with oblett border.
24,5 cm.

Besides cups were made with views on them which were to appear like steel engravings.

The Dresden academy used its influence with regard to the artistic treatment of china. By an order dated January 10th 1773 the Court painter and professor Joh. Eleazar Schoenau or Schenau was to supervise the painting. He was born in 1740, had lived for 12 years in Paris, was summoned to the Dresden academy in 1769 and acted as director of it for some time. He kept his residence in Dresden, but was obliged to come to Meissen from time to time and to work there altogether for three months during the year. He had to go round the studious, to correct the work and always to think of new designs; but his principal duty consisted in the supervision of drawing lessons. Schoenau is said to have been a good teacher, it is certain that he made a large number of drawings after which Meissen painters and sculptors worked, still under his surveyal the factory did not show any striking improvement artistically speaking.

He was assisted on one side by the chief artists on the other by the drawing master. There were three chief artists:—two — Richter and Walther — for coloured and one — Colmberger — for blue painting. Richter's place was taken by Kuehnel then by Birnbaum and when the last-mentioned was pensioned off in 1804 Donat took his place. When Walther died in 1780 C. Gottl. Grahl and afterwards Tiebel worked in his stead. Colmberger the chief of the painters in blue died in 1779; he was succeeded by Hahnefeld then by Zschentsch who died in 1802. Foerster who came after him filled this post but a short time as he was drowned in the Elbe in the same year. In 1803 Moebius took his place. The apprentices of the factory had already been taught drawing in the thirties, the lessons had, it is true been discontinued for a couple of years, but were again taken up at Kaendler's initiative in 1740. In 1743 Fehling and Hofmann were engaged as special drawing masters. As these died in 1753 and 1751 respectively, the chief painters had to give the drawing lessons (see page 48). These however were so much occupied with performing their ordinary duties, that they — in their opinion — had not the necessary time for teaching the apprentices, therefore these lessons quietly dropped out of existence. When in 1764 the Court painter prof. Dietrich, in taking over the management of the artistic part of the works, became principal of the art school as well (see page 59f.), he insisted upon serious teaching of drawing. He probably soon saw that not much could be done in this respect with the management, he saw to the installation of new drawing masters. The following men were engaged for this purpose:—in 1766 the court artist Borstichen, in 1767 Joh. Chr. Dietrich (a nephew of the court painter's) who died in 1799 — as well as the artist Haeuer to teach the women and girls. At the same time the school was enlarged, so that young people who had not been taught at all before now received preliminary instructions in the school. The following painters were made drawing masters:— Grahl in 1771, Lindner in 1779 (died in 1806), Ehrlich in 1782, Heinr. Gotth. Schaufuss in 1796, Mehner in 1796 and Arnhold in 1806. It is said of Schaufuss that he brought the figure painters to such a state of perfection as "to make them outshine all the other painters in the factory".

Generally speaking, we may take it for granted that the artists mentioned above were the most important men in the artistic life of Meissen. As has been mentioned above in 1776 and 1786 the painters had been divided into categories according to their abilities, so that it is possible in going by the documents to make a distinction between them[323]. Besides the chief painters and the drawing

Page 79.

Fig. 196. SALVER, perforated, painted with battle scene.
30 : 43 cm.

Table 26

Page 88.

Works by Leuteritz.

1. Bacchus group, C *35*.   2 and 3. Cooks (man and woman) as menu holders, K *116, 117*.   4. Centre piece, D *196*.
30 cm.   14 cm.   40 cm.

5. Grandfather and grandchild, M *192*.   6. Grandmother's birthday, M *184*.
21 cm.   21,5 cm.

Table 27

Pages 97, 98, 100.

Cupids.

1—3 by Schwabe, L *118, 126* and *124*.   4 and 5 by Pollack, M *115* and *114*.
18 cm., 17 cm., 18 cm.   20 cm., 18 cm.

6—9 by Stellmacher, Q *162, 161, 160* and *159*.   10 and 11 by K. Hentschel, R *133* and *130*.
11 cm., 11,5 cm., 15 cm.   12 cm., 11 cm.

12 and 13 by Fischer, O *193* and *192*.   14 and 15 by Hoelbe, N *196** and *195**.
16 cm.   43 cm., 41 cm.

16 and 17 by Schwabe (afterwards altered), P *119* and *121*.
18,5 cm., 19,5 cm.

masters the following of them deserve particular mention:—as figure painters Joh. George Loehnig, Chr. Fr. Matthaï, Schuetze, Thile; as painters of cattle, landscapes, architecture, hunts and battles Ehrlich, Chr. Fr. Kuehnel, Joh. Karl Mauksch; for painting of birds Mann; for fruit and flower painting Aug. Ferd. Dietrich, Gotsch, Grossmann, Heynemann, Roegner, Schmidt, Thiele and Winckler.

On April 1st 1796 Schoenau laid down his office in Meissen. In his place Joh. Dav. Schubert was created general supervisor of the painters.

Although at this time some skilful painting had been done, still the general artistic ability of the factory gradually decreased. Meissen had lost its world-wide reputation and had been excelled by several other factories. It could not keep pace with the rival factories either in the elegance and novelty of form and ornamentation, or in the low prices which the latter set upon their goods. As besides this other untoward circumstances came in its way, nothing could be done to stay the decay of the factory.

VII. PERIOD:
INFLUENCE OF THE NAPOLEONIC WARS
(1814–33).

The Russian Imperial General Government under Count Repnin[324] took over the administration of Saxony in 1813. On December 18th it set a commission on foot[325] for investigating the working conditions of the factory. At this time Marcolini was still manager. On March 17th 1814 the leadership of the factory was given into the hands of Counsellor of mines von Oppel, a member of the commission; at the same time the factory was connected, for a while, with the stone-ware works of St. Hubertusburg and the "Pottery" of Doehlen[326].

Oppel introduced several noteworthy innovations into the factory. For instance he had less painting in blue done because this work was connected with loss to the factory; he only had articles with this kind of painting made to order. Then he obtained for samples a great many casts of classic ornaments in Etruria (the Wedgwood works) and Saarburg (?). As gold ornamentation was at that time in great demand, he took it so far into consideration as to depute the arcanist Holzwig to seek a cheap method of producing it. The latter succeeded in making a very "useful, rather fluid gilding by the addition of red mercury oxide".

When King Friedrich August returned home to reign in his country on May 27th 1815, he called a new investigation commission[327] according to the propositions of which the factory was to be managed. The local commission in Meissen was now turned into the "local administration". Oppel, though living in Dresden, filled the post of director, Steinauer who had been a member of the managing commission had taken his leave owing to old age, von Wedel was deputed to act as overseer of the employés until he, as well, was pensioned off in 1816. In 1814 Heinr. Gottlob Kuehn was made inspector, manager of the technique and a member of the board of administration. With his entrance the keeping in secret of the arcanum was suppressed. Finally the merchand Martini was appointed member of the administration in 1816. After his death in 1824 he was replaced by Maertens. In 1824 the arcanist Koettig was made the third member of the "local administration".

All these men did their utmost to put the working of the factory which had become antiquated in its art, technique and ways of business on a new and orderly footing. It was possible to attain some measure of success but very gradually. It should not however be forgotten that at that time Meissen laboured under a burden of particularly unfavourable circumstances. As a result of the devastation of Germany by Napoleon's troups, the german people were impoverished and the demand for an article of luxury such as chinaware was existing almost nowhere. The cheap stone-ware had entirely supplanted it in the market. It is true that England, one of the most dangerous competitors was made harmless by the fact that the connection between the continent and all other countries

Page 84.

Fig. 197. TEA SERVICE, wreath of vine leaves in green under glaze.

Tea pot, Q o. Plate, F 135. Sugar basin, F 135. Cup, N 91. Milk jug, O 65.
22 cm.   24 cm diam.   12,5 cm.   7,5 cm.   20 cm.

was for a time severed (1807—13). Still Meissen was not able to draw much advantage from this because in Germany itself a great many stone-ware factories had sprung up. They sought to satisfy the demand for cheaper ware. When Napoleon was driven back over the Rhine the severing of all connection with the continent came to an end. England very quickly and skilfully managed to regain what it had lost in not having been able to deal with Germany for so long a time. It also knew how to make its stone-ware highly attractive by the use of tasteful models, excellent bronzing and copper-engravings. Besides the factories in Thueringen knew how to make good use of the demand for cheap productions. Meissen had too long

Page 84.

Fig. 198. WEDGWOOD WORKS.

O19
21,5 cm.

O96
Cup 10 cm. high, saucer 14,5 cm. diam.

depended upon the excellence of its goods and the fineness and durability of the paste. As it did not work so cheaply and did not show the "elegance" and novelty of form and design, it soon remained behind its rivals.

First of all the prices were reduced on the Leipsic fair and later on auction sales were held in the country, the sale of the white second class goods which seems to have been mostly sought was permitted and in 1822 a third class paste was used for making chemists boxes and such like.

The most important way of cheapening the "Refining" of china was the introduction of the slight or lustre-gilding discovered by Kuehn. It was applied in liquid form and came bright and shining out of the baking (see page 127 f.). At first fault was found with it because it had a greenish shade, but this was soon set right. Trials were made as to the durability of this gilding, it did not however stand the test and could only be employed on articles which were but little used. At any rate Kuehn could in 1836 boast of the fact that Meissen delivered the best and most durable gilding which could be baked together with enamel colours.

In 1828 the Lithophanien or lamp-shades of quite thin transparent china were introduced. They were often painted with subjects of a slightly sentimental nature and were exceedingly popular. In 1831 forms for sugar basins, fruit dishes etc. were made from casts of pressed glass. This was not by any means laudable, as it produced cheap china but the shapes did not suit the material.

With the assistance of the painter on glass and the copper-engraver Schubert an attempt was made to use copper-plate printings. The latter sent the two plates first etched by Hammer with representations of Schandau and the cow-shed to the factory. In a short time the factory successfully adopted this technical plan and soon "border decorations, letters, landscapes, figures, animals and portraits" were made in this way. This must have continued till the seventies. In 1832 copper-plate printing was once used on unglazed porcelain. In 1824 the painter and seal-engraver Carl Gottl. Boettger succeeded in lithographing gilt ornamentation on china, while in 1827 he used lithography and copper-plate printing under glazing on china. Lastly the inscriptions on porcelain which before had to be made with a paint brush could now be written with a pen. This made the chinaware much cheaper and the man who had first hit upon the idea was engaged at the factory as a "writer in china".

In this period chrome colour came into general use instead of the copper colour used before (see

Page 84.

Fig. 199. WEDGWOOD WORK, P35.
34 cm.

Page 84.

Fig. 200. WEDGWOOD WORK, Q93.
19,5 cm.

Page 84.
Fig. 201. PIPEHEAD
AS NAPOLEON'S
BUST, 26.
8,5 cm.

Page 84.
Fig. 202. BUSTS OF LUTHER AND MELANCHTHON.
U 19   U 18
12,5 cm.   12,5 cm.

page 129). It is reported in 1817 that trials with chrome-green had been very successful. Hereby a new colour for use under glazing was obtained. It was first used only for "turkish designs on turkish vessels", afterwards it was very much used for german flower painting. A pattern in this style with a wreath of vine leaves was very popular (Fig. 197).

Through all these innovations the goods improved and met with a more ready sale. Painting in blue which had been almost entirely given up had to be in 1819 again taken up and young people were employed for it, while in 1821 it could be reported that the demand for copper-printings had risen.

As the old artists had remained to oversee the forming, things here had gone on pretty much in the old way. For instance chinaware in Wedgwood-style was even now very popular (Fig. 198—200, O 19, 96, P 35 and Q 93). Juechtzer remained at the factory till his death on October 25th 1823.

The chief work in the modelling department seems, in this period to have been done by Schoene. He modelled "Napoleon's bust as a pipehead" (Fig. 201, 26), as well as the busts of Napoleon (U 17), Luther (Fig. 202, U 18) and of Melanchthon (Fig. 202, U 19), probably those of Gellert (Fig. 203, 5), Homer (Fig. 204, U 8) and Gutenberg (Fig. 205, S 65) as well. The bust of the King (Fig. 206, P 100) he created in 1817. In 1818 he made the figure of the Queen in relief and in 1828 a portrait of Prince Friedrich August. In 1821—22 he modelled four hunting scenes in relief (they represented hunting after does, stags, pigs and hares), in 1825 two groups of peasant children with oxen and cows (R 78—79) and in 1833 he made busts of Christ and the Virgin as well as a child sleeping on a pillow and a dog lying on a pillow. Of Weger's productions the following are mentioned:—a bust of the Court rector Reinhardt, a letter-weight with a sphinx and a lion and a pipehead in the shape of a turk; while of Schiebells work it is only said that he made wax-models for screens, especially for one with the King's portrait. Carl Gotthelf Habenicht was a very able apprentice who secretly went away to the stone-ware factory in Pirna, but was again employed in Meissen from November 1823. He made principally screens, then pipeheads, besides a watch case with an eagle, a goblet in the shape of a fox's head etc. Goethe's head represented on Fig. 207, Q 48 was made by him after a model that had been sent to the factory.

Page 84.
Fig. 203. BUST OF GELLERT, 5.
21 cm.

Director von Oppel was particularly anxious to improve the painting which he considered very imperfect. He complained in 1816 that Meissen had only four artists who were capable of doing good work. They were Schaufuss and Arnoldt — who were employed as teachers as well — and Richter and Wollmann. Schaufuss was said to be very skilful in producing "rich artistic grouping in serious style"[328]; while Wollmann excelled in figure painting "especially as far as pleasing and life like representation was concerned". Arnoldt was a landscape painter, Richter a flower painter. As it was greatly feared that the factory would be quite without good painters, it was decided to seek new artists. As a result of this Georg Friedrich Kersting was brought to Meissen in 1818 to supervise the painters. He had been educated at the academy of art in Dresden and Copenhagen and had lived as a free artist in Dresden

Page 84.
Fig. 204. BUST OF
HOMER, U 8.
7,3 cm.

Page 84.
Fig. 205. BUST OF
GUTENBERG, S 65.
12 cm.

Table 28

Pages 97, 98, 100, 101, 106.

1. Psyche and Cerberus by Hultsch, M *176*.   2 and 3. Paris clothes dealer and book-seller by Hoetger, T *163* and *162*.
38 cm.   28 cm., 25 cm.

4—6. Soldier groups by Andresen, P *181, 182* and *180*.   7. Capture of the water fairies by Herter, Q *195*.
23 cm., 24,5 cm., 23,5 cm.   29 cm.

8. Dying warrior by Roeder, N *140*.   9. Cupid and a water fairy by Haehnel, M *199*.
27 cm.   35 cm.

Table 29

Pages 97, 98, 100, 101, 106, 109.

1. Loreley by Offermann, O *153*. 2 and 3. Loreley and Omphale by Schwanthaler, N *109* and *108*.
34 cm.   19 cm.

4. Cupid and a water fairy by Otto Koenig, G *148*. 5. Venus and cupid by Eras, O *161*.
16,5 cm.   20 cm.

6. Gentleman and lady by Goeschel, M *183*. 7. Chocolate girl, T *5*. 8. Genevieve by Otto Koenig, E *187*.
18 cm.   18 cm.   19,5 cm.

9. Concert by Kramer, T *186*. 10. Cinderella by Hirt, M *171*.
22 cm.   17,5 cm.

until he joined the Luetzow corps as a volunteer and went to war. Before coming to Meissen he had been engaged for several years in Warsaw. In Meissen he is supposed to have influenced the drawing and the combination of colours for the better. The grandest piece of work made under his direction was a table-service painted with battle-scenes. The King had it presented as a gift of honour to the Duke of Wellington[329]. Kersting died in 1847.

Pages 84 and 87.

Fig. 206.   BUSTS OF KING FRIEDRICH AUGUST I, FRIEDRICH AUGUST II AND JOHANN.
P *100*   V *80*   B *177*
26 cm.   28,5 cm.   26 cm.

The landscape painter Carl Scheinert was permanently employed at the factory after a trial engagement of three months. Later he acted as a drawing master as well. In 1823 Strassberger of Leipsic and in 1824

Page 84.

Fig. 207. BUST OF GOETHE, Q *48*.
21 cm.

Eberlein of Thueringen came to Meissen as artists. In 1827 Carl Aug. Mueller a gifted apprentice received permanent employment at the factory. In 1823 the chief director of the painters professor Schubert died in Dresden, in 1826 the painters overseer Donath and in 1828 the court artist and drawing master Arnoldt whose place was taken by Ludwig Richter. The last mentioned was engaged in Meissen on March 1st 1828 as a master of drawing and received a salary of 200 talers yearly for the tuition of a drawing class. He kept this place until the school of art was abolished in 1835. It can only be conjectured, but not proved[330], that the influence of the great miniature painter was important to the factory. Richter himself speaks of this time and of his work in Meissen with a certain sadness. Here he missed the fresh and stimulating artistic circle of his Dresden friends. Schaufuss seems to have been a narrow-minded and whimsical old person so that Kersting and Scheinert alone could have been considered as fitting companions for him, but they were not able to take the place of his Dresden artist-friends. Besides his state of health at that time left much to be desired[331].

On October 1st 1814 the art school was so separated from the factory, as to obtain permission to be directed by the Dresden academy of Fine Arts; this state of things lasted until the abolition of the school.

VIII. PERIOD:
KUEHN (1833–70).

In 1816 the management of the factory consisted of the Director von Oppel who was living in Dresden and the local administrative board in Meissen. It had been in the previous period put in authority by the ministry of finance and was, to a certain extent, superintended by it. The factory which had till 1831 been the property of the crown was in that year declared as belonging to the state. This did not bring any great alterations with it. Changes, however, were brought about by von Oppel's death two years later. At first the factory remained without a director at all, but was managed by the Administrative board in Meissen alone. Inspector Kuehn who has already in the former period been favourably spoken of stood at the head of this board. He acted skilfully and energetically in doing his utmost to keep the factory in the foremost ranks of its competitors. In acknowledgement of his fruitful work, he was appointed director. This post he filled till his death in 1870. On page 126 f. will be found all the changes wrought by him in the working of the factory i. e. the improvement of the kilns, the investigation of new china pastes the introduction of a motor, the alteration in the use of fuel (coal instead of wood) and the introduction of chrome-colours.

Kuehn was supported by Maertens, the chief manager and Koettig the manager of the chemical laboratory. On the strength of the invention of the latter the fabrication of ultramarine known as artificial was begun. This brought considerable gain to the factory. When Koettig was pensioned off in 1863 (Maertens had died in 1843, his place remaining unoccupied) the arcanist Crasso and the general manager Raithel were made members of the administrative board in their place.

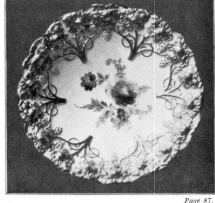

Fig. 208. DISH with lustre-gold and flower painting, Z 94b.
21 cm.

The modelling department was directed by Joh. Gottfr. Dressler from 1812 to his death in 1836. He does not seem to have stepped forward with any work of his own. His place was taken by Habenicht — who as above mentioned was soon after drowned in the Elbe — and who in his turn was succeeded by Ernst August Leuteritz. The latter was born in 1818 near Meissen, came to the factory in 1836 as an apprentice, studied under Rietschel and was engaged in Meissen as a modeller in 1843. From 1849 to 1886 he held the post of one of the managers. During these many years he did great service to the factory by his extraordinary activity and skilfullness.

The following acted as managers of the painting department in this period:—Kersting 1818—47, Scheinert who in time was well known as a painter in glass 1848—60 and

Fig. 209. VASE with rose painting, X 74.
30 cm.

Fig. 210. BASKET, perforated, with forget me nots, 66.
12 cm. height.

Page 87.
Fig. 211.
CUPID WITH A LYRE, Y91.
21 cm.

Page 87.
Fig. 212. ARIADNE, X34.
24 cm.

Page 87.
Fig. 214.
NAPOLEON, W58.
28 cm.

Page 87.
Fig. 216.
BUST OF BEETHOVEN, Y72.
13 cm.

Page 87.
Fig. 213. KING FRIEDRICH
AUGUST I, U16.
42 cm.

Page 87.
Fig. 215.
SCHILLER, S95.
32 cm.

Carl August Müller 1860—80. All three have already been spoken of above.

Owing to the peculiar circumstances described above the aim in view at that time was to cheapen the production and ornamentation of chinaware. The discovery of "lustre-gilding" (a cheap yet bright gilding) by Kuehn has already been spoken of. This discovery proved very important, as it was principally owing to the varied uses made of it that the Meissen factory again found a better sale for its goods. In 1833 Kuehn reported that a new pattern in "greco-gothic" style had been designed. It was made "en bas-relief" and "would in its execution show much colouring as well as gilding by the method peculiar to the Meissen factory[332] i. e. lustre-gilding". This is the chinaware which may still be seen in the old cup-board of grandmother's time (Fig. 208, Z94[b]). It is plastically ornamented with dead and bright gold and colours. Although this kind of chinaware and the kind made after glass-casts may seem very coarse to us, it should not be condemned without investigation of the circumstances which accompanied their appearance into the world; after such investigation we shall find their existence justified.

Copies of famous paintings of the Dresden picture gallery seem to have been very popular as well. At any rate the documents report of many dishes of this description which were put up at the large exhibitions.

In 1852 a further discovery of Kuehn's — which was soon taken up by other factories in the same way as lustre-gilding — came to be used in painting. This invention consisted of painting with changeable (fickle) colours (technical explanation on page 132). They were very thinly applied, appeared very iridescent and were used for producing coloured grounds as well as border decorations and other ornamentations.

The forms in empire style were in many cases, still made (Fig. 209, X74), older models were used only in very few instances at first at any rate (Fig. 210, 66). In Meissen as well as in all Germany an unsuccessful attempt was made to ressurect the gothic style. Now and again particularly favourite models were copied or reduced in Meissen. For instance of a Cupid with a lyre by Thorwaldsen (Fig. 211, Y91), Ariadne by Dannecker (Fig. 212, X34); Fig. 206 the busts of the Kings Friedrich August II and Johann (V80 and B177), then Fig. 213 Friedrich August the Righteous (U16), Fig. 214 Napoleon (W58), Fig. 215 Schiller (S95), Fig. 216 bust of Beethoven (Y72), Fig. 217 that of Mozart (Y76) as well as the ballet dancers Fig. 218 Fanny Elssler as a spanish dancer and Maria Taglioni in her favourite role of sylph (V60 and 62). Independent work was done in the same style as well Fig. 219 the fisher boy by Leuteritz (Y95) may serve as an example.

With the increasing sale of chinaware the demand for greater variety of shapes and forms again arose, so that Meissen went back to the old style which was so rich and varied. It is a great credit to the manager of the moulders Leuteritz that he so well and energetically did the duty laid upon him by circumstances in resurrecting the old styles. Fig. 220 shows an example of the renewed empire style. It is of complicated shape and colouring and has beautifully

Page 87.
Fig. 217.
BUST OF MOZART, Y76.
13 cm.

Page 87.

Fig. 218. ELSSLER AND TAGLIONI.
V 60   V 62
37 cm.   35 cm.

Page 87.
Fig. 219.
FISHER BOY, Y 95.
27,5 cm.

arched handles shaped like snakes (A 148). The vases Fig. 228—229 are in the same style.

It was the Rococo-style, however, which was principally renewed. This was due not only to the taste of the time but to the fact that the models — which had been created in this style and had added so much to the world wide renown of the Meissen factory — so excellently adapted themselves to being copied. Leuteritz was untiring in making the rich store of Rococo forms fit for use in his time or in creating entirely new models in the same style. Table 25 shows several old forms which had been treated in the way just spoken of:—a tureen with Ozier pattern; on its cover a cupid (the work of Eberlein) strewing flowers is seated, a large serving dish (P 174*) with Watteau painting and a coffee service with blue scale-like border. In the case of Fig. 221 and 222

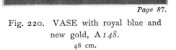

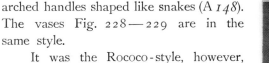

he has used old baskets and created new figures (D 176 and H 166). In the case of the two candlesticks (Fig. 223, F 155 and 156) he has used figures already existing while the rest was independently modelled by himself. The fruit basket (605) which is placed between them on the illustration seems to be entirely his work, as well as one of the two candlesticks (Fig. 224, E 128 and I 197) and the centre pieces (Fig. 225—226, 2772 and E 141). The vase of complicated form in Barock-style (Fig. 227, B 194) was made by Leuteritz in 1860 and placed on the table as a decoration at the Jubilee-banquet.

Table 26 shows six further examples of his work. The two small figures at the top (K 116 and 117) are intended as menu holders. The Bacchus group (C 35*) was made as a counter-piece to the "capture of the Tritons" (C 35) spoken of on page 65. The grandfather and his grandchild (M 192) and "grandmother's birthday" (M 184) are made to resemble Acier's work, the large centre piece D 196 is in Rococo-style.

Fig. 220. VASE with royal blue and new gold, A 148.
48 cm.

The Rococo-style as it appears in the productions of Leuteritz does not appeal to us at all as it is dry and shows shapes artificially borrowed from another age and mostly superficially conceived. As it, however, entirely suited the taste of the time the increased sale of chinaware was greatly due to it. This conception of art in Meissen did not by any means remain unchallenged. For instance the ministry of finance — probably as the result of an opinion formed at the Dresden industry exhibition in 1845 — in 1846 advised the administration not to make an exclusive use of Rococo forms and not to neglect a "pure and noble style". It was also put down as necessary to "educate skilled modellers and to acquire new tasteful designs and sketches". For this purpose it allowed the Dresden sculptor Anton Seelig jun. to influence the modelling of chinaware and pointed out to the administration that it would

Page 88.
Fig. 221. CENTRE PIECE, D 176.
42 cm.

Page 88.
Fig. 222. CENTRE PIECE, H 166.
20 cm.

Table 30

Pages 99, 100.

Works by Andresen.

1. Saxon grenadiers, P 183.   2. By the seaside, Q 127.   3. In the park by Romanus Andresen, Q 149.

27 cm.   34 cm.   45 cm.

4. The Night, P 108.   5. A declaration of love, P 132.   6. The Evening, P 107.

36 cm.   31 cm.   39 cm.

be advisable to consult the professors of the Dresden Academy of Fine Arts in artistic matters. In 1850 the ministry wished to invite artists not connected with the factory to hand in sketches for designing artistic china; it gave up this project, however, at the urgent request of the administration. In 1851 a commission was appointed "to criticise the old and the new style of painting and modelling and to supervise the execution of the work". This commission consisted of the director and the two leaders of the artistic branches and three professors of the academy[333] of fine arts.

Page 88.

Fig. 223. CANDLESTICK, FRUIT BASKET, CANDLESTICK.

F 156   605   F 155.
52 cm.   54 cm. height.   52 cm.

Although nothing can be directly proved to be the work of this commission, we may take it for granted that the Dresden artists must have given many a good advice to the administration. Their proposition to employ the architect Wiedemann at the factory, going by his work, was not accepted by the ministry. Besides the artists of Dresden occasionally made sketches and drawings of their own for the factory. Among the chinaware sent to the exhibition in Munich in 1854[334] there were three vases which had been sketched or modelled by Rietschel, Nicolai and Gottfr. Semper. The one by Semper had been painted by the Dresden artist Sachse after sketches by Schnorr who principally gave artistic advice to the factory with regard to this exhibition. I should like to mention as well that Ludwig Richter delivered two pencil drawings for some of the work exhibited.

Page 88.

Fig. 224. CANDLESTICKS.

E 128   I 197
45 cm.   52 cm.

In 1853 the Meissen painters were reproached with having allowed themselves to be surpassed by some of their Dresden colleagues, but a trial made with two Dresden painters proved favourable to Meissen[335].

At the Muenchen-Exhibition the Nymphenburg porcelain factory put up a large picture in mosaic representing the Sixtian Madonna. It was greatly praised notwithstanding the fact that it was disfigured by a large joint; so that in Meissen as well, it was attempted, through Scheinert, to make something resembling this. It was 113 cm. high and 56 cm. wide and represented the Bendemann painting of the Emperor Charles the Great which had a place in the throne room. In 1858 the painter Zimmermann made another picture in mosaic which represented Saxonia after a sketch by Schnorr.

One of the most important events of this period was the London Exhibition of 1862, at which the Meissen factory took part with a very good and varied collection[336]. Schnorr had designed

Page 88.

Fig. 225. CENTRE PIECE, 2772.
50 cm.

two vases à la Majolica and had arranged the painting for another (the Bath of Diana by Albano). The four seasons and the golden age had been painted after Huebner, Nicolai was the originator of the vase with flower application, and two vases had been painted with flowers by Braunsdorf (see page 110). Besides this a candelabra nearly 2 m. high after Wiedemann, a fountain 1 ½ m. high and a collection of 69 animals (probably such as were made in Kaendler's time) in their natural colours were sent to England.

Page 88.

Fig. 227. VASE of 1860, B *194.*
70 cm.

The Exhibition afforded the Meissen administration an excellent opportunity, not only of distinguishing itself, but of obtaining information as to the productions of other factories. According to its own judgement "the painting on small articles in Meissen was more delicately done than in any other, even in those of Sèvres and Berlin". A less favourable judgement was, however, uttered on a meeting held in Dresden under the chairmanship of von Friesen the minister of finance, besides Kuehn the two leaders of the artistic branches from Meissen were present as well. The minutes of this meeting read as follows:—

"1. that the Royal factory is able to stand the competition of the german and french factories in every respect, but that the english china industry had progressed with such giant strides that its rivalry could not be left unnoticed. As an incentive to the production of new designs the purchase of various models was decided upon.

2. · The following observations had been made with regard to the judgement of the public:—

a) The artistic decorations did not always appear to advantage.

b) In prospect painting almost always views of Dresden and of Saxon Switzerland had been used. In future the Rhine country and Italy etc. should be considered as well.

c) Figure painting should show a greater variety of subjects.

d) Only a limited number of white groups and figures should be produced, as the coloured ones had met with greater approval of the public. The Saxon commissioner of the exhibition has been on all sides assured that the most perfect execution of the painting especially in valuable pieces was quite indispensable for preserving the good name of the factory. The minister gave express orders that this should be observed as well as possible in the future."

Page 88.

Fig. 226. CENTRE PIECE, E *141.* PEDESTAL, *1047.*
21 : 53 cm.   12 : 48 cm.

Pages 88 and 91.   *Pages 88 and 91.*

Fig. 228.   VASE in Limoges painting, F*199*.   Fig. 229.   VASE in platinum painting, G*117*.
85 cm.   52 cm.

Of the innovations seen in London which Leuteritz recommended as particularly worthy of imitation the following may be mentioned:—the painting "paste upon paste" of Sèvres and the Limoges enamel-painting of Worcester.   The first mentioned was not successfully imitated till the next period (see page 93).   But Limoges-enamel painting was already in 1865 used on a dish shaped vase 56 cm. tall. "The procession of Alexander" after Thorwaldsen was represented on it in the above-mentioned enamel on blue ground (Fig. 228, F*199*). The vase (Fig. 229, G*117*) shows another new painting technique of this time.   On it may be seen Haehnel's Bacchus procession from the old court theatre in Dresden in platinum painting on tortoise-shell ground.

IX. PERIOD:
MODERN TIMES (1870—1910).
GENERAL MANAGEMENT.

he many bleeding wounds which had been inflicted on the german people by the Napoleonic slavery and the war for liberation had healed by degrees to about the middle of the 19th century. As herewith the general prosperity began to increase, gradually people became anxious to surround themselves as in former times with valuable household goods. This circumstance excellently suited the Meissen factory and it was succesful in increasing the sale of china-ware from year to year by making use of them. Shortly after the war of 1866 and more especially after that of 1870/71 quite large profits were delivered at the state treasury.

The man to whom, in the first instance, the credit for bringing the factory to a more flourishing state from 1814—1870, is due is the Privy counsellor of mines Kuehn. After his death on January 10th 1870 Raithel who had to that time been general manager was appointed director. At the end of 1894 he was pensioned off after having been connected with the factory as director for 25 years. Raithel guided the affairs in Meissen with firm hand and advanced in the path which he considered right in a steadfast manner, never deviating an inch from it. He steadily kept to a system of saving which brought an increasing sum of money to the factory each year.

The ordinary utensils painted mostly in blue under glaze were particularly popular. Since 1878 we notice the exportation of chinaware in increasing quantities to America. It has kept pace with time and stands high to this day. It was possible to discontinue auction sales altogether in 1876. They were however again taken up in 1887, but now only chinaware which was slightly damaged or which had been unavoidably overproduced was sold by auction.

All this led to such an improvement in the state of affairs that the new building of 1863 was not sufficiently large for the needs of the factory. Already in 1873 and again in 1884—85 these buildings had to be extended and the kilns were increased in number from four to seven i. e. almost doubled,

Page 93.

Fig. 230. TWO VASES in pâte-sur-pâte painting.
G 59   F 26
29 cm.   27 cm.

Page 93.

Fig. 231. PLATE, BELONGING TO THE CABINET.
25 : 35 cm.

Table 31

Pages 101, 107.

1—3, 8 and 9 by Ringler, 4—7 by Helmig.

1 and 2. Cupid on the shooting of deer and on stable-stand, Q *182* and R *148*.   3. A forbidden kiss, O *181*.
15 cm., 12,5 cm.   24 cm.
4 and 5. Cupid fettered and unfettered, R *123* and U *148*.   6. Seller of cupids, Q *184*.
18 cm., 19 cm.   24,5 cm.
7. In spring, S *166*.   8. Titmice, F *125*.   9. Starlings and sparrow, F *148*.
19 cm.   18 cm.   24 cm.

Page 94.
Fig. 232. VASE with crystal
glazing, S 180.
36 cm.

Page 94.
Fig. 233. TWO VASES with melted glazing.
R 102   R 195
27,5 cm.   24 cm.

Page 96.
Fig. 236. SINGERS (woman and man).
G 105   G 104
35 cm.   35 cm.

filter-presses, bullet-mills, batting-machines and other such like innovations[337] were introduced into the factory in consideration of the general extension of the working as a result of the larger sale of chinaware.

In the chemico-technical working Kuehn was assisted by the inspectors Crasso and Brunnemann. The former retired in 1876, the latter was appointed director in 1895. This position he filled till 1901.

During the time of Raithel's directorship a great number of successful attempts to improve the refining of china were made[338]. For instance in imitation of chinese productions an especially thin china known as "muslin-china" as well as the "crinkled" china with many little tiny cracks was first made. In 1878 Dr. Heintze, (he is a pupil of Kolbe's and was called to the manufactory from Freiberg in 1873) who fills the post of director of the technical and chemical departments at present was successful in making the painting "paste upon paste" which the factory had been anxious to produce in the former period. In 1883 he produced red protoxyd of copper on hard porcelain which the men working in ceramics had so often sought to make before him.

Decoration in colours which might be exposed to the high temperature necessary for the baking of china was closely connected with the "paste upon paste" painting. From about 1880 Heintze increased the number of colours which could be used in this way on hard porcelain by teaching how to lead the run of the fire. On Fig. 230 (G 59 and F 26) two vases of rather ancient form are illustrated; they were decorated by Kretzschmar after 1900 in "paste upon paste" painting, Fig. 231 shows a picture sketched by Sturm and intended for the wall of a cabinet. Its centre is executed in the same technique.

Page 94.
Fig. 234.
VASE with melted
glazing, R 150.
32 cm.

Page 97.
Fig. 237. ALBRECHT DUERER,
D 148.
40 cm.

Another manner of ornamentation which principally requires a particular managing of the fire consists of crystallised glaze and molten glaze. The principal thing in this work is to lead the reduced fire. In this manner peculiar colouring and crystallisation can be brought forth, to a certain extent, according to the estimation of the chemist, not being only left to chance.

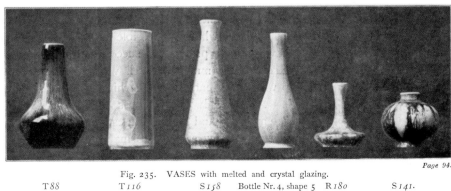

Page 94.
Fig. 235. VASES with melted and crystal glazing.
T 88   T 116   S 158   Bottle Nr. 4, shape 5   R 180   S 141.
21 cm.   23,5 cm.   25 cm.   23 cm.   13 cm.   10,5 cm.

Page 97.

Fig. 238. MORNING, NOON, EVENING AND NIGHT.

H 195   I 187   I 186   H 191
45 cm.   56 cm.   60 cm.   45 cm.
        Sizes including socle. Socle 14 cm. high.

Page 97.

Fig. 239. RAFFAEL AND MICHELANGELO.
K 174   K 173
43 cm.   44 cm.

Page 97.

Fig. 240
KALLIOPE, M 117.
51,5 cm.

This species of technical work is produced according to the investigation of Dr· Foerster. Fig. 232 (S 180) shows a vase made after and old model but ornamented with crystal glaze. Fig. 233—234 show three vases with molten glazes, of these R 195 was made by K. Hentschel. Fig. 235 represents, in the two outside pieces (S 141 and T 88), two vases with molten glazes, models by Grust, and in the rest (T 116, S 158, Nr. 4, R 180) are made with crystallized glaze; the models being by Grust and both Hentschels.

The years 1895—1901 when the factory was managed by Brunnemann can be described as a particularly difficult chapter in its history. For it embraces the time when in the world of German artistic industry opinions vigorously clashed and modern ideas sought to break through and gain the upper hand. The Meissen factory was obliged to hear criticisms from sources worthy to be taken notice of. It was blamed for not taking the lead of the modernising movement and for following it but slowly. Perhaps in an artistic sense such a mode of action was worthy of regret, but from a business point of view it is quite comprehensible. It is certain that by this keeping back at the beginning many a mistake natural at the initiation of a new artistic era was avoided.

Great zeal and energy animated Brunnemann. He had shown great understanding for the advanc of the movement and had done what was possible under the circumstances without achieving any prominent success. His successor the Privy counsellor of commerce Gesell was entrusted with the directorship when the finances of the china manufactory were at a low ebb. As a result of the Paris Exhibition of 1900 more men were employed and higher wages were paid them. The financial position was now such as to make it necessary either to dismiss some of the employés or — in order to keep them all — to lower their wages. As they showed no dissatisfaction at the last mentioned measure being taken, their salary was lowered,

Page 97.

Fig. 241. MEDECINE, BACCHANTE.
N 145   L 155
42 cm.   43 cm.

Page 97.

Fig. 242. BOY WITH BIRD'S
NEST, M 150.
45 cm.

Page 97.

Fig. 243.
LYRICAL MUSE, M 155.
49 cm.

Page 97.
Fig. 244. CUPID, M 159.
45 cm.

Page 97.
Fig. 245. FIGURE OF
GRETCHEN, N 151.
52 cm.

Page 97.
Fig. 246. PERCEVAL, N 163.
38 cm.

Page 97.
Fig. 247. HAPPINESS, M 188.
61 cm.

Page 97.
Fig. 248. MINSTREL, N 165.
33 cm.

so that there was no need for any dismissals. Owing to the energy of the old artists who in common with the younger men succeeded in answering all the requirements which the new artistic era set upon their ability the factory was soon able to keep pace with its competitors. The years between 1901—10 show a picture of increasing success artistically and financially which reached its acme in the Jubilee year of 1910 — which was the 200th anniversary of the foundation of the factory. As a result of the steady exertion of the workers as well as of many modern reforms, the Royal Manufactory again obtained the lively interest of the whole world in its successful working. The numerous orders which literally flooded the factory required an extension of its works. A laboratory, a new building for the enamel colour furnaces and a new building for models were erected in 1907—10, while the construction of a third story in the wing occupied by studios A, as well as of a kiln for final baking 8, and a large museum-like building for exhibiting purposes was considered for the near future.

It has been said above that a drawing school had been attached to the factory in the middle of the eighteenth century, that it had been under the supervision of the Dresden Academy of arts from 1814 and was abolished in 1835. The next year, however, saw the re-organisation of the drawing school which existed till 1893 with varied success. Then it was again dissolved. In place of the drawing-school the more able men were now, for some time, sent to the Dresden school of art and industry. As this arrangement did not prove suitable, in 1906 a new drawing-school was founded at the factory. This school exists to this day based on modern principles and is a kind of preliminary school whose aim it is to give young people varied artistic

Page 97.
Fig. 249. TWO FRAMES.
L 192   L 193
22 cm.   22 cm.

Page 98.
Fig. 250. CUPID ON A PANTHER, M 196.
40 cm.

instruction. The pupils are set to drawing, painting, modelling; they receive a preliminary technical education and are encouraged to seek to develop their abilities in all directions. They do not only work from nature but exercises in stylisation and composition are set as well. After spending two years in the drawing-school, the pupils are directed to such departments as they are deemed most fitted for and are there employed as apprentices. The pupils who are particularly gifted go to study at the School of Art

Page 99.

Fig. 253. BUST OF BISMARCK, P110c. 43 cm.

Page 98.

Fig. 251. MARIA ANTOINETTE, K118. 50 cm.

and Industry or at the Academy of fine arts, without thereby losing their connection with the factory.

I have not thought it necessary for many reasons to treat the trade-mark system here in its particulars. Any one who would like information on this subject and who thinks that what Privy counsellor Gesell has written about it in this book[339] is not exhaustive enough, I should refer to the book on Meissen china, page 153 f. In it he will, on two tables, find illustrations and explanations of all the trademarks.

THE MODELLING.

As, under Raithel's directorship, Leuteritz had still kept his place as leader of the modelling department, the work in that department proceeded in the old manner. They kept returning to the Rococo-style altering it to suit the taste of the time. Fig. 236, G105 and G104 shows two statuettes of this description. They are a singer and a songstress which have been created by the modeller and worker in plaster Ruedrich who was working at the factory. Besides the Rococo-style, the style of the Renaissance came into vogue in Meissen as well as in all Germany. It is, for instance reported that Meissen flooded the Exhibition of Art

Page 99.

Fig. 252. WISDOM, CONQUEROR OF OLYMPIA, WOTAN, ART, VIGILANCE.

O154	O179	O156	O183	O169
29 cm.	42 cm.	28 cm.	45 cm.	28 cm.

Table 32

Page 104.

Works by Pilz.

1. Kicking donkey, Y 156.   2. Italian gray-hounds, A 236.   3. Desert foxes, X 142.

24 cm.   23 cm.   15 cm.

4. Yacks, X 141.   5. Peasant with cows, X 123.   6. Group of cats, X 103.

17,5 cm.   28 cm.   20 cm.

and Industry in Leipsic in 1879 with china-ware in Rococo- and Renaissance-styles. The models for these productions had been partly created by artists employed at the factory, partly by Haehnel, Schilling, Schwabe, Schreitmueller and others. A great number of forms came from abroad at that time, even a greater number than in the period before.

Pages 99 and 100.

Fig. 254.   BUSTS OF THE KINGS ALBERT, GEORG AND FRIEDRICH AUGUST.
P 197   V 117   V 116
60 cm.   59 cm.   60 cm.

The statue of Albrecht Duerer by Rauch (Fig. 237, D 148) and the figures representing "Morning", "Noon", "Evening" and "Night" by Schilling which stand at the foot of the staircase of the Bruehl Terrace (Fig. 238, H 191, 195, I 186—187) have been — the latter in 1870 — produced in china in greatly reduced size. The factory purchased rather a large number of models from E. Haehnel:—in 1878 Raffael and Michelangelo (Fig. 239, K 174 and K 173) — in 1881 Kalliope, one of the Muses intended for Vienna (Fig. 240, M 117) and a bacchante (Fig. 241, L 155)— in 1883 Medecine (Fig. 241, N 145) and in 1884 Cupid and a water fairy (Table 28, M 199). The following pieces of china were executed after the models of Prof. Hirt in Munich in 1881 the boy with the bird's nest (Fig. 242, M 150), the lyrical muse (Fig. 243, M 155), a Shooting Cupid (Fig. 244, M 159) — in 1884 a figure in the costume of Gretchen (Fig. 245, N 151), Perceval (Fig. 246, N 163) and Cinderella (Table 29, M 171). Professor Schwabe of Nuern-berg produced the following:—Happiness (Fig. 247, M 188) and several Cupids (Table 27, L 118, 124, 126 and P 119, 121). Schwan-thaler of Munich sent Loreley and Omphale (Table 29, N 108—109), Pollack of Munich two Cupids (Table 27, M 114—115) and lastly Koenig of Vienna:— Geneveva and a cupid with a water fairy (Table 29, G 148 and E 187). Of the Dresden sculptors besides the above mentioned, Schreitmueller sen. de-livered in 1882 a minstrel (Fig. 248, N 165) and two mirror-frames (Fig. 249, L 192—193), Roeder executed in 1884 a

Page 100.

Fig. 256.   TABLE-CLOCK, O 126.
110 cm.

Page 100.

Fig. 257.   MIRROR-FRAME, P 157.
87 cm.

dying warrior (Table 28, N *140*), Hultsch — Psyche and Cerberus (Table 28, M *176*), Rentsch in 1883 Cupid on a panther (Fig. 250, M *196*), Offermann a Loreley (Table 29, O *153*), Hoelbe — Cupid and Psyche (Table 27, N *195—196*).

During this period King Ludwig II of Bavaria wished the Meissen factory to participate in the decoration of his magnificent castles Herrenchiemsee, Berg and Linderhof. In 1866 he ordered a group representing "Lohengrin", in 1876—77 a figure of

Page 100.

Fig. 258.   TABLE-CLOCK, R *200*.
82 cm.

Page 100.

Fig. 255.
MIRROR, O *106*.   FIRE SIDE, O *111*.   TABLE-CENTRE, M *175*.
250 cm.   140 : 180 cm.   63 cm.
TWO CANDLESTICKS, M *172—173*.
57 cm.

Maria Antoinette[340] (Fig. 251, K *118*), in 1873 one large service for a wash-stand and in 1884—85 another as well as two peacocks, two candlesticks for the table a large and a small chandeliers, a mirror-frame with an occasional table and eight painted large china-plaques for doors. The sketches for the shapes and partly for the painting were sent from Munich.

When Leuteritz was pensioned[341] off in 1886 Emmerich Andresen was appointed to succeed him. He had studied sculpture first in Hamburg than in Dresden under Haehnel. We are obliged to him for several monuments such as Hoelderlin's in Tuebingen, Gutzkow's in Dresden and Boettger's in Meissen. The bust of the last is executed in china as well (illustrated page 119). He was very successful in creations the subjects for which were borrowed from allegory and ancient and norwegian mythological legends. It is probable that he was thought fit for the position in

Meissen, owing to several decorative groups made by him; such were he four seasons as groups of children, the figure of a boy with a frog for a fountain, as well as the plastic decorations of the yacht Hohenzollern[342].

Andresen geniality based upon monumental plastique and could never quite free himself of it. His models were not — as we to-day think right — made especially to suit the material. He simply transferred the forms intended for stone or bronze into china. It is true we should not make this a particular subject of reproach to him, as it was a mode of action then generally adopted and had been applied many a time before him. Under him Rossmann in 1889—90 copied the following groups in reduced size:—the two sand stone groups in the Large Garden, "the ravishment of Beauty" by Pietro Balestri and the Psychevase by Corradini. In 1892 he made "Vigilance" (Mattielli) (Fig. 252, O 169), a figure standing at the entrance of

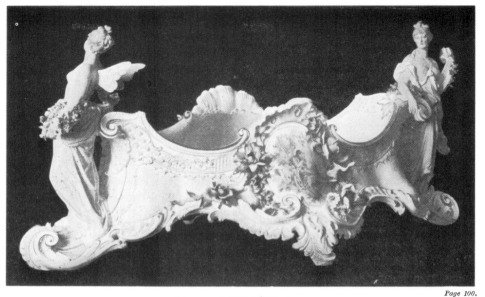

Fig. 259. JARDINIÈRE, S 117.
Length 76 cm., height 35 cm.

Page 100.

Fig. 260. MEZZETIN, COLOMBINA, COVIELLO, PAGLIACCIO, FRITELLINO.
S 126   S 128   S 123   S 121   S 122
14 cm.   15 cm.   15 cm.   14,5 cm.   15 cm.

Page 100.

the Bruehl-palace which has now been pulled down. Richard Koenig copied "Wisdom" the "pendant" to the last-mentioned figure (Fig. 252, O 154).

Andresen himself made the three pieces of porcelain in the middle of Fig. 252 i. e. the figure of Wotan (O 156), the conqueror of Olympia (O 179) and "Art" (O 183). The world of allegory which was so dear to him, we find represented in "Evening" and "Night" (Table 30, P 107 and 108), while the "Declaration of Love" brings us back to the Rococo-style (Table 30, P 132). Of the portraits made by him the bust of Bismarck (Fig. 253, P 110c) and of King Albert (Fig. 254, P 197) may here

Page 100.
Fig. 261. TEUTON, Q 187.
27 cm.

Fig. 262 AFTER THE BATH, T 185.
26:33 cm

Page 100.

Page 100.

Fig. 263. AESOP, R *164.*
24 cm.

Page 101.

Fig. 264.
FORTUNE-TELLER by Rehm, R *120.*
25 cm.

Page 101.

Fig. 265. LADY WITH CAT
by Ungerer, T *173.*
23 cm.

Page 101.

Fig. 267. HUN, Q *197.*
30 cm.

be mentioned. The last-mentioned has been modelled by him with the help of Helmig partly from life. The other two busts on Fig. 254 i. e. the Kings Georg and Friedrich August (V *117* and V *116*) owe their existence to Hoesel.

The enthusiasm called forth by the war of 1870/71 finds an echo in the three groups on Table 28. They represent two wounded Prussians — a hussar and a cuirassier (P *181*) as well as two bavarian artillerists which form a group named "Heroic death" (P *182*) prussian hunters on the outposts (P *180*) and two saxon grenadiers — a group which is called "the entry of the conquerors" (Table 30, P *183*). Here the attempt to depict the people and events of the time has been to a certain extent successful; this is not the case of the figure of a lady in bathing costume (Table 30, Q *127*).

The form which Andresen preferred to all others in his artistic work may be seen in Fig. 255. A fire side with a mirror is here represented (O *111* and *106*). It was sketched by Andresen, executed by Ringler and sent to the exhibition of art and industry to Munich in 1888. This work shows a mixture of Barock and Rococo forms, but nothing original. It is treated in a strict, stiff and dry manner. On the mantle piece candlesticks and an table-centre (M *172—173* and *175*) modelled by Hirt are standing, they are made insimilar style. The following productions of Andresen all show imitated Rococo-style:—a table-clock crowned with the fates (Fig. 256, O *126*), a mirror-frame (Fig. 257, P *157*) ornamented with three cupids and modelled by Helmig after a sketch of Sturm's, as well as the table-clock (Fig. 258, R *200*) made by Helmig and copiously ornamented with symbolic figures. The jardinière (Fig. 259, S *117*) was made by Boermel in 1899 in Berlin and shows the same style.

During the last year that Andresen was employed at the factory his son Romanus as well made several models for Meissen. Thus the love group "In the Park" (Table 30, Q *149*) the figures of which are dressed in the costume of the time and six of the twelve figures from the Italian Comedy. He has made two of the five figures illustrated on Fig. 260 (S *126* and *128*), the others were made by K. Hentschel (S *122*), Koenig (S *121*) and Helmig (S *123*). In Andresen's time the following originated as well:—The Teuton returning from the chase (Fig. 261, Q *187*) and "After the bath" (Fig. 262, T *185*) by Ockelmann, Aesop bestriding a donkey and relating fables (Fig. 263, R *164*) by Heinr. Mueller, besides Table 27 the "Cupids":—Spring (Q *162*) and "Autumn" (Q *161*), Cupid with a tambourine (Q *160*) another with a cymbal (Q *159*) by Stellmacher. The chase (R *133*) and Winter (R *130*) as cupids by Hentschel and, lastly, Cupid as a singer (O *192—193*) by Fischer, Munich. To this belong the following as well:—gentleman and lady by Goeschel (Table 29, M *183*), Venus and Cupid by

Page 101.

Fig. 266. PLAYER AT BOWLS (WOMAN),
Q *180.*
35 cm.

Page 101.

Fig. 268. FIGURES IN NATIONAL DRESS.

Q 190 v	Q 190 r	Q 190 t	Q 190 u	Q 190 m
16 cm.	17 cm.	18,5 cm.	14 cm.	14,5 cm.

Eras (Table 29, O 161), Fishing for water-fairies by Herter (Table 28, Q 195), the uppermost and the lowest row of the figures illustrated on Table 31 (Q 182, O 181, R 148, F 125 and F 148) by Ringler, the fortune-teller by Rehm (Fig. 264, R 120), the lady with the cat by Ungerer (Fig. 265, T 173), a mother teaching her child to walk by Schreitmueller jun. (R 169), by Arthur Lange "Satyr in trouble" (Q 191) as well as a "girl in a storm" (T 2) by Philipp Lange; the last three productions on Table 36.

About this time the above-mentioned tendency to modernisation set in and the new views were fighting a hard fight with the old-fashioned ideas. It is quite right for an institution like the Meissen factory to keep a certain amount of tranquility and not to be swayed hither and tither by the storm of changing opinions, but it would have been just as inappropriate for it to remain altogether indifferent i. e. not to take part in the new movement:—Thus, Meissen, although it at first acted with circumspection, took part in this important battle as well. Models were, at that time (1895) bought from french sculptors such as Deloye and Bourgeois in Paris, or from belgian sculptors such as Ch. Samuel in Brussels (Ulenspiegel et Nèle). Two more works of art were purchased at the Dresden art exhibition of 1897, there were "the player at bowls" (a woman) by Walther Schott of Berlin (Fig. 266, Q 180) and the "Hun on horseback" by Erich Hoesel in Dresden (Fig. 267, Q 197).

In agreement with a lively interest for the history of nations which was rife at the time, various figures in national dress were modelled to order by Spieler in Dresden. Some of then are illustrated on Fig. 268 (Q 190 m, r, t, u, v).

Extraordinarily great pains were taken in Meissen with the articles which were to be dispatched to the Paris world's exhibition in 1900. The greatest stress was here laid upon the employement of the rich old store of forms and models. Hardly anything can be said against this; the public at large to this day has a preference for chinaware which originated in this manner. But the way these old forms were employed is not

Page 102.

Fig. 269. CHANDELIER, 2718.
118 cm.

Page 102.

Fig. 271. WALL-BRACKET, belonging to the swan service, *348.*
50 cm.

Page 102.

Fig. 270. CHANDELIER, Z *92*.*
70 cm.

now recognised as correct. At that time they did not make use of the old forms as they found them, but attempted to improve them by modelling everything very sharply, by executing everything very correctly and by observing the most minute details. As a result of such a trivial conception the chief of the whole was lost sight of and an unpleasant type and stiff forms were created. This was a misconceived imitation of the good old models. The following may be here shown as examples of this kind of chinaware:—a chandelier by Kaendler which was altered to suit electric lighting (Fig. 269, *2718*), another one resembling it made by Leuteritz (Fig. 270, Z *92**), a wall-bracket, belonging to the "Swan service" (Fig. 271, *348*), a copiously ornamented tureen in Barock-Rococo-style (Fig. 272, *350*) — the model for the last mentioned also probably originated in the eighteenth century — and a Rococo coffee service (Fig. 273, *138*) but slightly altered from the original.

When the modern views gradually began to find greater favour and gained a firm footing, Meissen thought it inadvisable to keep back any longer, but found it necessary to graft a new branch on to the old tree-trunk. This change of opinion brought the intention to go

Page 120.

Fig. 272. TUREEN, *350.* TUREEN-SAUCER 1
45 cm. high.   60 cm. long
(Altered 1899.

Table 34

Pages 104, 105, 107, 108.

1 and 2. Girl with cat, Lady with foxboa by Ph. Lange, Y *153* and A *201.*

19 cm., 31 cm.

3. St. Bernhard dog by Oehler, X *117.*   4. Embroideress, X *116.*   5. Parisienne, X *183.*   6. Danceuse, Y *111.*

19,5 cm.   23 cm.   22 cm.   24 cm.

7. Girl with a child, W *130.*   8. Figure for a centre piece, A *250,9.*   (4—8 by Eichler.)

21 cm.   32 cm.

9. Brahma-chickens by Zuegel, X *148.*   10. Snow owls by Fritz, X *184.*

21 cm.   20 cm.

with the time and give the new ideas their due. This is made apparent in the fact that both positions of artistic leaders were given to Hoesel and Achtenhagen — men vowed to modern ideas.

Even now the old forms and models which have made Meissen famous are being largely used, only the manner in which this is done differs entirely from the way described above. To day a new model is made after the old shape. It is made in all its details as far as possible like the original and, wherever possible, a good old piece of china is used to compare it with. According to this the forms for use in making china are produced. In the ornamentation as well as in the modelling it was sought to follow the old models as closely as possible. The parts intended for colouring are not — as has been to this time usual — entirely covered with paint or made realistically to imitate flesh-colour, the colours are only indicated and single parts relieved in colour; this airy style adapts itself beautifully to china.

Page 102.

Fig. 273. COFFEE SERVICE, design *138.*
Plateau, Milk pot, Coffee pot, Cup, Saucer, Sugar basin.
48 cm. 16 cm. 20 cm. 6 cm. 15 cm. 10 cm.
(Altered 1899.)

Not only imitations of old models are being made in Meissen ut present, quite the contrary, new ideas are very extensively used at the factory. In such independent work the chief aim is to create new forms entirely adapted to the material, where the great amount of shrinking in the baking, the peculiarities of the glaze etc. are considered.

Page 103.

Fig. 274. TEA SERVICE by van de Velde.
Sugar basin, Cake plate, Tea pot, Milk ewer, Cup, Saucer.
6:14 cm. 17,5 cm. 14:25 cm. 6:11 cm. 5,5 cm. 18,5 cm.

It is quite natural that many a mistake was made here at first. For china is an extraordinarily brittle material which can not be easily mastered. Everyone who works with it must have a great deal of practise before he learns to manage it at all well and to consider it in all its complicated nature. When therefore the renowned industrial artists were requested to make models in modern style for Meissen they achieved by no means brilliant results. The dinner service which was sketched by van de Velde in 1904 (Fig. 274 shows the tea service belonging to it) seems not at all successful in form. It is not well adapted to china and would be more fit for making it in metal. The dinner service designed by Riemerschmid in 1905 (Fig. 275 shows the coffee service) appears more appropriate for rustic majolica and the cutting of the edge is not exactly happy in its design. The chandelier and the wall-bracket (Fig. 276—277, W *199* and X *115*) which were designed by Kreis for the exhibition of art and industry in Dresden in 1906 are much too monumental for the material, although highly original in conception. The little vase by Gross (Fig. 278, W *136*) betrays its origin as designed for tin.

Animal plastique was a branch which Meissen was the first factory

Page 103.

Fig. 275. COFFEE SERVICE by Riemerschmid.
Coffee pot 1, Dinner plate 1, Milk pot, Cup, Saucer, Sugar basin.
21 cm. 26 cm. diam. 11 cm. 8 cm. 16,5 cm. diam. 10 cm.

Page 103.

Fig. 277. WALL-BRACKET
by Kreis, X *115*.
30 cm.

to put on an important footing. With regard to this Pilz and Fritz of Dresden must be mentioned of all the workers outside the factory. Table 32 shows several of the best works of the former:— the humourously conceived group of a kicking donkey (Y *156*), the slim italian grayhounds (A *236*), the bold long-eared desert foxes (X *142*), the shaggy yacks (X *141*), the farmer with the team of cows (X *123*) and the group of cats (X *103*). The two giraffes and the mandrill (monkey) (Table 33, X *162* and *143*), the girl sitting on the back of a tortoise (Fig. 279, X *163*) were designed by him as well.

Page 103.
Fig. 278.
VASE by Gross, W *136*.
19,5 cm.

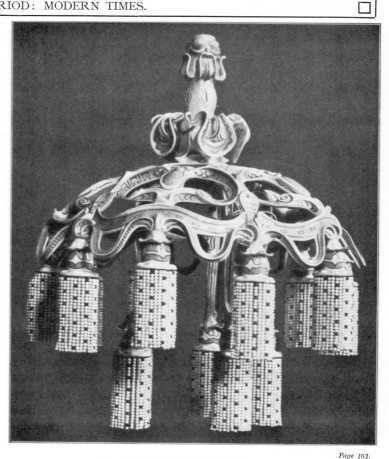

Fig. 276. CHANDELIER by Kreis, W *199*.
65 cm. high, 54 cm. diam.

Page 103.

Fritz made the two white owls (Table 34, X *184*) — which are particularly effectful because they are so flatly made — and the falcons (Table 37, X *185*). The following artists delivered models for the factory as well:—Hartung of Berlin the wild boar (Fig. 280, S *133*), an excellent study from nature in the Berlin zoological garden, Willi Zuegel of Munich a polar bear with its young (Fig. 281, X *147*) and Brahma chickens (Table 34, X *148*), Paessler of Loschwitz english goitre pigeons (Fig. 282, W *180*), Roth a polar bear (Fig. 283, W *137*) and Katz of Berlin the genettes (grinster cats) (Fig. 284, A *231*).

Jarl of Vienna was occupied in Meissen for some time, he created a series of original models; of these the following may here be mentioned:—the sea-lion, particularly well observed (Fig. 285, U *122*), the two pointers which are being led on a cord (Fig. 286, U *164*) with the hunter leading them (Fig. 287, U *160*), the kitten (Fig. 288, U *146*), the polar bear (Table 33, T *182*) and the writing stand with owls and a bust of Dante on the ink-pot cover (Fig. 289, U *200*).

Page 104.
Fig. 279.
GIRL AND TORTOISE by Pilz,
X *163*.
14 cm.

When Andresen died in 1903, Erich Hoesel was appointed director of the plastic department in Meissen. He had studied at the Dresden academy, first painting under Pohle then sculpture under Schilling and Diez. After a voyage to the Orient for purposes of study, lasting two years, he was employed from October 1899 as a teacher at the Academy of Cassel. It has already above been spoken of that his "Hunn on horseback" had been bought for the

Page 104.
Fig. 280. WILD BOAR by Hartung, S *133*.
25 cm. high.

Fig. 281. POLAR BEAR WITH ITS YOUNG
by W. Zuegel, X *147*.
17 cm.

Fig. 282. GOITRE PIGEONS by Paessler, W *180*.
20:42 cm.

manufactory on the Exhibition of Art in Dresden in 1897. Meissen has to thank him for the extraordinarily difficult opening of the treasure house of shapes and models, as well as for the plastic and artistic treatment of these old models which has already been described above. Besides he has very successfully worked at the initiation of the spirit of modern art into the Meissen factory.

Of his own works the following may be here shown:—a brown bear and four collar-bears (Fig. 290, V *102, 112, 106, 123*), an oriental musician (Table 37, V *129*), a rooster (Table 37, V *130*) and a group named "North America" (Fig. 291, V *120*) as a token of artistic studies made in America.

A large number of artists gathered round Hoesel and were influenced by him in attempting to solve their varied problems in modern style. This brings with it the necessity of making studies from nature; for the sake of this some of the artists went abroad for some time.

Fig. 283. POLAR BEAR by Roth, W *137*.
6:26 cm.

Fig. 284. GENETTES by Katz, A *231*.
9:15,5 cm.

Ph. Lange had been twice in Holland. A proof of the studies he made here is offered in his excellently conceived group of the Dutch (Table 33, Z *193*). The management of the factory afforded Eichler the opportunity of studying in Paris, Koenig in Ostende, Walther and Barth (the latter is a painter) in the zoological gardens of Berlin and Stellingen.

The works in animal plastique are extraordinarily numerous and will be here first spoken of. Walther designed the slinking fox (Fig. 292, X *170*), the mandarin duck, the cacadoo and the little screech owl (Fig. 293, Y *129*, A *208* and A *225*), a baboon in a saucer (Fig. 294, A *226**), guinea fowls (Table 37, Z *155*), a toucan (Table 37, Z *188*) and on Table 38 a pelican (W *142*), an ash tray with maki (a kind of monkey) (X *127*), swans (Z *102*), owls (W *146*), a peacock on a pillar (W *145*), an elephant with a cosmak (W *148*) and a mock-eagle (W *150*); by Bochmann the kangaroos (Fig. 295, Y *105—106*), the cormorant in a saucer (Fig. 296, Y *163**) and on Table 38 the girl with rabbits (Z *148*), the group of zebus (Y *162*) and the child with a sheep (Z *134*); by Oehler a lady with a parrot (Table 36, A *277*) and the St. Bernhard dog (Table 34, X *117*); by Tillberg a bonbon-box ornamented with mice sitting on it (Fig. 297, X *144*),

Fig. 285. SEA-LION by Jarl, U *122*.
14 cm.

Fig. 287 HUNTER by Jarl, U *160*.
29 cm.

Fig. 286. POINTERS by Jarl, U *164*.
10:28 cm.

Fig. 288. KITTEN by Jarl, U *146*.
9:17 cm.

Fig. 289. WRITING STAND by Jarl, U 200.
12 : 20 cm.
Page 104.

Fig. 290. BROWN BEAR AND COLLAR-BEARS by Hoesel.
| V 112 | V 102 | V 106 | V 123 |
| 7,5 cm. | 13,5 cm | 10 cm. | 6 cm. |
Page 105.

Fig. 291. NORTH AMERICA by Hoesel, V 120.
33 cm.
Page 105.

Fig. 292. SLINKING FOX by Walther, X 170.
7,5 : 25 cm.
Page 105.

rice-bunting (Fig. 298, Y 103) and the english rabbits (Fig. 299, X 177); by Arthur Lange the duck with a frog (Fig. 300, T 179) made already in Andresen's time.

Besides the animal plastique the rest of the figure plastique gained more and more ground in Meissen. In this case as well many models were obtained from outside the factory.

Fig. 293. MANDARIN DUCK, CACADOO, OWL
by Walther.
| Y 129 | A 208 | A 225 |
| 10 cm. | 11 cm. | 11 cm. |
Page 105.

The two Paris street types of dealers in books and clothes by Hoetger, Paris, (Table 28, T 163 and 262) I should describe as charming but too sketchy for being made in china. The "Piqueur" (Fig. 301, T 102) modelled by Kramer of Munich may, in my opinion be classed with the best work of the present time. It is conceived in old style and executed in a modern manner. An excellent pendant to this is the lady hawker (Fig. 301, V 132) by Hoesel. Besides the Piqueur Kramer modelled the Concert (Table 29, T 186) as well.

Fig 294. BABOON IN A SAUCER
by Walther, A 226*.
13 cm. high, 14,5 cm. diam.
Page 105.

The artists employed at the factory produced, however, a still greater number of models. Of these artists I shall first speak of

Fig. 295. KANGAROOS by Bochmann.
| Y 106 | Y 105 |
| 9 cm. | 15,5 cm. |
Page 105.

Fig. 296. CORMORANT
by Bochmann, Y 163*.
11,5 cm.
Page 105.

Fig. 297. BONBON-BOX
WITH MICE by Tillberg, X 144.
10,5 cm. high, 11 cm. diam.
Page 105.

Fig. 298.
RICE-BUNTING
by Tillberg, Y 103.
11,5 cm.
Page 106.

Page 106.

Fig. 299. RABBITS by Tillberg, X *177.*
16 cm.

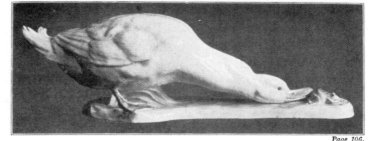

Page 106.

Fig. 300. DUCK WITH FROG by A. LANGE, T *179.*
17 : 48 cm.

Helmig whose work has already been mentioned under Andresen. His strong point probably lies in eclectics.

The following figures in old style represented on Table 31 may be given as examples of this:—two cupids (R *123* and U *148*) and the vendor of cupids (Q *184*) and "spring" (S *166*). Helmig has however gone to the trouble of making himself at home in the new style as well; as proof of this we mention the saucer with a wave in the shape of a water fairy (Fig. 302, R *176*) and the clock-case slightly showing modern style (Fig. 303, U *189*).

Konrad Hentschel was one of the artists who was quick and apt in catching the modern style. But he was unfortunately snatched away from his work at an early age in 1907. His "playing children" (Table 35, W *118, 117, 124* and Table 36, W *166, 120, 165*) and the girls with flower wreaths (Fig. 304, W *126, 128*) are treated in a style adapted to china and seek to picture well-observed scenes from the life of to-day. The figure with the sea-shell was also made by him (Table 36, P *144*). His brother Rudolf Hentschel should be noticed principally as a painter, still Meissen has to thank him

Page 106.

Fig. 301. LADY HAWKER by Hoesel, PIQUEUR by Kramer
V *132*   T *102*
39 cm.   39 cm.

for many a model conceived in the same style; such are the lady in riding habit accompanied by a greyhound (Table 33, Z *187*), a lady putting a glove on Table 36, A *205*) and the lady tennis player (Table 36, Z *113*).

The girl with the child and the embroideress (Table 34, W *130* and X *116*) were made by Eichler, a pupil of Diez. The Paris lady and the danceuse (Table 34, X *183* and Y *111*) as well as the Dresden

Page 107.

Fig. 302. WAVE IN THE SHAPE OF A WATER FAIRY
by Helmig, R *176.*
15 25 cm.

Page 107.

Fig. 303. CLOCK-CASE by Helmig, U *189.*
21 : 45 cm.

Page 107.

Fig. 304.   GIRLS WITH FLOWER WREATHS by K. Hentschel.
W *128*   W *126*
14 : 28 cm.   23 cm.

Page 108.

Fig. 305.   BUST OF THE SOLO DANCER HESS
by Eichler, Y *196*.
37 cm.

ballet dancers (several of whom he has modelled) show the influence of his studies in Paris. Fig. 305, Y *196* represents the bust of Miss Hess, Table 35, W *115* a group called blind-man's buff and Table 34, A *250* a figure which belong to a rather large centre piece.

Of the work of A. Koenig two ladies dressed in Empire-style and a couple of lovers (Table 35, A *257—259*), are illustrated as well as a group of skaters (Table 37, Z *196*); while Phil. Lange is represented in the already mentioned dutch group (Table 33, Z *193*), the girl with the cat and the lady with the fox boa (Table 34, Y *153* and A *201*).

THE PAINTING.

Page 109.

Fig. 307   PLATE, red border and fruit painting,
design *157*.
22,5 cm.

Ludwig Sturm was the leader of the painting department in Meissen for the longest time in this period i. e. from 1880 to 1905. He had received his education as an artist in a Bamberg china factory, then in the academies of Munich and Dresden. After having lived in Dresden as a portrait painter for several years, he came as a young, fresh artist to the Meissen factory. Here he did away with some irregularities in the painting branch and breathed new life into the ornamentation which from the Marcolini period downwards had gradually grown pale and stiff. As the opinions of what is true and false in artistic industry have since then thoroughly altered, we can not, on principle praise many of his productions. He had a preference for copying oil-paintings on china plaques. This is a procedure which we to-day reject as not adapted to china. For this purpose the painter

Page 109.

Fig. 306.   THE RAVISHMENT OF EUROPA
after Grosse, O *170*.
69 cm.

Page 109.

Fig. 308.   PLATE in altered Rococo-pattern, T *22,2*.
22,5 cm.

Table 36

Pages 101, 105, 107.

1—3. Playing children by K. Hentschel, W *166, 120* and *165.* 4. Lady with parrot by Oehler, A *277.*

14 cm., 17,5 cm., 12 cm.   19 cm.

5. Mother with child by Schreitmueller jun., R *169.* 6 and 7. Ladys by R. Hentschel, A *205,* Z *113.*

17 cm.   26,5 cm., 23 cm.

8. Figure with shell by K. Hentschel, P *144.*

25 cm.

9 and 10. Satyr in danger by A. Lange, Girl in a storm by Ph. Lange, Q *191,* T *2.*

38 cm., 29 cm.

Fig. 309. DISH by Braunsdorf, M *130*.
46 cm.

Page 110.

Page 111

Fig. 312. CHILD'S CUP, *41.* MOCCA CUP, O *49.*
Cup 7,5 cm. high.   Cup 10 cm. high.
Saucer 16 cm. diam.   Saucer 13 cm. diam

Frenzel was principally engaged in copying the paintings in the Dresden picture gallery. After one of these productions, the copy of the "chocolate-girl" by Liotard a small figure was modelled in Meissen and afterwards executed in porcelain (Table 29, T *5*).

In Sturm's time as well artists from outside were employed in painting for Meissen. So in 1884 reproductions of Schwindt's wall-painting in the Vienna operahouse were purchased, while the painting on the principal pieces of chinaware which Meissen sent to the exhibition of art and industry in Leipsic in 1879, had been designed by Grosse, Bendemann and others. A dinner service painted in blue under glaze had been designed by Graff. The drawing of the "ravishment of Europa" on the vase represented on Fig. 306, O *170* is the work of Grosse as well.

Page 110.
Fig. 310. VASE by Grust, R *192*.
26,5 cm.

In single cases they went to work in the same way under Sturm. For instance in 1886 the artist just-mentioned delivered drawings for the painting to be executed on two vases, in 1897 Zwintscher made a drawing for "paste upon paste" painting, in 1897—98 Grust drew

Fig. 311. VASES, X *59*.
25 cm.

Page 111.

water-fairies dancing with centaurs to be executed in colours which could be exposed to the high temperature necessesary for the baking of porcelain. But here as well Meissen felt the need of not only doing the painting on china, but of having the drawings and designs for it executed within the walls of the factory by its own artists.

The manner in which the old style was at that time used may be seen in Fig. 307 and 308. The former shows a plate (*157*) which is painted with a Rococo-pattern, red border and fruit, the latter figure shows a plate (T *22,2*) in which the Rococo-pattern has been

Page 111.
Fig. 313. OVAL TUREEN, *3*.
18 : 28,5 cm.

Page 112.
Fig. 314.
LADIES WRITING-CASE by Walther, Z *154*.
18 cm. diam.

Page 112.

Fig. 315. MOZART-VASE
by Grust, S *147**.
34 cm.

Page 112.

Fig. 319. BONBON-BOX, Z *111*, Z *109* and Nr. 2 by Hentschel, Z *107* by Stein.

Z *111*	Z *107*	Z *109*	Nr. 2
7 cm.	6 cm. high, 11,5 cm. diam.	5 cm. high, 10 cm. diam.	5 cm. high, 7 cm. diam.

modernised under Sturm.

Besides I should like to mention that Sturm wished to open new vistas to the porcelain industry.

For instance he often had plaques of china painted which were intended for inlaying furniture and doors (Fig. 231) and for ornamenting walls. It was owing to Sturm's initiative that Braunsdorf — the able painter in water colours — studied the art of flower painting to perfection (Fig. 309, M *130*) Braunsdorf's artistic importance as a flower painter should not be depreciated, although at present this naturalistic painting on china does not appeal to us any more, neither do we now find it appropriate. A short time after Braunsdorf's installation in Meissen as a flower painter, his artistic ideas were shared by the other painters; we find for instance, the vase designed by Grust — who was employed in Meissen in 1898 — (Fig. 310, R *192*) entirely in Braunsdorf's style. New means of decoration were put at the disposal of the Meissen painters by the laboratory; it made new gold and platinum which appeared transparent and effectful when applied to china baked at a high temperature;

Page 112.

Fig. 317. VASES, AUTUMN AND SPRING, S *147*.
Shape by Grust, painting by Hentschel.
35 cm.

besides variegated covering enamel and colour grounds which could be exposed to the high temperature required for baking china as well as coloured glazings. These coloured grounds, for instance blue and yellow, were often used for flower painting in natural colours as well. The figure painter Julius Hentschel successfully painted the white and coloured chinaware (with "paste upon paste" painting) which was continually produced after 1880 according to his own sketches or those of other artists.

Page 112.

Fig. 316. VASE by Grust, P *146*.
104 cm.

Page 112.

Fig. 318. DISH by Hentschel, W *182*.
30 cm. diam.

Fig. 320. OVAL DISH by Hentschel, SAUCERS by Voigt.

Pages 112 and 113.

4	N 112	Z 125	Z 120
13 : 18 cm.	11,5 cm.	14,5 cm.	13,5 cm.

Page 113.

Fig. 324. CUP by Olbrich, W 198.
Cup 5,5 cm.

The modern tendency, although but slowly came forward in the painting in Meissen as well. It has already been above intimated in what way the ornamentation of the forms made according to the old models was altered and how the artists sought to equal the old work in lightnes and grace of painting as well as of the formation of the original models. Fig. 311 shows three vases (X 59) of old form which are painted in this fashion, with designs of the yellow lion, with butterflies and "german flowers". On Fig. 312, 41 and O 49 two cups are represented. One of these is painted with the yellow-lion pattern, while the other shows festoons in Biedermeier-style and a silhouette portrait.

It has been above pointed out that the development of the "paste upon paste" painting brought with it a great increase in the number of colours which could be used for painting on china and which could bear the high temperature required for the baking of it. Through the use of these colours Meissen's relation to modern art was made possible. Therefore most of the chinaware described in the modelling has been relieved or painted with the last mentioned colours, which excellently sustained the effectfulness of the form by their soft brightness.

The oval tureen illustrated on Fig. 313 shows a manner of decoration for which good old models had been referred to.

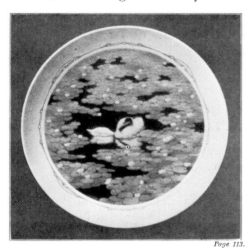

Page 113.

Fig. 321. DISH by Voigt, Y 169.
42 cm.

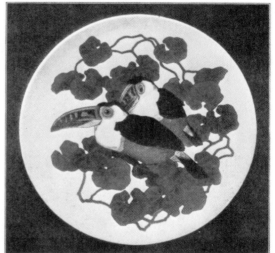

Page 113.

Fig. 322. DISH by Voigt, A 229.
31 cm.

Page 113.

Fig. 323. PRESENTING PLATE by Barth, oval, I.
29 cm. long.

Page 113.

Fig. 325.
VASE by Hoest, T 72.
15,5 cm.

Page 114.

Fig. 326. CHRISTMAS CANDLES by Hentschel, A 265.
25 cm.

Page 114.

Fig. 327. STAR OF BETHLEHEM by Hentschel, A *280*.
25 cm.

Page 114.

Fig. 328. WOMEN'S CHURCH IN MEISSEN by Voigt, A *279*.
25 cm.

We do not here find a painting of flowers in still-life on china but an appropriate decoration of the porcelain with flowers instead. The painting here consists of five sharpfire-colours which could bear the high temperature required for the baking of china, thus the stalks and the outline were painted brown, the small blossoms blue, the large ones red, the fruit yellow and the leaves green; another example for this manner of ornamentation is the ladies writing-case by Walther (Fig. 314, Z *154*).

Under Grust who in 1905, for the time being, represented Sturm's place after the latter had left the factory the change in the artistic conception above spoken of took place. He created the shape and the painting of the Mozart-vase (Fig. 315, S *147**) as well as the enormous vase with "the dance of the water fairies" (Fig. 316, P *146*) which was exhibited in Paris in 1900 and brought its author the silver medal. The forms of the two vases representing "Autumn" and "Spring" (Fig. 317, S *147*) have been made by him as well while the painting was done by Hentschel who has above been mentioned as a sculptor. Of the work of the latter we give illustration in three plates painted with landscapes (Table 33 T *22,₆* and Fig. 318, W *182*), in most of the bonbon-boxes (Fig. 319, Z *107* and *109, 111*, Nr. 2) and the oval dish (Fig. 320, *4*).

Page 114.

Fig. 329. EASTER PLAQUE by Baring, A *298*.
25 cm.

Page 114.

Fig. 330. PRIZE PLATE, T *22,₁*.
27 cm.

Page 114.

Fig. 331. MEMORIAL PLATE by Hentschel.
New cu⁺ 1.
25 cm.

Page 114.

Fig. 332. JUBILEE PLATE by Voigt, N *117*.
25 cm.

Page 114.

Fig. 333. JUBILEE PLATE by Voigt, N 117.
25 cm.

Page 114.

Fig. 334. JUBILEE PLATE by Richter, N 117.
25 cm.

Voigt and Barth deserve to be particularly noticed as painters in colours which bear the high temperature required for the baking of china. We get an idea of the style of the former from the three saucers (Fig. 320, N 112, Z 125 and 120) and the two large dishes (Fig. 321, Y 169 and Fig. 322, A 229); of that of the latter artist from the oval presenting plate (Fig. 323).

The artists mentioned have at different times designed new patterns for dinner or coffee services. The following may be mentioned as examples:—by R. and K. Hentschel the crocus, wing and arnica-pattern; by Grust the shamrock and the Misnia-design; by Voigt the so-called Saxonia, rose wreath and glycinia-pattern and the primula and the dame's violet pattern by Barth. In several instances artists not employed at the factory have had chinaware executed in Meissen after their own designs, these designs afterwards becoming the property of the factory. As examples of this I mention the toilet set with the roses-pattern by Vogeler, of Worpswede and a tea-cup with copious plastic gold-painting by Olbrich of Darmstadt, which is here illustrated (Fig. 324, W 198). Miss Hoest has worked at the factory for some length of time (Fig. 325, T 72).

The Meissen factory has besides all this created various pieces

Page 114.

Fig. 335. JUBILEE PLATE by Richter, N 117.
25 cm.

Page 115.

Fig. 336. COMMEMORATIVE PLATE by Barth, A 245.
25 cm.

Page 115.

Fig. 337. COMMEMORATIVE PLATE by Barth, Z 133.
25 cm.

Page 115.

Fig. 338. COMMEMORATIVE PLATE by Barth, Z 137.
25 cm.

Page 115.

Fig. 339. COMMEMORATIVE PLATE by Barth, A *244*.
25 cm.

Page 115.

Fig. 341. COMMEMORATIVE PLATE by Barth, A *237*.
25 cm.

Page 115.

Fig. 343. COMMEMORATIVE PLATE by Barth, Z *105*.
25 cm.

of china which were intended for general or especial festivals; thus the coronation plates, the Christmas plaques (Fig. 326, A *265* by Hentschel, Fig. 327, A *280*, "Star of Bethlehem" by the same, Fig. 328, A *279*, "Women's church in Meissen" by Voigt) and the Easter plaques by Baring (Fig. 329, A *298*). Some other plates were intended for the following purposes:— as a prize of the "society for advancing the traffic in Dresden and with foreign countries" (Fig. 330, T *22,1*) designed under the direction of Professor Naumann by Kamke; for the consecration of the artists' house in Dresden (Fig. 331, by Hentschel), for the jubilee of the infantry regiments 102 and 104 (Fig. 332—333, N *117*, by Voigt) and of the "Trainbataillons" Nr. 12 (Fig. 334—335, N *117*, by Richter). For its own 200th anniversary the Meissen factory has made a plaque as well (Fig. 349, N *117*, by Grust).

The mementoes of Saxon towns and castles in the form of plaques which have only of late been first made by Barth have gained exceedingly great popularity. There is already a great number of these plaques in existence and more can be made if required. The outlines are slightly pressed on to the plate

Page 115.

Fig. 340. COMMEMORATIVE PLATE by Barth, A *240*.
25 cm.

Page 115.

Fig. 342. COMMEMORATIVE PLATE by Barth, A *238*.
25 cm.

Page 115.

Fig. 344. COMMEMORATIVE PLATE by Barth, A *242*.
25 cm.

Page 115.

Fig. 345. COMMEMORATIVE PLATE by Barth, A *243*.
25 cm.

Page 115.

Fig. 346. COMMEMORATIVE PLATE by Barth, A *241*.
25 cm.

out of the form and the painting is made in blue under glaze thus (Fig. 336, A *245*, Meissen, Fig. 337, Z *133*, the Meissen Cathedral, Fig. 338, Z *137*, the same, Fig. 339, A *244*, Dresden, Fig. 340, A *240*, Moritzburg, Fig. 341, A *237*, Freiberg, Fig. 342, A *238*, Pillnitz, Fig. 343, Z *105*, Bautzen, Fig. 344, A *242*, Chemnitz, Fig. 345, A *243*, Plauen i. V., Fig. 346, A *241*, Zwickau and Fig. 347, A *239*, a bastion bridge).

In 1909, as has already been above intimated, August Achtenhagen was appointed leader of the painting department in Meissen. He received his artistic education in the school of art, the school of art and industry

Pages 115 and 116.

Fig. 348. JUBILEE VESSELS. Designed by Achtenhagen.

B *160*	B *113*	Q *131*
12 cm. without garnishes.	13 cm.	25 cm. without garnishes.
17 „ with „		30 „ with „

and the academy of fine arts in Berlin. Then he perfected his knowledge under Bracht and Kampf, worked for some time practically at the Royal china factory in Berlin, travelled in Italy for purposes of study for two and a half years and lastly filled the position of teacher at the art school in Berlin for seven years. Lately Hentschel has under him made attempts to use copper-red for painting under glazing. These attempts must be noted as very successful thanks to the excellent technical execution under the guidance of the Counsellor of mines Dr Foerster. Of Achtenhagen's original designs the following are here shown:—the beer jug, wine jug and goblet in painted blue under glaze which were made to commemorate the jubilee of the factory

Page 115.

Fig. 347. COMMEMORATIVE PLATE by Barth, A 239.
25 cm.

Page 114.

Fig. 349. JUBILEE PLATE by Grust, N 117.
25 cm.

in 1910 (Fig. 348, B 160, B 113 and Q 131) and the decoration of the old vase BC. which may be seen on Fig. 114, page 52.

I believe here to be able to draw attention to the fact that the factory, now under the direction of the Privy counsellor Gesell, has during the last years done a great deal that will redound to its credit. It has been successful in completely keeping at the height of technical perfection and in putting a number of artists in its employ, artists who work in modern style and seek to adapt themselves to the excellent qualities of the material and not to cover it with painting but to paint it in order to show the china itself to better effect.

To day we find a rather large number of component parts united in Meissen, which give cause to the hope, that the factory will in future as it has done in the past prove worthy of its old renown by recognizing the modern demands with regard to technique, art and commerce.

Table 38

1—3 by Bochmann, 4—11 by Walther.

1. Girl with rabbits, Z 148.   2. Group of Zebus, Y 162.   3. Child and sheep, Z 134.   4. Pelican, W 142.

12 cm.   13 cm.   16 cm.   16 cm.

5. Parrot, A 207.   6. Matchstand and ashtray with maki, X 127.   7. Swans, Z 102.   8. Owl, W 146.

10 cm.   20 cm.   21 cm.   13 cm.

9. Peacock, W 145.   10. Elephant, W 148.   11. Fancy cyclist, W 150.

31 cm.   With socle 34 cm.   29 cm.

Table 39

ROYAL CHINA FACTORY IN MEISSEN.

ROYAL CASTLE OF ALBRECHTSBURG IN MEISSEN,
PLACE WHERE THE FACTORY WAS FOUNDED.

THE DEVELOPMENT
OF THE CHEMICO-TECHNICAL MANAGEMENT
FROM THE BEGINNING TO THE PRESENT TIME.

BY DR. HEINTZE.

When Johann Friedrich Boettger, in the first decade of the eighteenth century, made systematic investigations with regard to the fire proofness of the free combinations to be met with in nature such as ore, minerals, earth and stones, he found that all these bodies may be divided into groups of greater or lesser fire proofness. Originally Boettger made these investigations in connection with a question which was rife at the time i. e. with the transmutation of the baser metals into precious ones. Although he had an unattainable aim in view, great credit is due to him for having been clever enough to make good use of the results of his work on another field. Boettger was than under the protection of the King of Poland and Elector of Saxony Friedrich August I who compelled his protegé to work at experiments in alchemy, that is to seek a way of making gold. When the King became interested in the mercantile policy of his country he ordered Boettger to invent a new industry where the raw materials that were lying waste in the country could be exploited. In case of failure to do this, he was to introduce an industry already known in other countries into the Saxon lands. After Boettger had unsuccessfully worked in alchymistry in Dresden and elsewhere, he was able in 1707 by making use of his preliminary studies to solve one of the problems above mentioned in a satisfactory manner. The course of the work itself will be here but shortly described. (Compare Heintze, Archive for history of natural science and technics, vol. II, 1910.)

Under the burning reflector produced by Tschirnhaus Boettger melted lead, tin and silver and transmuted pinewood into charcoal under water. He made investigations as to the relation of gold and other metals, of stones, ore, coloured and other earth. He then went further and tried the various bodies in the muffle-furnace and the melting oven, in a fire of beech wood and of charcoal. Here he found that the bodies did not remain in their anterior state, but were destroyed by the fire in order at last to bring forth a new product. In examining the coloured earths — which were at that time much used in manufacturing various articles —, he found that some changed their colour in the fire while others passed unchanged through it, also that there is earth which burns white or as we now say:—clay which turns white in the baking. He made use of this observation first with clay which he found near Dresden and which turned white in the baking and succeeded in producing what was at that time called "Delft ware", as well as "Dutch china". As far as we can ascertain he made this discovery in 1707 at the fortress of Koenigstein. Here he was kept in safety together with his three assistants in the laboratory for over a year, during the invasion of Saxony by the Swedish army. When Boettger reported his discovery to the King, the latter had a factory of Delft ware erected in Altstadt Dresden at his own cost. Here household utensils and vases were made. They were still but clay vessels which were covered with a glaze containing easily melted-soda and lead ashes and painted with cobalt blue under the glaze. After a few years this factory was joined to the Meissen china works but the management was soon discontinued. In the further course of his investigations, Boettger produced red china or, as we must now call it, red stone-ware. He had mixed red Nuernberg clay with a red bolus and had baked it at a temperature which is used for melting silver. In place of the Nuernberg clay he soon used another which was yellowish, but turned red in the fire and was found in the neighbourhood of Zwickaw in Saxony. As it was soon evident that fire influenced the colour of the vessels, he put them into double saggers and filled the interstice with fine quarzy sand. In order to be able to judge of the heat in the kiln, he put small clay cylinders into the peepholes and observed the brilliance as it arose.

Now that Boettger had ascertained that, besides the coloured earths, clay existed which became white in the baking and that besides such bodies as melted in the fire, fire-proof ones existed as well, it was but a step to the production of white china. This was done by analogy of red porcelain with the aid of the clay which turned white in the baking and of a medium of flux — he chose gypsum. For perfecting it he required a glaze fit for using, which it took him a year to produce. It had to be brilliant, hard and suit the body and was not to crack when baked with the china. His first attempts to produce a glaze consisting of quarz, caolin and borax were not successful. Only when he used lime instead of borax did he meet with a meed of success. He at first made the white porcelain paste out of Colditz washed clay and glowbaked, washed and finely ground alabaster. In 1709 Schnorr sent him white clay from Aue near Schneeberg. The clay came out of a mine which had been worked since 1700. The union of white clay workers of St. Andrew had already delivered clay to the Schneeberg cobalt works which when baked in connection with oxide of cobalt gave forth a blue colour. This white clay was caolin or porcelain clay and that was the first place in Europe where it was found. Its exportation from Saxony was prohibited in 1729. In 1745 the prohibition had to be renewed. This caolin from Aue was a very lucky finding as it was a material excellent in every respect; plastic and durable in its raw state and highly fire-proof in the high temperature necessary for the baking of china.

On March 28th 1709 Boettger reported to the King the result of his work at great length. After a sort of a trial factory had been worked on the Venus bastion in Dresden for a year, the King gave the Albrechtcastle in Meissen to be used for the new works. A factory for red china, white china and for Hessian crucibles was here installed. Only the production of white china was kept up permanently. Although the board of directors remained in Dresden, Dr. med. Heinrich Nehmitz — who had for long years collaborated with Boettger — was made an arcanist and transferred to Meissen. Besides him Boettger's three constant assistants:—Koehler, Stoeltzel and Schubert were removed to the new factory. The new industry was veiled in mystery as a state secret. The officials were vowed to secrecy, yet had great freedom afforded them in the execution of their work and were obliged with regard to any means employed in the works but to sign a certification. As a result of these orders we have very little authentic information as to the arrangements of the factory and as to the construction of the kilns. The working was at first divided between Meissen and Dresden. The paste was made, the vessels were turned and moulded and baked in Meissen, but Boettger ordered the glaze to be made and ground in Dresden. This organization can not be looked upon as convenient. Valuable pieces of china were mounted with gold or silver by the goldsmith Funke in Dresden. The china was baked in single, half-cylindrical, tunnelshaped rather small kilns which were horizontally placed and had a single chimney at the end. On the upper front side of a kiln of this sort a fire with Boettger back flame was built, which was fired with dry logs of wood. This way of firing is interesting and is worthy of being here noted (see illustration 351). A pit 1,5 m. deep is dug. It is of rectangular shape, being 60 cm. long and 30 cm. wide. At a distance of 30 cm. from the opening two benches 10 cm. wide are arranged as sets-off, on these the logs of wood, spoken of above, are heaped up. At various heights of the shaft, openings are made which are closed with stones exactly fitting them and serve to convey the air. The flame is now drawn downwards and enters thus the kiln itself. Here at first small pedestals of shamott stones were put up on which the vessels enclosed in shamott saggers were placed. Chinaware when being made requires two kinds of baking. The vessels when ready turned, moulded and dried by air are first put into the biscuit-baking kiln and baked by heat as great as is required for melting gold. The introduction of this baking is a peculiarity of Boettger's fabrication. The biscuit-baking and the final or sharp fire baking are done in two separate kilns, as two different procedures. In the biscuit-baking the china loses the mechanically and chemically bound water of the caolin, the paste becomes hardened and after it has cooled it can be drawn through the fluid for glazing and glazed without becoming soft again. After the primaly baked china has been glazed it receives the sharp fire baking at real white heat. The chinaware shrinks greatly in this baking, the glaze which has been applied before gets vitrified, combines itself chemically with the body and becomes transparent with it. The creation of porcelain glaze was in its turn a great step forward from a hygienic point of view. It was the first glaze made for clay vessels which was altogether free from lead. In order to bake these fire-proof pastes and glazes until they were perfectly fired through a very high

Johann Friederich Böttger

temperature was required. It was therefore a "conditio sine qua non" that the kilns and saggers should be of a very fire-proof material. The red lime bricks which were alone known at that time could not bear such heat. Therefore Boettger among his inventions put that of the white fire-proof clay bricks; this was really the essential consequence of his pastes and glazes. The fire-proof clay bricks as well as the saggers which had been broken in use were at once again crushed in a mortar. This powder was afterwards mixed with

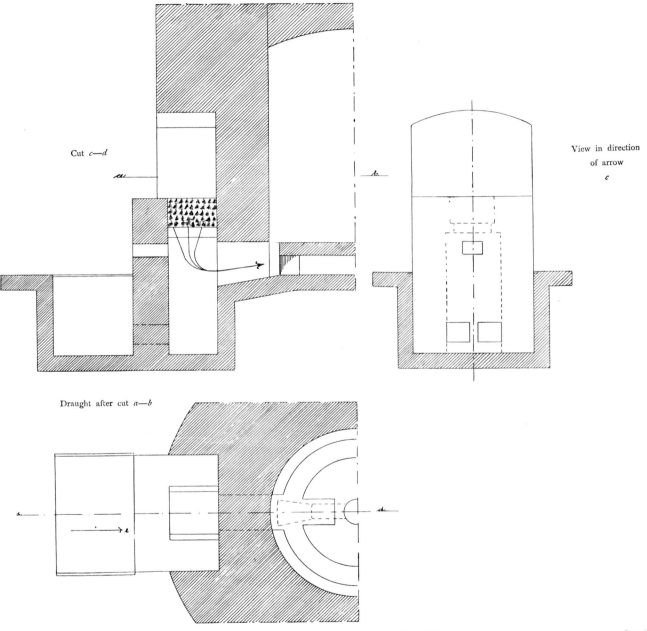

Cut c—d

View in direction
of arrow

c

Draught after cut a—b

Illustration 351. BOETTGER'S BACK FLAME FIRING.

Page 118.

new clay and made into new stones and saggers. These productions are at present called with the collective name of "chamotte". Afterwards a very important branch of industry developed from this.

As the painting on porcelain greatly improved when Hoeroldt — particularly spoken of on pages 9 f. and 14 f. — was employed in Meissen; the arcanists produced a large variety of colours for china-enamel colours as they were then called. They were applied to the china when it was quite ready and baked in muffel-furnaces at a temperature great enough to melt silver. The production of these colours was a very difficult task. It is wonderful how the chemists of the time with their scant knowledge of the science managed by careful observation and trials to produce the necessary combinations and auxiliary preparations in the chemical purity and pro-portion required. They were obliged to prepare for themselves nitric and sulfuric acid, besides tin salt, sulfate of iron, salts of copper out of verdigris, various combinations of gold etc. When we take into consideration the fact that neither the managers nor the employés had any experience in the well-ordered working of a large factory we must admit that, notwithstanding many difficulties a great deal was done already at the beginning of the fabrication, while the second decade brought brilliant success with it. It is therefore interesting to describe the old way of fabrication.

The white clay from Mehren and the Colditz clay which was brought by the district peasants were used for the production of the highly fire-proof saggers. The clay was first of all pounded and wetted in tall barrels with water, then it was trodden or beaten and divided into single bales. These were mixed by being cut and again combined into clay chips, mechanical dirt being removed at the same time. Now the clay was put with the sagger sand; the latter was made by pounding the well baked broken saggers which now produced in pounding machines, the coarser bits being removed by sifting. Clay chips and sagger sand were put in alternative layers and sprinkled with water. Four layer were laid on top of one another and had to be thoroughly wetted. After having stood for rather a long time, the paste was digged out and the workmen trod on it the way potters do. When the clay was being trodden fine quartz sand in the proportion of one barrel of clay (= 3 Treten) to 12 troughs of sand. The sagger clay which had been trodden several times and mixed to an even paste. It was trodden into a square and cut into rather long pieces which were rolled into longish bales. After a great deal of treading the clay-balls were ready and could be used for making all sorts of saggers, wads, headings, sagger-covers, muffles, moveable covers, pipes, slabs, pillars, crucibles and small kilns.

The fire-proofs ovenbricks were made by a similar proceeding. The clay was pounded and mixed with sagger sand by the addition of water. Large and small bricks as well as wedge formed bricks for the vaultings and cleft bricks were known at that time. Instead of lime Colditz clay was used for the making of kilns. The bricks came into the biscuit kiln and were baked according to requirement from 17 to 19 hours, or in larger kilns for 32 to 34 hours. The bricks were used either in a glowed condition or were finally baked in sharp fire in certain places of the kilns for the sharp fire baking of china. In the last-mentioned the various zones of heat were sharply differentiated and the vessels were divided according to them. White plates and cups were baked in another place then brown glazed china or such as was painted in blue under glaze. Grooves were made in the kilns in order to give the flame sufficient room. It was found that the vessels were either blistered or of yellow colour according to the way the flame went.

The preparation of the raw materials for the china pastes and glazes themselves must be noted as very careful as well. Soon the best caolin of the 18th century, that found in Aue near Schneeberg in the Saxon Erzgebirge, entirely supplanted the Colditz clay. It was taken out of the shafts and packed in barrels in a raw state for delivery at the factory, it cost 1 taler 16 Groschen per hundredweight, but contained only 40% of fine caolin. For washing the clay was soaked in water in large pots. Then it was put into a large vessel for stirring, where as sediment of coarse sand and stones which had not become decomposed settled at the bottom. The clay minus the sediment — was then placed into tossing tubs and lastly drained and stored. The clean clay free from sand obtained in this manner was dried in chamott saggers partly on the stoves, partly — in summer — by fresh air. The clay balls thus dried were pounded in a mortar and sifted through a hair sieve before being used.

In the caolin from Aue Boettger had found an insurpassable raw material for his china production. As a medium of flux he added oxide of calcium to his glazes and pastes. Soon after his death a more perfect medium of flux was found in a kind of stone which was brought into use under the name of "Sieben-lehner gestein". It was praised as a mineral between quartz and fluor spar and said to be vitrifiable and to give a white flux which in so far differed from fluor spar as not to hurt the crucible or other instruments used for melting it, even when melted in the sharp fire. The Siebenlehner stone was felspar, a good orthoclase. The stone was baked in especial calcining furnaces. One baking required 4—5 hours, whether it had been sufficiently baked was decided by drawing out single bricks and examining them. The baked stone was parted, pounded in the stamping mill and then sifted. The "fine good" was put into a mill and ground for 24 hours. A few words about the mill and the stamping machine bear a certain technological interest. A drawing has been preserved of the mill and the polishing machine made by Boettger. It was driven by the water of the Weisseritz in the Plauen valley near Dresden. After this pattern the mills in the Albrechtsburg were made as well. Only instead of water to drive it, a whimsey drawn by a horse was put up in front of the cellar of the castle. The glaze, stamp, and stone grinding machines were very cleverly made machines (see illustration 352). The works of the mill are driven by a horizontal wave B and the

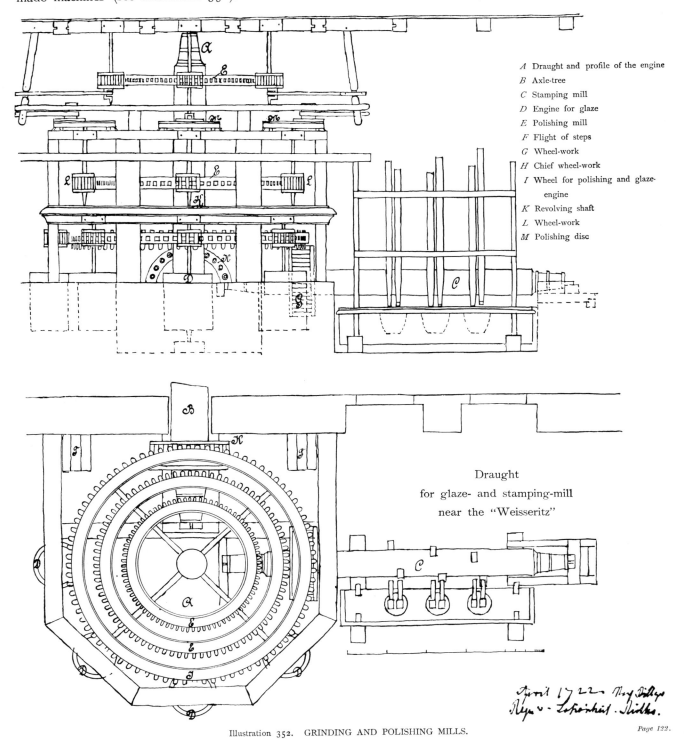

A Draught and profile of the engine
B Axle-tree
C Stamping mill
D Engine for glaze
E Polishing mill
F Flight of steps
G Wheel-work
H Chief wheel-work
I Wheel for polishing and glaze-engine
K Revolving shaft
L Wheel-work
M Polishing disc

Draught
for glaze- and stamping-mill
near the "Weisseritz"

Illustration 352. GRINDING AND POLISHING MILLS.

Page 122.

driving power is carried over to the vertical wave K through the driving wheel H—I. Through the driving gear I—G the stamping mill C is set in motion, while the wheel I drives the four glazing mills. Over it the polishing disks were lying and were sent in motion by the horizontal wave K and the driving gear E—L, as well as by the cogged wheel E arranged over it which, in its turn, set the stone-grinding machine into motion. All the parts of the machine were made of hardwood and stone.

For the fabrication of divers articles and for various modes of decoration different china pastes were used, thus for blue painting, for brown glaze and for pure white porcelain and lastly coarse pastes for extraordinarily large pieces. They varied in the degrees of their fluidity and were made fluid by the addition of a quantity of felspar which varied from 20 to 30 % and by the additions of materials for thinning it of varying fineness to lessen the shrinking. Although they worked altogether empirically we must admit that they had great power of observation and found ways which must be considered right and conformable to the purpose. The same recognition must be paid to the arcanists of the second period, when we turn to the branch of painting which had been introduced to Meissen since 1720. For soon after Boettger's death the manner of decorating china rather copiously in colours developed in a fairly rapid manner. Up to that time only seldom china had been ornamented in colours. The history of the blue colour under glazing (see page 49 f.) may serve as proof of the fact that the arcanists Dr. Nehmitz, Stoeltzel and Koehler of the Boettger school as well as Hoeroldt acted systematically and on scientific principles, as far as was possible with their scant knowledge of chemistry. In the history of the blue colour under glaze, a remark is made that it was "made in an expensive and very troublesome manner". This probably refers to the preparation of "the lovely blue out of the Reguli Cobaldi". The way it was made is noted in the "description of such colours as were made and used in the Royal Polish and Electoral Saxon china manufactory in Meissen". It is described as follows:—"I put $2\frac{1}{4}$ lbs of aqua fortis into a cucurbit and gradually added '12 Loth' of finely ground Reguli Cobaldi; thus, in the morning a small tea-spoon full, at noon the same quantity again and in the evening another tea-spoon full of Reguli Cobaldi, proceeding in the same manner until all the '12 Loth' of Reguli Cobaldi had been put into the aqua fortis. After this solution had stood for a few days and had been often shaken, I carefully poured it off into a large 'sugar glass', so that none of the residuo came with it; afterwards I diluted the solution I had poured off with a few canfuls of distilled water. Then I again put 1 lb '4 Loth' of aqua fortis on the Reguli Cobaldi remaining in the cucurbit and put it on a warm stove, so that the colouring particles should be drawn out. When this had happened I poured this solution off into the large 'sugar glass' with the first solution and diluted it with more distilled water; afterwards I filtrated the solution and first precipitated the metals which were mixed with it by aid of a pure vegetable alcali solution. Here it was seen what the Regulus was mixed with, as I often obtained iron, copper and bismuth etc. I noticed that when the first sediment 'souci' was of a brown colour, I received the most beautiful blue sediment with less trouble. The cobalt which was mixed with bismuth always gave me the greatest trouble in purifying by precipitation. When the first precipitate of the metals mixed with it, fell to the bottom, I let it run through a clean strainer made of double white filtering paper, afterwards I continued precipitating and filtering until at last blue cobalt precipitate appeared; now I let it stand still for some days, so that it should set thoroughly and the solution could be again dissolved with the blue and absorb it. Now I again filtered the solution through double white filtering paper into a large clean 'sugar glass' where the solution appeared a pretty rose-red colour, then I took a small glass and poured some of the cobalt solution into it and precipitated the solution in the small glass with pure vegetable alcali in order to see if a pure blue precipitate would settle. If the precipitate does not appear of a pure blue colour, it must be again precipitated and filtered until the solution is quite pure. When this is quite certain the whole cobalt solution is altogether precipitated with the above mentioned alcali. On the next day the water standing over the sediment is carefully poured off so that none of the blue sediment goes with it into the glass. Now I poured pure fresh water on this blue precipitate till the glass was quite full and stirred it well with a clean wooden rod, after the sediment had again entirely sat I again poured the water standing over it carefully off and again poured fresh water on it. This purifying with clean fresh water I have done 8 times morning and evening, so that in four days' time, no salt could be tasted in the water. Now I filtered this blue precipitate with white filtering paper and let it gradually dry; now the blue precipitate was ready for use."

This "blue precipitate" served as a basis for the production of blue enamel colours and the author of the "description" quoted above knew judging from further information that by the addition of "precipitate of zinc" the beautiful blue shade was greatly improved. He also when describing the preparing of enamel colours, he speaks of the flux necessary for it as:—Composition of lead ashes, lapis sillicis, potash and tin ashes etc.

A favourite way of decorating china was with the mother of pearl lustre. For this "aurum fulminans" or fulminating gold was used. It was made through a precipitate of a solution of gold in a mixture of nitric acid and ammonia through potash. The sediment was filtered, washed and dried in a place as far as possible removed from the stove where it could not be touched by inexperienced hands. It was not however thoroughly dried but remained damp and was stored in a well-closed glass vessel where care had to be taken that none of the "Gold lime" remained adhering to the sides and especially to the neck of the bottle because when the small particles were thoroughly dried the slightest touch resulted in an explosion and the proper name of the preparation became known.

For the production of red colour, gold was dissolved in a mixture of nitric acid and common salt. In the same manner a solution of tin salt and chlorate of tin was prepared. Finest english tin in small portions was added to the aqua regia. Gold and tin solutions were then poured together into a large quantity of water.

The various iron red shades were produced by strong heating of sulfate of iron. An old recipe for producing dark red runs as follows:—"It is made out of the colcothar of aqua fortis. It is well washed in lye and edulcorated so that no taste can be felt on the tongue and then dried. Various materials could be here used which give a red colour but they are not equal to calamine and vitriol, I therefore find it unnecessary to use them." It was soon recognised that crude sulfate of iron contained copper and that the purity of the shade of the sulfate of iron made of such raw material suffered. The vitriol was therefore dissolved, iron rods put into it to precipitate the copper and pure sulfate of iron obtained. Brown shades were at first produced out of "real english umber", yellow out of "Naples yellow" i. e. antimoniated lead, green out of oxide of copper. The last was obtained by "mild heating of french verdigris". Black colours resulted from well mixed precipitate of cobalt, umber and manganese ore.

In the years from 1760 to 1770 and from 1780 to 1790 the colours used were greatly improved and increased in number and variety by the chief mining assessors Klinkhammer and Wentzel. They did not any longer content themselves with using Naples yellow for making yellow vitrifiable pigment but used preparations of antimony of their own fabrication. Klinkhammer in 1769 describes the way it was obtained as follows:—"1. The preparation of the antimony regulus:—1 lb of iron is put into a crucible placed in the fire and allowed to heat. Then 2 lbs of antimony are thrown in and the crucible covered first with a clay lid then with coals. When it is melted it is all well stirred up and allowed to stand for a short time. After the crucible has been taken out of the fire and allowed to cool the antimony regulus is found at the bottom and the dross is easily separated from it. This regulus can be again melted with 8 to 12 Loth of antimony which has not been used before, so it is free enough from iron for this work. If we wished to have it quite pure the melting could be repeated with a little saltpetre. 2. Production of lime of antimony. Crushed regulus and pure saltpetre are mixed and heated on a mild fire and the salt separated from it by washing in lye, so the lime of antimony is left over in a white state. 3. 1 part of this almost insoluble acid metaantimoniate of potash and 2 parts of red lead are rubbed together and mildly heated, so the mixture becomes yellow and is ready for further precipitation."

Tin-ashes, lead-ashes, oxide of mercury, oxide of uranium, oxide of bismuth, oxide of nickel, oxide of zinc, manganese ore were all either produced in the laboratory out of the raw-materials or cleaned after particular recipes.

The old colours umber, ochre and "green-earth" still played the principal part as ingredients of new colour-combination. The first-mentioned is written about in the following manner:—"Umber is an excellent clayey fossil which is penetrated with and coloured by manganese ore and oxide of iron and may be used particularly well for dark colours brown, black and blue. It is finaly crushed, calcinated for a short time in a crucible in order to give it a reddish brown colour and to allow some stuff mixed with it to evaporate; lastly it is again finaly ground." The "green-earth" was also first subjected to baking and turned, by this process into a green paste with a brown shade in it. In connection with antimonial lead it gave forth a straw coloured paste; this was the "paille" so much used at that time.

We find directions for the making of non-metallic preparations as well, such as common salt, saltpetre, pottash, tartaric acid, borax etc. "How to convert sal tartari into oleum tartari":—"Large pieces of tartaric acid must be used — it may be either white or red, this makes no great difference —. I fill three or four saggers with it and put them in the oven to calcinate the tartaric acid; afterwards I put the calcinated tartaric acid into a large vessel, for instance into a butterpot and pour boiling water over it, stir it a few times with a stick and let it stand for a day until the faeces have set a little. Then I pour the clear and light-coloured lye into another vessel and pour hot water again on the tartaric acid, so that all salt is drawn out of it. When it has again stood for 4 to 6 hours and the lye has become light, I pour it into the first lye. —

Whether there be much salt in the baked tartaric acid, can be tasted by putting a drop on one's tongue — I pour hot water over it and let it stand for a day, stirring it several times. When it has become clear I pour it into the other lye as well. Only another vessel must be at hand into which all the lye must be filtered by means of a strainer made of double filtering paper, the sediment can be filtered as well and can be again calcinated in the oven in order to see whether there be any salt in it; if it has been thoroughly washed in lye it is not necessary to calcinate it again. Now a kettle of sheet-iron shaped like a saucepan must be at hand as well, it should be put on the fire and filled with the lye made of tartaric acid, when the lye is half boiled away more lye is added to it; this is done until all the lye in the kettle has half boiled away. It must not boil on a large fire, so as not to boil over, as in boiling over the salt would run off and it would be a pity to lose any of it. Therefore when the lye has boiled away and the salt can be seen, there must be but a small fire in the stove; when most of the dampness has steamed away and the salt does not rise so high any more, the fire can again be better heaped up and the salt kept on it till it becomes white and almost dry. It is to be well closed up and stored in a warm place." "Oleum tartari is prepared in the following manner:—I either take the first lye poured off from the tartaric acid and let it run two or three times through a fine strainer and store it in a glass, or I take tartaric acid, put it into a broad and open vessel and put it in a damp place or into the cellar and let it become fluid; this is filtered and put in a glass so as not to get dusty. With this oleum tartari various solutions can be precipitated. It is especially required for precipitating the blue out of the regulus cobaldi as has above been mentioned."

Oxide of chromium was first used only as a colour which could bear the high temperature required for the baking of china after inspector Kuehn was employed at the factory. This will be spoken of more particularly below.

Examples like the above could be found in great number, they serve to show the high standard of the chemical work. Those given are sufficient to picture the state of the technical work in producing the colours during the 18th century. Muffel-ovens were introduced which were heated with wood-fire. They must have worked carefully and with great circumspection, as for a number of years charcoal was used for colour baking — the use of charcoal as fuel was as expensive as it was troublesome — afterwards wood again took its place.

Aften 1739 Hoeroldt added baked and finely ground bits of china to the paste. Through this the paste shrunk less. In 1731 another biscuit-kiln was build. In 1740 two new machines for turning oval and striped vessels, as well as oval dishes for roasts and fish, were erected with very good results. They had been erected by the organ-builder Haehnel at the initiative of the Counsellor of mines von Heynitz.

In 1744 the King ordered all the manuscripts written by the arcanists about the technical and chemical working to be delivered to the commissar, the Counsellor of the chamber von Nimpsch. The manuscripts were now lost sight of and were only a short time ago found in Dresden packed in a box and partly sealed. Their contents have been overtaken by time.

In 1747 a vineyard in Naumburg a. S. in which there was a plaster quarry was bought. The gypsum for the forms was baked out of this plaster in the kilns of the factory. As the works extended themselves further and further, the castle mount was soon too small to hold them. During this time 1800 hundred-weights of paste and 1000 trestles of wood were used yearly. In 1751 von Heynitz came forward with the complaint that there was too little room for enlarging the fabrication — the washing houses were too small — there were too few drying rooms, baking houses, moulding-rooms, glazing and grinding mills. In 1752 a new plant for stamping mills was put up.

After the intermission in their work caused by the second Silesian and the seven years' wars the arcanists set to work with redoubled energy. In 1765 seven new kilns for sharp fire baking partly in place of those destroyed during the war were erected under the direction of the arcanist Elsasser. In the following year dry wood was again used as fuel instead of charcoal in the muffel-ovens which were used for baking the painted chinaware. As some vessels lost their circular shape in the baking, rings and lintels came into use to prevent this. As a result of the continual striving to improve the working in 1764 a discovery of greater importance was added to the rest. The painter Hahnefeld discovered a white clay paste in Seilitz, a village near Meissen. The arcanist Schertel first made experiments with it and decided that the Seilitz earth was a raw material equalling the caolin of Schneeberg with regard to colour and plasticity. Already at that time difficulty began to be experienced with the caolin from Aue. The clay was dug up in nests of iron stone. As the upper strata of clay had already been removed it was necessary to go deeper, but the clay was here not pure but contained iron. The King had in the meantime become part-proprietor of the shaft. At first the Seilitz clay was not believed to be very good, but it was experimentally made use of for pastes and glazes. Only in 1770 the newly-appointed arcanist the Counsellor of mines Dr· Poerner undertook investigations as to the chemical and physical structure of the clays and earths then in use and compared some well-washed Seilitz clay with the caolin from Aue finding them of equal quality. Besides the price of the washed Seilitz clay was 3.2 marks for 50 kg., while the same amount of Aue-clay cost 13.2 marks. The cost of conveying the latter was great owing to the distance of the shaft from Meissen. Notwithstanding this the greater part of the cux of the St. Andrew mine was bought from the court administration in 1790. Probably for this reason the use of the Seilitz caolin was again discontinued in 1789, but from 1801 it was again continually used. The kilns for biscuit baking and for sharp fire baking of china which had been erected in 1765

Illustration 353, R 139.
175 cm.

Page 136.

according to a new system did not give satisfaction for any length of time and the old system was again reverted to in 1774. In 1773 the sagger room, some studios and part of the white stock were destroyed by a large fire. The fire was supposed to have started in the packing hay. In the years from 1780 to 1790 the Chief mining assessor Wentzel from Freiberg was often employed for chemical experiments. He produced a new blue paint in a novel-fashion which afterwards came into general use under the name of "royal blue". While the preparation of the colour is being spoken of, it may be mentioned that it had to be baked in a peculiar fashion which was also invented by Wentzel.

In 1798 it was tried whether coals would not make better fuel than wood for heating the stoves. They attempted heating the kilns for biscuit baking and sharp fire baking with coals as well, but met withfailure, at first at any rate.

For some decades instead of the Siebenlehner felspar some from Braunsdorf near Tharandt was used. But in 1789 the Siebenlehn felspar was again preferred. Probably it had proved inadequate because of the iron and mica contained in it; afterwards this material was altogether done without.

In the last decade of the 18th and in the first decade of the 19th century nothing worthy of notice in the technical and chemical working can be mentioned. It appears that they had not been lucky in awarding the higher offices and that many obstacles were put in the way of the progress of the factory, by the wars, the unfavourableness of financial circumstances and the difficulty in finding a sale for the goods. In order to be able to sell cheaper, a second class china paste was introduced. Only a limited quantity of this sort of chinaware was to be manufactured. This however proved impracticable and soon large quantities of second class china were put on the market. Only afterwards did the management see what a mistake had been made in introducing a second quality of chinaware and stopped the production of same. The articles made out of this kind of paste G. R. were marked with a II under the Electoral swords.

From the time that Kuehn entered the factory a new era of its existence was opened. First of all he sought to introduce improvements and innovations into the factory which had been kept at a stand-still in this respect for some time.

He found that the use of the existing kilns which were still of the old horizontal, half-cylindrical shape, required an extraordinarily large amount of fuel and were by no means perfect in their construction. He declared that it would soon be impossible to obtain as much wood as these kilns required. He therefore received permission to build a kiln for sharp fire baking several stories high; after a model of the kilns used in the porcelain manufactory of Berlin. At the beginning of the 19th century in England round kilns had been used for baking stone-ware. As it was found that these did not answer the purpose and could not be used for baking china; the experiments of the employés of the factory itself led to the discovery of cylindrical ovens several stories high. The Berlin kiln was three stories high and of circular shape. After some resistance on the part of the officials and the workmen in 1819, this system was put on so firm a footing as to keep up its existence in Meissen nearly all through the 19th century. Great progress was made by the introduction of these kilns because the biscuit baking and the sharp fire baking of the chinaware were through it united into one process. In the lower story the baked and glazed china receives its sharp fire baking. The freshly turned or modelled china is biscuit baked in the first story. In the second story the rate saggers and chamott-stones are baked, so that none of the heat should be wasted.

There had been for years many reasons for complaining of the caolin from Aue Schneeberg. Not-withstanding all endeavours and investigations made, the fact that the shaft was worked out could no longer remain unnoticed. Several times suppositions as to the finding of caolin were brought forward. A caolin from Kaschka which was at first thought reliable soon proved to be unfit for producing china. But an excellent material was found in 1817 in a caolin from Sornzig near Muegeln in Saxony, under the fields of the lands of the monastery of Sornzig. There colonel Flachs had found a white clay over which the factory soon obtained rights of possession. They did not however begin working a shaft at once. Only from 1840 they began to work the shaft regularly, after having built a washing house next to the pit. At any rate rather a long time passed before a substitute for the caolin from Aue was obtained. For when they had begun to think of giving up the working of the shaft in 1814 in 1821 at a greater depth a new stratum was found which was supposed to be able to supply sufficient caolin for 28 years at the of 1200 cwt. yearly.

Page 136.

Illustration 354, R 140.
235 cm.

In 1817 besides the porcelain paste from Auer caolin two productions of inferior quality were introduced. They were made of Kaschka clay and caolin from Seilitz and were especially marked and used for apothecaries' utensils. But it was soon noticed that this had been made a very ill use of by the dealers and customers who, because Meissen had produced an inferior sort of china, sought to depreciate and discredit all the productions of the factory. Therefore in April 1824 an order was issued by which it was decreed that inferior pastes should no more find a place in the Meissen factory. These pastes were chemically combined in the same way as the old ones, only the caolin used was not as chemically clean as the caolin from Aue. As a result of this the china suffered in appearance, although the faults were only slight. Nothing was altered in the high temperature used in baking it which was as that used for the best sort and which had so rightly made the Meissen china famous for its great power of resistance against jolting and knocks as well as against chemical influences. Trials of caolin lasted for years and a new sort was introduced with great circumspection. Besides the newly introduced Seilitz caolin, the caolin from Aue was used for various purposes as well until the Sornzig caolin was introduced in the middle of the 19th century. Indeed in some instances it is being used even now. This is however a matter of small importance as at present so many places are known where good caolin is to be found.

In 1827 Kuehn, after many years work found a new mode of decorating china which became a matter of very great importance in the development of the factory. Heinr. Gottl. Kuehn had received scientific education as a craftsman at the mining academy of Freiberg. After having passed his examinations the practised at the Freiberg smeltinghouses. Later he studied jurisprudence for several years at the university of Wittenberg, afterwards taking his degree as Prussian auscultator in Berlin. He was employed at the Freiberg mining office as a mining referendary. He received command of the militia regiment of the Erzgebirge in the war for liberation and was employed at the factory in 1814 as managing inspector. After some preliminary work he succeeded in producing a gold preparation of remarkable quality.

In the new preparation the gold was united in fluid form as sesquichloride of gold in oily solution to balsam of sulphur. When it was applied to porcelain with a paint brush, broad spaces were gilded as evenly and well as narrow lines were drawn. When it was baked on the porcelain in the muffel-ovens the gilding appeared of a bright metallic lustre, while the gilding applied by means of a fine powder had to be rubbed with an agate stump in order to regain its original brightness. By making use of Kuehn's new invention the affairs of the factory improved. The new manner of decoration required new forms; new patterns in vases and coffee and dessert services were produced. Besides this coincided with the time when after the economical decay of the former period the commercial intercourse became more lively owing to the German Customs-Union which then originated (1831). It should be mentioned however that the new gilding could not bear baking at so high a temperature as the colours and that less heat had to be used for it.

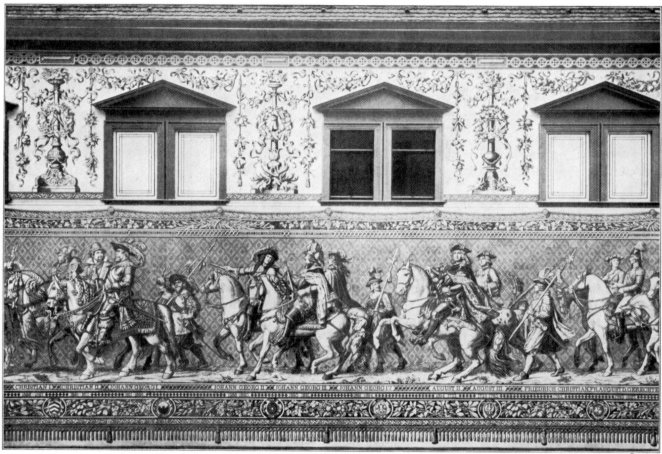

Illustration 355.

Page 137.

Therefore no chemical combination took place between the china and the gold and the durability of the gilding left much to be desired. Only during the last decades has it been possible through the introduction of a harder gold allay to make the gilding fire-proof and thoroughly adhering to the china. Although the secret of the method of manufacture of this gilding had at first been carefully kept, lustre gold was, after a few years, produced in other places as well and the ceramique of the whole cultured world soon made successful use of it. But for more than two decades the use of the new gilding had decided the trend of the affairs of the factory and had greatly increased its revenue. A period which was inimical to the Rococo- and similar styles was tided over.

    Another invention must be here mentioned which, although it did not concern the manufacture of china itself, was of great use to the factory. The leader of the chemical laboratory Friedrich Aug. Koettig was in the spring of 1827 engaged in attempts to produce a fluid glaze which should be free from lead. He formed natrum salicilicum and by adding pure clay to it he found, after heating it, a blue earthy substance sprinkled in the frit. After repeating the experiment and studying the mutual influence on each other of the materials employed, namely:—sulfate of soda, powder of quartz, charcoal and clay, he, after heating, received the body of a blue colour. As it was known from existing analyses that natural ultramarine consisted of clay, silicic acid, soda and sulphur; it therefore struck Koettig at once that in his blue colour he had discovered artificial ultramarine. His experiments were ended in autumn 1828 and the goverment in spring 1829 attached a factory to the Meissen works in which the artificial ultramarine was produced under the inappropriate name of "blue of lapis-lazuli". The manufacture of this artificial ultramarine greatly increased

the revenue of the factory only it was gradually overreached by private undertakings until in 1877 it ceased to exist for reasons outside its scope of working.

(Compare Heintze, History of the ultramarine, Journal for practical Chemistry, vol. 43, 1891.)

As the manufacture had two branches of production attached to it, greater attention was paid to the composition and use of enamel colours and the colours for sharp fire baking. In April 1816 already Kuehn had, through the intermediation of the Imperial china factory of Austria in Vienna, imported 50 vienna lbs of chromschlich out of which oxide of chrome was obtained as a new body of colour useful in china industry. Experiments with saxon serpentin for production of chrome green had preceeded this step; they can be traced back to 1815. The fire-proofness of oxide of chromium was soon recognised and already in September 1817 the first plates

Illustration 356.

Page 137.

decorated with a wreath of vine leaves and painted in chrome green under glaze were put on the market. The new design caught on and kept its popularity for a long time. Oxide of chromium is only entered in the index of combination of colours in 1837 as a colour for enamel painting, in the same index of 1823 only colours of oxide of copper are noted.

To obtain oxide of chromium chromschlich (Chrom-iron minerals) was very finely powdered and well mixed with equal parts of equally finely crushed saltpetre, the mixture was placed into a crucible and thoroughly baked in an air furnace. "It is baked for about an hour until no saltpetre vapours which brighten and colour. the flame escape from the crucible any more. After it has cooled it is washed in hot water a few times until the water is but slightly tinged. The combined residue is allowed to stand for a few days. During this time the manganese ore which absorbs the oxygen in the water and in the atmosphere and is mixed with the chromium of iron falls out of the solution as brown oxide and can be easily separated by being carefully poured off. What has remained in the crucible is dried again and with an equal quantity of salt-petre, treated in the same way as before, baked and washed in lye until — after this has been repeatedly done (about twice) — (in this case the sediment has been weighed and the equal parts of saltpetre determined) the green colour of the water has become quite pale and of a more yellowish colour. The combined and filtered residue which has been separated from the manganese ore is steamed so that the silicic acid should evaporate and again filtered." They proceeded with the fabrication in one of the three following ways:— 1. Evaporating

Illustration 357.

Page 138.

with hydrochloric or sulphuric acid; "during this process the oxygen in the chromic acid settles and the hydrochlorid and sulphuric acids evaporate". "As soon as the process of removing the acid begins to colour the fluid green the sediment of silicic earth is taken away by filtration, the oxide of chromium is precipitated a solution of carbonate of potash out of a solution more or less resembling the colour of leeks. The sediment after it settles is edulcorated several times with cold and hot water and is calcinated in a wall covered crucible in an air furnace after having been thoroughly dried, or, to save coals, it may be put into the kiln for sharp fire baking. Through this calcination of the oxide the volatile and acid bodies attached to it are evaporated, this makes it easier to apply to the china and — from many experiments we know — that it adheres better to the china." (August 1816.) In a supplement of the same year we find an improved method of obtaining oxide of chromium ly· using alcohol for the reduction of chromate of potash. The methods No. 2 and 3 described below fall out of use as being too complicated. 2. The impure solution of chromate of potash was neutralized with nitric acid and precipitated with a solution of nitrate of mercury. For half a pound of chrome-ore a pound of mercury was used. The bright red washed and dried precipitate of chromate of mercury is put into a retort which is placed in sandbath able to stand a strong fire. At its neck a receiver which does not shut but fits almost closely is placed and is cooled with water. It is heated until all the mercury vapours have evaporated and the oxide of chromate remains at the bottom of the retort. It is then of beautiful dark-green colour. 3. The solution chromate of potash obtained as before is neutralized with nitric acid and precipitated with a solution of nitrate of lead. The sediment is lemon coloured chromate of lead; it is filtered and dried.

In 1819 a new motor in the shape of a large whimsey drawn by horses and having a clapper 32 yards long was erected. It was worked by three or four strong horses and served to set the stamping mills and grinding machines in motion.

Illustration 358.   *Page 138.*

In order to become acquainted with the way porcelain factories were worked in Germany and France, Kuehn in 1823 undertook a journey lasting five months and visited the large china works at home and abroad. He brought a great many new ideas home with him and was able to act according to them. Besides small improvements in baking and turning he introduced the casting of single pieces. But the most important part is that his work became the foundation of the preparations of colours for china-painting with regard to their chemical combination. He altered the preparation of these colours and introduced many new shades. These colours are prepared in such a way that the painter can mostly combine the desired shades on his palet without having recourse to the chemical laboratory. As a result of these innovations chrome green took the place of oxide of copper. The chrome colours which were now introduced proved to be easier to work with, perfectly reliable in baking and could be mixed with the other colours in use. In the further elaboration of the porcelain enamel colours such brilliant results were obtained that when these colours in later years came on the market, a great number of private undertakings in the porcelain industry in Germany and Austria began to make use of them as well.

Although Kuehn introduced other improvements and alterations into the working viz:—the wet combination of pastes, new arrangement of mills, the turning of hollow vessels by free hand, the combination of large pieces of many separately made horizontal sections, still their description can not be here entered into. In 1827 a twelve hours' working day was introduced. The employés were to work from 6 a. m. to 6 p. m. and to have an hour free for dinner, half an hour for breakfast and a quarter of an hours' pause for tea. The workers in the artistic branches were working by the piece and had since the third decade of the 18th century been paid accordingly.

In 1833 the director, Counsellor of mines von Oppel, died in Dresden. His place remained vacant until in 1849 Kuehn in Meissen was appointed director.

Illustration 359.

Page 138.

In 1837 Kuehn was fortunate in making another step forward in his chemical researches. In connection with his fluid gold-combination he produced organic combinations with resins, oils and various metals such as bismuth, copper, lead, gold, silver and uran. These were applied to the china and were baked mostly in common with the so-called "lustre gold". In this way brightly iridescent ground-colours were produced they were original and pretty and were much liked. This manner of colouring was called chamaeleon or lustre colouring. This discovery of Kuehn's was later introduced everywhere, it was especially much used in private porcelain works. Only in 1858 J. H. Brianchon of Paris wrote in the "Technologiste" that he had discovered how to produce (chamaeleon) changeable colouring with bismuth, lead, silver, platinum, palladium, rhodium, antimony and uran. Kuehn who had long ago preceded him kept his rights of priority.

The working was extended owing to the various discoveries, so that more wood for fuel was required and a greater amount of money had to be spent on it. In 1839 Kuehn succeeded in constructing his kilns for sharp fire baking and in leading the process of baking china so as to allow of the use of coal as fuel. Generally speaking, it was only natural to think of using coal which was already being used for other purposes for baking china as well. In the 18th century already experiments had been made; the failure of these attempts was ascribed to the accessory constituent parts of the coal. With the deficient scientific knowledge of the process of the burning of wood and coals in a kiln, it was impossible to get at the real cause at first. At any rate it required great powers of observation to successfully bake the white and blue and green painted chinaware in a kiln for sharp fire baking. The kilns which were several stories high possessed five rather large fire grates laid at the periphery and an inward channel for leading the flame in the necessary direction. The cubic contents were still small. Between the place for biscuit baking and for sharp fire baking a dividing-wall was made, it was composed of layers of sand and was 1 m. thick. All the same this system saved a great deal of fuel.

Illustration 360.

Page 138.

Another step forward was made a few years later when in 1852 the oven for baking the colours, the muffel-ovens, were also built in several stories high, here as well the productions were improved and the consumption of fuel lessened. During this time experiments were made in Meissen, Berlin and Kloesterle in Bohemia to bake china with the aid of generator gas, this was after many failures successfully done, only especially constructed stories had to be used; but the difficulties overweighed the advantages so that this method did not become installed in the porcelain industry.

Up to the year 1853, the stamping mills etc. were set in motion by a whimsey worked by horse power, but in that year a steam engine was put up in the cellar of Albrechtsburg. Indeed the steam engine seems not to have given satisfaction, as it was asserted that the cellars of the Albrechtsburg suffered from the constant vibration caused by it. To this the thought must have been added that, as the china factory had since 1831 ceased to be the property of the crown and was given over into the hands of the state, the castle of Albrechtsburg would again be put to its original use. The works could not be extended as the room accorded to the factory was limited complaints of want of space had made themselves heard already in the 18th century; so that the King, the government and parliament accepted a proposition to remove the china factory out of the castle into a new building. In 1858 the amount of 300000 talers was voted for a new building which was to be erected in the valley of the Triebisch Meissen. The new factory was built in 1860—64 and it was entirely moved into in 1865. The plan, considering the time when it was made, can be praised as being rational and conform to the purpose and the large piece of empty ground adjoining the new building allowed of extension of the works should it become necessary later. In order to obtain a motor power, a piece of ground with a water mill in the valley of the Triebisch was bought as well and the water power adapted for use in the new works. Four large wings 120 m. long were built in a square. One of them contained four kilns for sharp fire baking, the number of which has since been doubled. After

Illustration 361.

Page 139.

the events of 1866 a great improvement in the affairs of the factory took place in 1871 they became more flourishing still. Kuehn who had lived to a very old age died in 1870. His place was taken by the leaders of technique Crasso and H. Brunnemann. As the sale of chinaware increased an extension of the works was soon required. In erecting the kilns for sharp fire baking extra walls were put in to afford the possibility of enlarging them according to requirement. Already in 1873 these extra walls had to be removed so that it should be possible to bake more china at a time. By this it will be seen that Crasso's foresight was very soon rewarded. G. Crasso was an able pupil of Liebig's, while H. Brunnemann had been well taught at the mining academy as a miner and smelter. In 1872 extensions were proceeded with which had already been planned in 1870, the new building which contained two kilns was ready in 1873. In this year the author of this was engaged at the factory to assist the leading officials in the laboratory as well as in the general management. During this period a great increase is to be noted in the production and sale of household utensils painted with cobalt under glaze (onion pattern). The difficult part of producing this kind of chinaware lay in the sharp fire baking. It was therefore a great step forward when the author of this managed in 1875 to put the baking process on a scientific basis by the examining the kiln gasses by aid of the new system of gasanalysis. For ceramic purposes this method of baking is of great value. Many difficulties and losses which were ascribed to other causes are now easily explained.

In 1876 Crasso left the factory; his place was taken by Brunnemann, while the author of this was appointed manager of the chemical laboratory and of the production of colours. The works were in this year further extended and various up to date machines and apparatus introduced; filter-presses took the place of sack-presses, rolling mills that of stamping mills, instead of the mass being beaten by hand a beating machine was introduced etc.

Illustration 362.

Page 139.

A new stimulus was given by the worlds exhibition in 1873; the National China Factory of Sèvres exhibited some beautiful work executed in a technically new manner, this was a kind of pâte-sur-pâte painting and nothing was known of the manner in which it was produced. As this chinaware is ornamented in novel fashion like cut of gems it is called cameo-china. It afterwards became generally known under the name of "pâte-sur-pâte" (paste upon paste) painting. In 1878 the author of this succeeded, after many experiments, in finding a technical method of imitating this painting; in order to make it practically possible, it was necessary to combine in an artistic and satisfactory manner a large number of colours which should be thoroughly reliable and able to bear the high temperature required for the sharp fire baking of china. The white pâte-sur-pâte painting was done on a coloured ground and it as well as the ground and the glaze were baked together in sharp fire. Although attempts to do this had been made before, they were unsuccessful as it was not known how to make the fire go in the way necessary for this work. The white and coloured sharp fire decoration which Meissen introduced in 1880 besides the painting in blue and green brought the factory gain and respect.

At first for a long time no large pieces were made with pâte-sur-pâte painting as it was technically rather difficult, only vases, dishes, plaques etc. being made, only after a great deal of practise was it possible to make large pieces. The world's exhibition in Chicago 1893 and the century exhibition in Paris in 1900 afforded the opportunity of bringing forward articles of a larger size. A large table with a top 1,5 m. long as well as four plaques for folding doors were ornamented with pâte-sur-pâte painting according to Sturm's design and put up at the Chicago exhibition. For the Paris exhibition two vases of exceptionally large size were painted with colours which could bear the sharp fire temperature required for the baking of china. The vase R *139* (illustration *353*) is executed after a sketch called "Spring" by E. Andresen. The ground of this vase which 1,75 m. high is coloured and decorated with flowers painted in colours which are able

Page 141.

Illustration 363.

to bear the high temperature required for the baking of china. The other "Water", R *140*, was sketched by R. Hentschel and painted only in the above mentioned colours; it was 2,35 m. high (illustration *354*). When the fragility of such large bodies in an unbaked and partly baked state be taken in consideration it must be admitted that it is technically a very difficult task to produce them; to say nothing of the painting. (Compare Zeitschrift für Architektur und Ingenieurwesen, Jahrg. 1898, Heft 5; Heintze, Zur Geschichte der europäischen Porzellanfabrikation.) In 1883 Meissen china was successfully painted with red protoxyd of copper a colour that was highly valued in old chinese ceramics. In Berlin and Sèvres in order to be able to apply these colours softer china — that is porcelain baked like that made in China, at a lower temperature than usual — was introduced. But it is an interesting fact that it is possible to paint with these colours on European hard porcelain. It is true that the use of the softer paste greatly facilitates the fabrication and Meissen has made use of it as well for this exclusive purpose. During the last two decades of the 19th century the colours which could bear the high temperature required for the sharp fire baking of china were used, in one and many colours, only on vases, dishes and table utensils but in this decade statuettes are being decorated in these colours as well. A more extensive use of this colour was made in an exceptional piece of work undertaken by the manufactory. (Compare Heintze, Zeitschrift für angewandte Chemie, Jahrg. XX, 1907, Heft 36—37.) On the outside of the royal castle in Dresden, on the side facing Augustus street, a huge painting 100 m. long and 10 m. high on which all the rulers of the house of Wettin were represented — 2 ½ times life size — with warriors and horses. This painting was in 1876 designed and executed in sgraffito-work by August Walther, but already by 1903 it was destroyed almost past recognition by the atmospheric influences of the large town. Owing to the proposition of the author of this the factory received an order — based on former experiments — to re-paint the whole picture exactly according to the

Illustration 364.

Page 141.

old design on tiles with colours that can bear the high temperature required for the sharp fire baking of china. The picture was painted and baked in 1905—06 and was put up at the castle in 1907. It consists of 25000 single tiles which exactly fit and are closely joined together (see illustration 355 and 356). The painting thus executed shows the possibility of producing in our climate in our large towns outside decorations on public and private buildings which fear not wind or weather and are not particularly expensive.

After having given a description of the development of the fabrication up to the present, it is an interesting matter to see into the

FABRICATION OF THE MEISSEN CHINA

of to day.

The most important material is at present caolin from Seilitz, a village situated seven miles away from Meissen down the Elbe. It developed out of porphyry and is obtained by mining and working shafts. In its raw state it is intergrown with quartz and sand and with more or less decomposed fragments of porphyry. In order to make it fit for use, the fine porcelain clay has to be extracted by a washing process.

The raw caolin is placed into a large drum which turns round its axis and in so doing is supplied with a constant stream of water and washes the caolin free from unnecessary substances. Under the influence of the water assisted by the dragging and shaking movements, the fine caolin is divided from the coarse and stony parts. A fluid satiated with particles of porcelain clay which are kept from running out by fine and coarse sieves, is formed (see illustration 357).

The fluid is led through large vessels and through horizontally placed channels in order to rid it of the quartzsand still mixed with it; lastly the now thoroughly cleaned porcelain clay is placed, with much superfluous water, into large tanks (see illustration 358). In this tanks the clay gradually sinks to the bottom, so that the superfluous water can be drawn off by syphons which are placed in them. The porcelain clay is now of mire-like consistency and almost chemically pure; it is precipitated by the addition of already

Illustration 365.

Page 141.

baked and finely ground felspar powder. In the mixing apparatus it is thoroughly mixed together by being stirred for several hours. As soon as this space of time has passed a membrane pump presses the paste — which is now fairly dense — into the departments of the filter-press for removing the superfluous water (see illustration 359). As the cakes in the filter-press are not of equal density, the paste is put through the paste-beating-machine where it is thoroughly mixed together in order to make it as even as possible. Besides caolin and felspar, several other minerals are used for the fabrication of porcelain, namely:—quartz, lime in the form of marble, limestone or chalk, as well as bits of china which have been baked before in biscuit or sharp fire. The last ingredient is added to lessen the shrinking of the mass. Illustration 360 shows drums and mills of various description.

Some statements might here be made about the mechanical power of the factory, as it as well is a matter of great importance, having been the cause of moving the works from the castle of Albrechtsburg. In the decision as to the place where the factory was to be moved to, weight was laid upon the fact that the water of the river Triebisch which promised to flow stronger yet could be used as a motor-power for the works. For it was already at that time intended to lead the waters of the Freiberg Oremines into the river Triebisch by a subterranean channel 13 kilometres in length. This was done and the motor-power of the Triebisch has almost sufficed for the working for several decades. In order to make it possible to keep up the more extensive working in 1903 it was sought to obtain more profit out of the water and a Francis twin turbine was put up. In 1907 electric motors began to be gradually introduced, but they were thoroughly established only in 1908. In that year a Deutz Dieselmotor combined with the turbine were put up as an electric motor for the general working of the factory (see illustration 361).

After having been kept for some time in the cellars for storing paste, the china paste which is by now ready for use, is drawn up in twisters into the workrooms of the turners, moulders and embossers.

Illustration 366.

Page 142.

Here the most varied work is undertaken, as the china paste is made into all sorts of articles imaginable (see illustration 362).

In order to obtain perfect and useful productions in the way of all kinds of table utensils, of all descriptions of artistic porcelain, as well as of china for chemical and physical purposes, the men must go to work in many and varied ways. After the moulding, the great difficulties which are connected with baking at the high temperature have to be contended with. During the 18th century the turning of the china paste in its soft state and its moulding over gypsum models was discovered; already in 1742 the machine for turning oval and striped vessels was used in connection with the ancient potter's wheel, later the moveable and firmly fixed stencil came into use, in the second decade of the 19th century a new oval machine was introduced while the end of the century saw the working of the potter's wheel by aid of machine. This was the cause of saving much human labour.

In the manner described table utensils and vessels of all sorts are made, but for a very important branch of the Meissen productions namely, the making of statuettes and ornaments, quite different methods have to be followed. Who does not know the groups, the chandeliers, the mirrors and artistic china of all descriptions, and all the charming articles which have been brought into existence by the Meissen artists of the 18th century, the artists who have really created the style of working in china! These china productions are first moulded over gypsum forms. A figure for instance is made in the following manner. The artist who models it first makes a model of clay which answers his purpose, suits his fancy and corresponds with the size required. He then divides the clay models into several rather small parts and covers them with soft plaster. After the plaster has hardened the forms of the clay model are sharply reflected by it; the

Page 143.

Illustration 367.

clay model is removed leaving an exact copy of it in plaster. Out of the plaster form thus obtained it is possible to model a large number of single pieces in soft pressed porcelain paste. As has already been mentioned the model is divided into several parts, therefore the reproductions in plaster also bear the same character and the parts must be again connected to form a complete model. This is done by the embosser who spreads fluid china paste over certain parts and connects the various parts by afterwards pressing them gently and carefully together. After this the figure has to be carefully gone over in order to give it character and expression which it can naturally not obtain by the ordinary moulding. In this way the numerous and very charming plastic figures and ornaments — which have done so much to further the renown of the Meissen china manufactory all over the world — are produced.

When the moulder, embosser and turner have done with the china, it is placed in saggers and goes into the kilns for so-called biscuit baking at a temperature of 1000 degrees C. — a temperature sufficiently high to melt gold. Through this biscuit baking a remarkable change is wrought in the china paste. Besides the water mechanically connected with it, the chemically bound water of the caolin disappears, so that the vessels obtain a certain hardness and firmness and can be drawn through water without softening. The china can therefore now be glazed. Before this is done, however, some technical work very much practised in Meissen is gone through, i. e. the vessels or figures are decorated in various colours under glaze. Blue cobalt colour and green chrome painting on table utensils are particularly popular; the former was already practised in the 18th century, while the latter only came into existence and use in the last quarter of the 19th century. During the last two decades of the last century the numerous colours which can bear the high temperature required for the sharp fire baking of china were added in nearly complete palette as well, and are being used for producing the many coloured chinaware with cameo painting. During the last decade groups and figures came to be decorated with these colours as well. All paintings of this description fully harmonizing with the material are particularly charming and very popular, as besides being pretty the colours on them are very durable, they are indeed indestructible being chemically united with the china. For executing this work, the painter must wield the brush with a sure hand, as the china absorbs the paint and does

not allow of much correction afterwards. Besides the painter has to reckon with another difficulty. The colours mostly develop in the baking so that it is not easy to know what the final appearance of the work will be like; the effect of the painting can be easily spoiled during the process of baking the china either by too strong a flame or by a mistake in leading it (see illustration 363 and 364).

All the chinaware can now be glazed, that is covered with a transparent glaze not easily melted. China glaze consists exclusively of natural products

Illustration 368.

Page 143.

and is combined in a similar way as the paste; it contains porcelain clay and mediums of flux, such as lime in various forms, felspar, silicic acid but no metallic oxyd. It never contains oxyd of lead like all glazes used for fayence, stone-ware etc. through this a very high temperature is required for baking china and its glaze, but the trouble is fully rewarded by the greater hardness and power of resistance against change of temperature against strong acids and alkali, shortly by the indestructibily of chinaware.

The workers draw each piece through the finely ground glaze to which water has been added (see illustration 365). The china itself which is very porous quickly absorbs the water and the powdered glaze settles on it in a thin and even layer while following all the forms and decorations exactly.

It is necessary to go over the china again in order to remove any faults in the glaze; only now the china is ready to receive its characteristic quality by being baked in sharp fire.

The Meissen kilns are, as has already been mentioned, of cylindrical form and three stories high. Kuehn's channel-like kilns with rising flame have been arranged by Brunnemann in 1885 on the principle of the flame turning downwards. They have six outside fire-places with plane and inclined grates for half-gas firing. In the ground flour of the kilns first place for sharp fire baking the highest temperature is obtained at white heat (a little lower than the temperature required for melting platinum) and the porcelain is here baked. In the story above it at a lower temperature — about sufficient for melting gold — the biscuit baking is done by aid of the hot gasses rising from below. In the upper story the chamott saggers and stones are baked, so the heated gas is made a final use of before escaping.

A very important part in the manufacture of china is played by the chamott saggers. As it is absolutely necessary to protect the chinaware from the direct influence of the heated gas, it is put into baked saggers made out of chamott paste. As the saggers crack through being constantly baked and become unfit for further use, they are ground and the powder wetted and mixed with fire-proof clay; new saggers are turned out of this paste, they are baked and used again. As has before been mentioned, the broken saggers were at the beginning of the fabrication pounded in mortars. The chinaware is put into the kiln in saggers that fit it, the saggers are then heaped on one another until the kiln is quite full (see illustration 366).

After the kiln has been walled up the baking begins. This process constitutes the most difficult part of the production of china and requires great care and circumspection. At first the management of the baking process was rather uncertain, but of late years, it has been possible to put this process on a sure and

Page 143.

Illustration 369.

reliable basis, so that we are in a position to do the most difficult part of the production of china surely and well. This is due to the gasanalytical examination of the kiln gasses and, lately, to the use of the thermoelectrical pyrometer.

White and coloured china as well as porcelain painted under glazing are produced in the sharp fire baking. After having been baked, the porcelain receives its characteristic qualities it is — except the coloured articles, — white, transparent and covered with a glaze as hard as steel and as shiny as glass.

The white chinaware now goes to the studios to be ornamented simply or copiously by painting. The painters paint the articles with metallic colours which are rubbed with turpentine and applied with a paint brush in order to melt upon the glaze in the muffel-ovens. In the same manner the metallic ornamentations such as gold, silver and platinum are applied.

During the time that the factory is in existence all manner of ornamentation has been arrived at and the paints of the muffel fire are used as well as those which can bear the high temperature necessary for the sharp fire baking. The faultless china the so-called "first choice" is only painted with artistically valuable decorations, while the articles which possess slight faults either in form or colour (so-called "second choice") are more simply ornamented and bear two cuts in the trade-mark (the blue electoral swords). The colours of the muffel-fire are very numerous and nearly all shades of the palette imaginable can be had. The colours for painting on china receive, however, brilliancy, depth and a proper effect only through being well-baked; the painter must, therefore, take the difficulty of judging before hand the effect of his colours into consideration and reckon with it while doing his work. The painting on glaze follows several directions:— figures, flowers and all manner of decorations are painted either in a simple manner or in perfect artistic style. But the painting under glaze allows also in our time of more elaborate use and artistic problems are undertaken in it with the certainty of success. All china painted on glaze goes into the muffel-ovens in the enamel-house (see illustration 367). The colours are smelted on to the china in especially arranged muffel-ovens at a temperature great enough to melt silver. The manufactory has a well fitted-up chemical laboratory attached to it (see illustration 368), where the Meissen colours for painting on china are produced for use in the factory as well as for sale. Since 1896 the management is in the hands of the working inspector Counsellor of mines Dr. Foerster. The Meissen colours for china are greatly valued by ceramic connoisseurs at home as well as abroad; they are known to be of equally good quality and to possess especially valuable properties. In the laboratory experiments are being made which tend to improve the technique of porcelain production from the point of view of chemistry, but especially are new manners of decoration and ornamentation of porcelain sought for.

After the china is ready for sale it is put up either in the principal store house in Meissen (see illustration 369) or in the Meissen depôts in Dresden and Leipsic.

When we, at the end of this history of the china manufactory look backward over the two centuries of its existence, we see how it has developed from works resembling an artisan's workshop into a factory which spreads its branches all over Germany and is renowned the world over for the sterling quality of its goods. It, in its time, was a model for the european porcelain industry of which it was the pioneer; a special industry has developed out of the chamott-saggers necessary for the baking of china. This branch, as well, now takes an important part among the industries of Europe. Shortly speaking, the world has received two industries at the hands of the Meissen factory which have become indispensable in the economical life of nations and have given employment and satisfaction to innumerable people. The china manufactory owes its existence to two men of genius, King Friedrich August I whose fertile mind had sought for means of enriching his country, and Joh. Friedr. Boettger whose fruitful experiments, under the auspices of the King, led to the discovery of china.

If at any time in the future there will be a gallery of eminent German discoverers erected a place of honour should be given to the discoverer of european porcelain

JOHANN FRIEDRICH BOETTGER.

ORGANIZATION.
FINANCIAL MANAGEMENT. SOCIAL STATISTICS.

THE ORGANIZATION.

he royal china manufactory was founded on June 6th 1710 by Friedrich August I, Elector of Saxony and King of Poland, called "the Strong". He made use of his own capital for the installation and the working. The factory as well as the territories, the estates, the forests, the mining and smelting works etc. belonged to the property of the royal house. After Saxony received a constitutional government, after the issue of the magna charta of September 4th 1831, the royal china factory with all the before mentioned estates became the property of the state-exchequer and was managed by the ministry of finance.

Thus the royal china factory had to keep its organization according to the wish of the wearer of the Saxon crown till 1831. August the Strong had shown an almost extravagant predilection for china even before the discovery of its production in Europe; this fondness for china increased after the great sensation created and the many hopes raised by its discovery in Saxony. It is therefore not at all surprising that the art loving monarch himself should have taken the management of the porcelain factory energetically in hand. Although the Counsellor of mines Nehmitz and the discoverer of china Johann Friedrich Boettger were appointed director and administrator respectively by royal rescript of March 12th 1710, still the King personally took part in the management and in the working even in details by stepping in and directly deciding doubtful questions. Nehmitz already in January 24th 1710 received an order by which the jurisdiction over the employés of the factory was given into his hands. As Boettger and Nehmitz both lived in Dresden, Steinbrueck, a brother-in-law of the former, was appointed local inspector of the works in Meissen. The chronic pecuniary difficulties experienced by the factory during Boettger's life time caused the frequent and unpleasant immediate interferences by the King. The painter Hoeroldt (1720) and the sculptor Kaendler (1731) have written their names large in the annals of the royal factory as far as artistic production is concerned, they brought various modes of decoration into existence and their work and influence are valuable to the present day. As long as the royal china factory was the property of the crown, its management lay in the hands of a commission appointed by the King and headed by a confidential person from the court and the Chief royal counsellors; questions of greater importance were decided by the King himself. After Boettger's death, the Privy counsellor Baron von Alemann, von Seebach and the Counsellor of the chamber von Lesgewang were made members of the commission. After the demise of August the Strong, Count Bruehl was appointed director in 1733, the post of vice-director was taken by Count Hennicke the 17th August 1739. An especial vigilance commando consisting of military invalids was instituted from November 17th 1726 to guard the manufactory. Among the persons appointed by the crown for the chief management of the factory at the beginning of its existence, Count Bruehl who was for a long time connected with it must be particularly mentioned as having exercised his influence over the development of the works. During Bruehl's management the Privy counsellor von Nimpsch had a great say in the affairs of the factory. After Bruehl's death which took place in 1763 at the same time as the demise of Friedrich August III, Elector Friedrich Christian gave the chief management of the factory into the hands of his spouse. In 1774 Count Marcolini became director and kept his post till 1814. The artistic leadership was in 1764 given over to the court painter

Table 40

HIS EXCELLENCY DD^{R.} VON RUEGER,
MINISTER OF FINANCE.

PRIVY COUNSELLOR D^{R.} JUR. WAHLE,
DIRECTOR OF THE MINISTRY.

PRIVY COUNSELLOR OF MINES FISCHER,
RECITING COUNSELLOR, REFERENT.

Table 41

PRIVY COUNSELLOR OF COMMERCE GESELL,
DIRECTOR.

COUNSELLOR SUPERIOR OF MINES DR· HEINTZE,
DIRECTOR OF THE WORKING.

SCULPTOR PROFESSOR HOESEL,
LEADER OF THE MODELLING DEPARTMENT.

Dietrich who introduced the classic artistic style in place of the Rococo-style which had to that time been popular in Meissen. Count Marcolini laid down his directorship in 1814, King Friedrich August I entrusted the general management of the factory to Herr von Oppel, under him inspector and later director Kuehn very successfully introduced a new organization. At this time the cost of production began to be more exactly estimated. In 1814 the Hubertusburg stone-ware factory and the Doehlen pottery works were joined to the Meissen china factory, but already in 1816 they were disconnected again. At the beginning the paste was made of porcelain clay from the St. Andrew mine near Aue, it was afterwards mixed with Seilitz earth; the best substitute for porcelain clay is found in a mine property of the monastery of Sornzig and was added in 1817. In April 1816 Koettig and Selbmann were created arcanists; in 1818 the artistic painter Kersting was called to Meissen. At this time the use of the stencil in connection with the potter's wheel, the casting of china articles and a machine for turning oval vessels were introduced. Instead of the moulders, turners, embossers and painters being paid by time, they received payment by the piece according to a set price. In 1849 the deserving inspector Kuehn was appointed director. Besides the selling depôts existing in Meissen, Dresden and Leipsic, a warehouse was in 1851 erected in Hamburg, but had to be given up in eight years time owing to the want of sufficiently large sale of the goods. An important change in the working of the factory was effected in 1839, when the kiln for sharp fire baking began to be heated by coals instead of wood. In 1853 a steam engine was introduced as a motor-power. Director Kuehn died in 1870 after having well and faithfully served the factory for 56 years; his place was taken by the chief manager Raithel who filled it until he was pensioned off in 1894. From 1894 to 1901 Brunnemann who was at first head inspector and afterwards Privy counsellor of mines was appointed director. By an order of June 5th 1849 the interests of the working staff with regard to the administration were taken care of by a committee of workmen. At the same time a new price-list for piece work was combined and the administration was allowed to grant exceptionally good workers a premium besides the money earned by piece work; this was later made dependent on the fact whether the workmen had reached a fixed age.

From 1831, that is from the time when the royal porcelain factory ceased to be the property of the crown and was given into possession of the Saxon government, various changes were effected in its organization. These alterations were well-considered and were made by the cooperation of government and parliament. At the close of the two hundred years which have passed since the founding of the factory, its organization in its principal points may be described as follows.

The royal exchequer is represented in the possession of the royal factory by the royal ministry of finance (see Table 40). The latter manages in his second department the royal china manufactory as a part of the mining branch and decides in all questions of importance. The direct management of the factory lies in the hands of an administrative board (see Table 41) appointed by the royal ministry of finance and consisting of several members; the director of the factory acting as chairman. The administrative board has to hand in a project of its budget to the ministry of finance every two years at the end of the bi-annual period for closing the government financial affairs. The list of employés includes officials who act as government servants, the employés of the factory and the workmen. The officials who act as government servants are appointed by the ministry of finance, while the workmen are engaged by the administrative board or the director. The royal porcelain factory embraces the most varied employments in its rounds:—Technique, art, chemistry, mining and commerce. The division of this varied work is so arranged as to have a superior officer as leader for each branch. There are three principal divisions:—Technique, art and commerce. To answer practical requirements the following divisions exist at present:—

1. General working (production of the raw materials, the direction of the baking process, of the machines, the buildings, ceramico-chemical experimentation etc.),
2. Chemical laboratory and the baking of the enamel paints (fabrication of colours etc.),
3. The modelling section (modelling, embossing, moulding, turning etc.),
4. Painting (sketches and their execution painted on or under glaze),
5. Commerce (three selling depôts in Meissen, Dresden and Leipsic),
6. Accountancy and book-keeping (see Table 42).

The managers of these divisions supervise them as well as the officials and workmen under them under the management of the director at their own responsibility and pretty independently. The latter is represented by the second member of the administrative board i. e. the director of the working. All important questions of finance and management meet with regular discussion between the director and the leader of the branches concerned, or between the director and the other members of the administrative board, or at a meeting of the upper officials under the chairmanship of the director. The administrative board reports all important business matters, whether they be extraordinary or in the order of the day, to the royal ministry of finance.

The order of business in general is regulated by the ministry of finance, the sphere of action of each official is made clear to him while the employés and workmen are managed according to the rules of work. The artistic employés who leave the factory owing to illness or death, — other causes need hardly be considered, as being of rare occurence — find fitting successors in men who have been especially trained for the purpose in the art school attached to the royal china factory. The pupils of this school receive drawing lessons for two years and are afterwards practically and theoretically instructed during the period of five years which follows as apprentices. In the first years of apprenticeship they are taught painting and sculpture equally, then it is decided which artistic branch the pupil is more adapted for. The teaching is done, under the management of the directors of both artistic divisions, by the artists of the royal factory who are most fit for this work. Particularly gifted pupils are afforded the time and the means of studying at art schools and academies of fine arts. The apprentices receive pecuniary assistance in the shape of board money increasing as the years of their appenticeship pass. The tuition itself is free. The school year begins at Easter.

As the royal factory belongs to the state, it is self understood that its arrangements have to fit in with the arrangements existing in the general government institutions. But the government gives the factory as much freedom as possible, so that it may manage its affairs as is customary in artistic institutions and as an industrial money earning concern. The commercial organisation is regulated in such a manner as to afford customers the opportunity of dealing directly with the factory. Each article ever made on the premises during the two hundred years of the existence of the works can at any time be again produced and substituted. The chinaware is sold all the world over. Besides the depôts which are managed by the factory, a large number of commission stores have been founded at home and abroad in order to make it an easy matter for customers to obtain the goods. Especial care has been exercised in the organization of the factory itself as far as the work and the workmen are concerned, so as to make it possible for it to keep its place as the first china manufactory in Europe — not only in an historic sense. The well-aired workrooms are provided with everything necessary for the safety of the employés, while the hygienic conditions of work are irreproachable. To safe-guard the buildings, machines and goods against fire the factory has organized a fire-brigade of its own and supplied it with all the necessary requirements.

Provision is made for the workmen by the royal factory, some of these assistance funds can be traced far back and will be spoken of more particularly further on.

FINANCIAL MANAGEMENT.

When the factory was founded the administration received 750 talers monthly from the King for its maintenance. According to a report of the chamber of revenue, the new factory with all its furnishings in Dresden and Meissen cost, up to July 15th 1713, the sum of 27 427 talers 21 gr. 4 pf. Half of the stock of china on hand in 1710 to the value of 3357 talers 7 gr. was brought to the Leipsic fair at which among other royal personages the King of Prussia Friedrich I accompanied by the Kronprinz, as well as the spouse of King August with the Duchess of Braunschweig from Torgau were present. The expenses here incurred amounted to 2700 talers and exceeded the takings which only amounted to 1993 talers. In 1714—15 already rather large orders came in from Paris, but they were entirely neglected by the director Dr. Nehmitz. From 1710—15 the goods had no fixed price but were sold as profitably as possible. They were sold in Meissen as well as in Dresden, Naumburg, Berlin, Cottbus and in other towns; no fixed depôts, however, existed at that time. Notwithstanding the high prices which the goods were sold at, pecuniary assistance was required by the factory; this was probably partly due to want of method in the management. From 1720 the aim of making the factory exist out of its own means was kept in view. The income for 1720 amounted to 9242 talers 21 gr. 6 pf. and the expenditure amounted to 7849 talers 2 gr. 6 pf., so that there was a surplus of nearly 1400 talers. The delivery of 2000 talers worth of chinaware to the King is considered as a deficit in the income. From the time that Hoeroldt was engaged in 1720, the quality of the work improved and the sale of the goods increased accordingly; this was so in a still greater degree from 1731 when Kaendler entered the factory as a sculptor. His imperishable productions have not been equalled to this day and are a joy to connoisseurs of art. The value of the stock on hand in Dresden and in the depôt in Warsaw amounted in 1737 to 100000 talers. The sale of the goods took a more lively turn from 1732. 18000 turkish cups were ordered to be produced and exported to Turkey; in 1742 the income rose to 82330 talers 13 gr. 6 pf., in 1752 to 224340 talers 4 gr. 9 pf. The cost of working amounted in 1725 to 15741 talers 15 gr., in 1750 the amount increased to 110653 talers 6 gr. 3 pf. The second Silesian war in 1745 brought with it the temporary dismissal of the workmen. The kilns were destroyed when the Prussians invaded Saxony, as it was feared that the enemy would penetrate the secrets of fabrication. Notwithstanding this precaution King Friedrich II managed to employ workmen from the factory and brought porcelain clay to Berlin. Some time later the Royal Porcelain factory in Berlin was founded. Although these disturbances were connected with financial loss, the factory soon again arrived at a more flourishing state. But the seven years' war 1756—63 brought the factory to the verge of ruin. After the invasion of the Prussians all the stock of china on hand was confiscated by them and sold for 120000 talers. The financial position of the factory was greatly shaken, as it had delivered now and in the Silesian war which had gone before

553336 talers 9 gr.

worth of goods to the King of Prussia as well as goods valued at

1572 talers 17 gr. 10 pf.

to the leaders of the prussian troops; besides the factory lost a large number of workmen who went over to the Berlin manufactory. The factory which had been bowed down by the storms of fate soon recovered again and reached the acme of its success in the 18th century in the years following the peace of Hubertusburg of 1763. Extensive journeys were made to the Netherlands, Portugal, Spain, Italy, Switzerland, England, Russia and Denmark, this resulted in large orders for the factory. In order to increase the sale of chinaware still more in 1764 auction sales were instituted. In 1765 there was a cash surplus amounting to 42000 talers. The income in 1766 rose to 221500 talers, but again decreased to 147334 talers in 1774. In the last years the factory has been and is still connected with 105 commercial houses including, 25 commissionaries. Because the sale of the goods kept decreasing, many ways to improve business were taken recourse to; among them a lottery was arranged, by order of the King, by the Counsellor of mines Poerner; here 60000 talers worth of chinaware that a sale could not be found for was disposed. At that time turkish and russian orders were of great importance therefore great loss was caused to the factory by the prohibition which was issued in 1806 to import goods into Russia. In the years between 1807 and 1813 the supply of the sum of 410000 talers was required in order to maintain the factory. By order of the russian general government the financial as well as the technical affairs of the factory were thoroughly gone into. In the time following this examination, the factory was unable to exist without the support of the King and required sums of money amounting to 20458 talers in 1829, 13484 talers in 1830 and 22853 talers in 1831—32 to help to keep it going. The unfavourable circumstances which the factory laboured under altered, by Saxony joining the German union of customs in 1834; now the factory entered upon a new era which has brought profits every year until the present day with but few exceptions. The profits amounted in 1835 to 20000 talers, in 1836 to 25000 talers, in 1837 to 30000 talers, 1840—47, 13500 talers yearly and in 1854—63 to 164400 talers. When inspector Koettig discovered the production of artificial ultramarine, works for producing it under the name of "lapis-lazuli blue" were adjoined to the china factory. This was carried on till 1877 and brought a clear profit of

314750 marks

to the factory. A favourable influence on the finances of the factory was exercised by the discovery of lustre gold by director Kuehn in 1828. This "lustre gold" is bright after baking, while the powdered gold must be made brilliant by a particular operation.

After the administrative board had been commissioned in 1852 to discuss the erection of new buildings for the royal china factory and to offer for consideration the suitability of modern improvements in its working, in answer to the expressed wish of his Majesty King Johann in 1858 a grant of 300000 talers for the erection of a new porcelain manufactory was accorded by parliament. The new building was erected in the valley of the Triebisch in Meissen in 1859—63 and in the last mentioned year the works were transferred to it. In this way the fears that the factory would be sold and turned into a limited company were dispersed. The war between Prussia and Austria in 1866 caused loss to the china factory as well. The financial position improved greatly however in 1867 when 223 000 talers work of goods were sold and a clear profit of 40 000 talers obtained. The profits rose still higher after 1870. In 1874 the factory already showed an income of 560 439 talers with a clear profit of 139 873 talers. In 1875—80

$$\left.\begin{array}{l} \text{the income amounted to . } 1\,500\,000 \text{ marks} \\ \text{cash surplus amounted to } \quad 260\,000 \quad \text{„} \end{array}\right\} \text{on an average.}$$

For the purchase of ground and the extension of buildings in 1871—76

439 199 marks

out of the factory monies were spent. Instead of the 900 000 marks granted by the government for the erection of new buildings, the state received in 1863—79 inclusive the sum of

3 302 400 marks

in clear profits. Besides this amount 400 000 marks were paid by the factory for new buildings. In 1909 the production was valued at a sum slightly over 2 000 000 marks; the clear profits amounting to 235 743 marks were delivered to the government besides 73 982 marks which were laid out on the erection of new buildings. The money delivered to the government in 1880—1909 amounted to 7 416 458 marks, while during this time 400 000 marks out of the income were spent on innovations. During the working year of 1909 the sale of the chinaware effected in different countries may be estimated as follows:—

967 032	marks	in	Germany,
71 730	„	„	Austria-Hungary,
24 223	„	„	Holland, Belgium and Luxemburg,
67 896	„	„	France, Switzerland, Spain and Portugal,
78 246	„	„	England,
41 658	„	„	Russia, Denmark and Sweden,
29 467	„	„	Italy, Turkey, Roumania and Greece,
110 197	„	„	America,
2 256	„	„	Asia, Africa and Australia,
644 015	„	„	Various retail sales.

The sale of colours for painting on china has brought rather a large income to the factory during the last decades. The colours produced — of which only a large number for muffle-ovens are sold — in the laboratory of the factory are much valued and sought after at home and abroad, owing to their good quality, incomparable purity and great durability. The high duty set upon china renders its exportation difficult; it unfavourably influences the sale and, through it, the financial success of the factory. The United States of America especially try to make the importation difficult by levying a duty of 60% of the value. As the royal factory only produces china of great value, it suffers more under this duty than the porcelain industry which makes cheap marketable goods.

As the foundation of the royal porcelain factory had been an object of envy for all Europe, so the discovery of china which it was based on was the object of energetically attempted imitation. The first of these imitators appeared in Plaue on the Havel in which place the president of the chamber von Goerne founded a factory which produced brown china in imitation of Boettgers red porcelain. Although the secret of making china (the arcanum) was strictly guarded and its betrayal threatened with the heaviest punishment, it was soon after the foundation of the factory betrayed by employés who thought that they knew it, or pretended to think so. The unfaithful employés betrayed their employer owing to the brilliant promises made to them by people who wished to worm the secret out of them. Gradually in this way china factories were founded in Vienna, Strassburg, Nymphenburg, Hoechst, Frankenthal, Petersburg and several states of Thueringen.

As the production of china which had been discovered in Saxony was from the very beginning eagerly imitated so the Meissen models and patterns created in the middle of the 18th century by the artistic ability of Hoeroldt and Kaendler were the object of zealous and numerous imitations. In order to deceive the

Table 42

COUNSELLOR OF MINES
DR. FOERSTER,
INSPECTOR
OF THE WORKING.

ARTISTIC PAINTER
PROFESSOR
ACHTENHAGEN,
LEADER OF THE PAINTING
DEPARTMENT.

MANAGER C. BARING,
ROYAL CHINA DEPÔT
IN LEIPSIC.

MANAGER A. TEITGE,
ROYAL CHINA DEPÔT
IN DRESDEN.

MANAGER C. WUERFEL,
CHIEF DEPÔT IN MEISSEN.

ARTISTIC PAINTER THEO GRUST,
INSPECTOR OF PAINTING DEPARTMENT.

CASHIER FR. GUENNEL,
PRINCIPAL CASH OFFICE IN MEISSEN.

Table 43

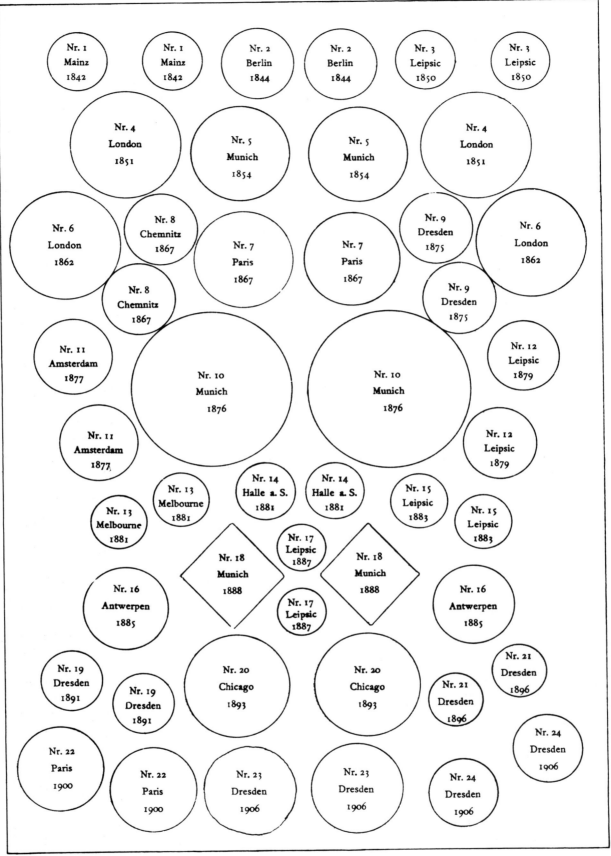

Table 43

uninitiated public and for their own gain these imitators of the Meissen models and designs made also use of the trademark of the royal manufactory or of marks strikingly similar. Several factories founded by renegades from Meissen in Thueringen came forward with these perfected imitations so that already in the second half of the 18th century prohibitions to export china with imitated trademarks into or through Saxony had to be issued by the King. As other porcelain factories were founded the necessity arose to make the productions of the Meissen factory cognoscible by a particular mark. From the very beginning the royal factory had made use of various trademarks, among them were the saxon electoral swords. By a royal decision of 1731 the crossed electoral swords were ordered to be used on all the chinaware which was put on the market. The question of trademarks however was only put on a lawful footing on November 30th 1874 when the first law for the protection of trademarks was passed in Germany. Through this the trademarks of the royal factory received an intrinsic value besides the extrinsic value they had before possessed. A great number of court cases at home and abroad were necessary, however, to protect the royal china factory from innumerable abuses which were made of its trademarks.

Drawings of the principal and registered trademarks used by the royal factory follow, they are accompanied by drawings of the principal trademarks of the other factories which are qualified to be confounded with those of Meissen.

TRADEMARKS OF THE ROYAL MANUFACTORY IN MEISSEN.

TRADEMARKS WHICH CAN BE CONFOUNDED WITH THOSE OF THE ROYAL MANUFACTORY IN MEISSEN.

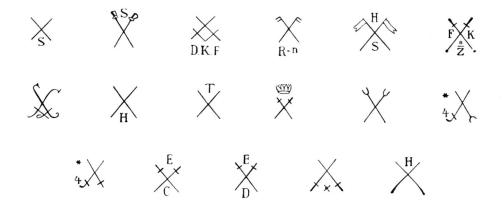

The royal china factory has made use of every opportunity afforded by the rivalry of nations in art and industry and has taken a prominent part in numerous exhibitions at home and abroad and has received the highest awards (see Table 43).

SOCIAL STATISTICS.

The employés of the royal china factory have, at all times from the beginning of the existence of the factory to the present day, been so well provided for as is only possible under the supervision of the crown or the state. This provision stretches over the education, the earnings, the health and all the needs of the employés, it even cares for the widows and children of deceased employés. Dismissal of the workmen even during the sad time of the retrogression of the factory, during the disturbances of war was, if possible, avoided. The employés have always appreciated the care that was shown for their welfare and have at all times rewarded it by fidelity and attachment. Owing to all this the employés only in very rare cases left the factory of their own free will and several successive generations of the same families have given the chief craftsmen of the factory into its service. Thirty men were employed in the year of the foundation 1710—11 of the works, among them were several arcanists, 8—10 pastemakers and bakers, 8—10 potters, 2 sagger-makers, 6—8 glass cutters and grinders, 1 artist, 2 gilders, 2 enamellers and 1 varnisher. The number of men employed during the two hundred years of the existence of the royal factory has greatly varied as will be seen from the following table:—

1720	1730	1740	1750	1765	1806	1828	1870	1890	1900	1909
33	49	218	378	731	515	354	400	741	718	717

The most important matter for a workman is the pay he gets. As has been above already mentioned the administrator Boettger received 750 talers monthly for paying wages and purchasing the necessary materials. The workmen received 4—12 talers monthly, the arcanists 20 talers, the local inspector Steinbrueck 20 talers and the director Nehmitz 30 talers. Boettger had to include the money derived from the sale of the goods in the allowance made him. In the year of Boettger's death 1719 the wages amounted to 2928 talers, in the year following it 4078 talers 4 gr. were paid out in salaries. In the royal factory, as in all industrial undertakings, the salaries of the employés rose and fell with each alteration in business, to say nothing of the natural change made in the value of money as time went on.

In the years 1720—32 the painters as well as 30 craftsmen and 10 apprentices were engaged and paid by the chief painter Hoeroldt. According to this Hoeroldt was with regard to the painters his own undertaker in the factory. Only in 1832 prices were set for piece work done by the painters and they were paid directly by the factory. During the war 1745/46 the work was altogether discontinued till January 10th 1746 and the employés were given leave on full pay. The years during which the seven years' war lasted were particularly unfavourable for the conditions of pay. Many employés left the factory while complaining of insufficient earnings and some of the most able workers were among those who departed — this was the direct cause of the foundation of some of the china factories in Thueringen. When the price of bread was high in 1771—72 and 1779—82 and in later times as well, the employés of the factory were supported by receiving corn at a cheap price. In 1778 the following amounts were paid away annually in wages to

embossers	178—294 talers
turners and moulders	179—294 „
painters	176—338 „
painters in blue	122—150 „
bakers of china	114—128 „
glazers and grinders	105—150 „
ordinary workmen	82— 98 „
apprentices	30 „

The war times of 1807—14 again brought the employés of the factory into straitened circumstances. It was possible to keep the factory going only by large supplies of money. The technical workers, in a petition in 1849, asked for higher wages; this was to a certain extent granted. They made a list of the expenditure of a family of four annually as follows:—

quarters	12 talers	— gr.
fuel	12 „	— „
clothing	18 .,	— „
taxes, washing etc.	18 .,	— „
school money for 2 children .	2 .,	12 „
food	58 „	— „

120 talers 12 gr.

At this time the ministry of finance ordered a committee to be chosen from the ranks of the work-men by the employés themselves. This committee was to care for the interests of the employés before the administrative board. This arrangement exists to the present to the satisfaction of all parties concerned. As the course of business increased and the cost of living became higher, the wages were in 1872 raised to correspond with these conditions. The increase of wages is made clear in the following table; they amounted on an average annually as follows:—

a) technical workmen

1869	1878
540	864 marks;

b) artistic workmen

1869	1878		
1448	2565	marks	modellers,
1242	1689	„	moulders and turners,
1734	1748	„	embossers,
1447	1772	„	figure painters,
1217	1448	„	flower painters,
1246	1349	„	decoration painters,
879	1045	„	painters in blue,
280	537	.,	women painters in blue,
549	668	„	women polishers,
372	656	„	apprentices;

c) workers in the commercial branch

1869	1878
828	1116 marks.

Generally speaking the wages of the employés rose from 1869 to 1878 from 774 marks to 1006 marks on an average per man; the total of the money paid out in wages rose from 200667 marks to 572832 marks and the proportion of the wages to the china production was increased from 35,38 % to 41,02 %. The working hours of the technical employés were fixed at 10 hours, from 6 a. m. to 6 p. m. with two hours' pause. From 1878 to the present the wages have been raised still higher. In a prospect for 1909 we find that in that year the following sums were paid away in wages. The average is given for each class of workmen.

Modellers, embossers, moulders and turners	2064	marks
Painters of figures, flowers and decorations	2183	.,
Male painters in blue	1373	.,
Women painters in blue, polishers and embossers of lace	860	.,
Technical workers	1164	..
and in total	976221	.,

The average pay for each of the workers amounted to 1540 marks in 1909 against 1006 marks in 1878.

The royal porcelain factory has from the very beginning of its existence founded and supported institutions to further the welfare of the employés and to provide for them in case of need; the benign influence exercised by these institutions has almost insollubly fastened the interests of the workmen to those of the royal china factory. During the years 1736—75 two burial funds and three funds for orphans and widows were founded at the initiative of the workmen themselves (these were the general- and the wood-yard burial funds and the painters, moulders and general widows funds). These funds are managed by the employés under the supervision of the administration board and have, during the 135—175 years which have elapsed since their foundation, done, under small contributions and costs, much towards brightening life during troubled hours for its members. The large insurance institutions founded by the state for the employés of the factory must be added to the above mentioned, private funds, of the employés who have created several especial supporting-funds for themselves. In the earliest times already, when the factory was still the property of the crown, pensions were granted to employés who had become unfit for work. The royal treasury arranged this matter in 1840 by founding the local institution for such of the pensioned off workers as were not considered as government officials. The members of this institution received a certain pension, according to a statute of it, when they became unfit for work, it was paid out of the contributions of the state and out of the contributions of the members as well as out of the interest of the capital of the institution. The contribution of the state amounted in 1840 to 2000 talers, up to 1878 it rose to 20000 marks, after that to 29000 or 25000 marks and was increased in 1910, until further orders, to the sum of 35000 marks. In 1878 the assistance of these funds rendered per man on an average has amounted to

> 662,4 marks from the local institution,
> 169,7 ,, ,, ,, general burial fund,
> 40,9 ,, ,, ,, wood-yard burial fund,
> 163,6 ,, ,, ,, 3 widows' funds.

The total capital of these institutions amounted to 331 678 marks.

To the above mentioned institutions the sickness-fund managed by the royal manufactory was added by order of the empire passed on June 15th 1883. The royal manufactory had granted money to its employés in case of illness already in 1740 and since 1884 gives the members of her sickness-fund more than is prescribed by law.

For supporting the employés in cases of particular need a special grant from the government is put at the disposal of the royal factory. In 1878 1337 marks and in 1909 7481 marks were paid out from these funds. In 1863 the Kuehn-fund in honour of the 50 years jubilee of the director, Privy counsellor of mines Kuehn was founded; it renders pecuniary assistance out of the interest on its capital (6922 marks in 1878, 35115 marks in 1909) to the widows of workmen at the end of each year.

The income and expenditure of the assistance funds of the royal china factory were for the year's end 1909 as follows:—

	Income	Expenditure
Pensioneers fund (including 25 000 marks government contribution)	61 407 marks	50 833 marks
General burial fund	21 978 ,,	14 311 ,,
Wood-yard burial fund	1 219 ,,	1 271 ,,
Painters' widows' fund	13 664 ,,	6 504 ,,
Modellers' widows' fund	7 925 ,,	6 062 ,,
General widows' fund	7 985 ,,	4 397 ,,

The total amount of money at the disposal of these institutions is reckoned at 1 097 544 marks.

The sickness-fund of the manufactory had 32 930 marks income (including 11 197 marks granted by the government), while its expenditure for the same year amounted to 32 913 marks. It possessed a capital of 32 963 marks. From capital of the sickness-fund the home for convalescents in Baerenfels was erected in 1897.

GESELL.

1710 – 1910

THE CELEBRATION OF THE 200TH ANNIVERSARY
OF THE ROYAL CHINA MANUFACTORY

ON JUNE 6TH 1910.

The celebration of anniversaries is an old custom resting on ethics and piety. Jubilees are the milestones on the highway of life which mark the progress on it of single individuals as well as the development of corporations of universal signification. These milestones are placed at the end of a long path trodden by the person or institution concerned; here the results of the large amount of work done, as well as the means by which these results have been attained with pains and care, are considered. With individuals the point at which the jubilee is celebrated is often the close of their career, while with corporations it can only be a turning point in the measure of experience gained in the years that have passed and the knowledge springing out of them. At present, when the conditions of life and the efforts of competitors make restless work in all branches strictly necessary, the word "jubilee" signifies a short resting space on an island of the blessed, where hearts beat high and are filled with the consciousness of work well done and at the thought of respite from labour and strife. Here modern man finds leisure to meditate, to cast a look backward at the past and forward at the future; here he has time to rediscover old ideals which had been lost in the whirlpool of everyday life, to foster old hopes and new creative powers. The committee of the celebration of the 200th anniversary of the day when the royal china factory was founded should like the participators of the festival to share their enthusiasm for it, as well as the honest endeavour of its initiators to glorify the oldest artistic institution of Saxony, to bear in mind its glorious history and to make it more harmonious and perfect in every respect.

The royal porcelain factory has already celebrated two jubilees ere now, viz. its centenary in 1810 and its 150th anniversary in 1860. The course of these festivities ran, briefly, as follows:—

CELEBRATION OF THE JUBILEE ON JUNE 6TH 1810.

On the eve of the jubilee the bells of all the churches in Meissen, Cologne on the Elbe and Zscheila with glad peals rang in the joyous day. In the morning shooting from small-cannon from the hills surrounding Meissen, a reveille played by the town shooters' band. 8 a. m. gathering of all the employés in the court-yard of the castle of Albrechtsburg, parade of the civil guard, procession to divine service in the cathedral. The royal guards (2 non-commissioned officers, 2 drummers, 12 grenadiers) parade with drums beating. Festive sermon by superintendent Dr. Donner. At 10 a. m. cheering of His Majesty the King and the director Count Marcolini and of the royal commissioners, in the courtyard of the castle. At 11 a. m. procession on the market square in honour of the magistracy and the citizens, procession to the place of festivity on the citizens' shooting lawn. Rendering homage to the bust of King August the Strong and Friedrich August, later to those of Marcolini and Boettger. At midday banquet laid in three pavilions. 944 persons (among them 513 wives of the employés, their widows and such of them as had been pensioned off) take part in the banquet. After the banquet dance and social at which the citizens of Meissen take part. The chronicler reports that no accidents occured and no excess disturbed the pleasant feast.

The administrative board headed by Count Marcolini subscribed 542 talers and 12 gr., the officials and workmen 254 talers 20 gr. 8 pf. towards the expenses incurred for the feast.

CELEBRATION OF THE JUBILEE ON JUNE 6TH 1860.

On the eve of the jubilee the management was honoured with a torch light procession in the court-yard of the Albrechtsburg. Shooting from small-cannon from the Meissen mountains announce the festive day. Gathering of the employés at 10 a. m. in the courtyard. Speech by director Kuehn. His excellency the Minister of finance von Friesen (supported by the Privy counsellors of finance von Broizem and Freiesleben) makes a speech, welcomes the assembly in the name of King Johann and hands director Kuehn a decree by which he receives, by order of the King, the title of Privy counsellor of mines, inspector Koettig receives the order of King Albrecht and the manager Leuteritz the cross of the same order. At midday gathering on the shooting lawn of the citizens. Rendering homage to the bust of August the Strong, King Johann and Boettger, as well as to a huge statue of Saxonia. Banquet in decorated pavilions at which the minister of finance and his counsellors take part, as well as all the employés of the factory (900 people among them 568 wives, widows and pensioneers). A concert and ball in a beautifully lighted room closed the festival for which the royal ministry of finance had granted 360 talers.

The celebration of both jubilees of 1810 and 1860 have served as forerunners in the planning of the celebration of the 200th anniversary of the royal china factory; the arrangements of the former festivities could be considered worthy of imitation as they had proved satisfactory to all parties concerned and had given brilliant results. Taking into consideration the change of the times and the increased number of employés from 900 to 1500 an essential difference had to be made in the proceedings and the whole affair had to be worked on a larger scale. The festival bears an ideal significance and thousands of people, expecting a great deal from it participate in the rejoicings so that immense mental and physical energy had to be spent in its planning and preparation. Great care was taken to make sure, as far as was humanly possible, of the success of the undertaking within the means afforded for it. From the very beginning the planning of the festival was furthered by the lively interest manifested by His Majesty the King, by the royal ministry of finance and by the houses of parliament. On June 6th 1710 the castle of Albrechtsburg, a beautiful German building in gothic style, was given over to the china factory to make use of as it a place for its works*. The royal porcelain factory can therefore look with well-justified pride upon the castle of Albrechtsburg as its birth-place. Here its cradle stood, in its high and beautiful halls it made its first uncertain steps into life, under its protection it grew to be the young giant-daughter of ceramic art. Its beauty and power, enlivened by the genius of a Hoeroldt and a Kaendler, filled its contemporaries all the world over with astonishment. The waters of the Elbe which flow at the foot of the Albrechtsburg seem to have been destined to bear the work and the glory of the young factory over the sea into far and distant lands. For over 150 years the royal porcelain factory has had its proud and happy home under the roof of the Albrechtsburg, then the beautiful and hospitable halls became too narrow for its growing limbs; a new building approved by government and parliament was then erected in the valley of the Triebisch, furnished with all modern improvements and offered to the factory as its new home. When the place for the celebration of 200th anniversary had to be chosen nothing was simpler than to decide on the Albrechtsburg. The Albrechtsburg, that jewel of the architecture of the middle ages from whose proud height the charm of flowering fields and the idyllic peace of quiet valleys enchant the view, being the home of the factory was a most fitting place for this festive occasion. A great step towards the fulfillment of the arrangements of the festivities was made by the choice of the Albrechtsburg as their site. His Majesty the King gave his consent to the project promising at the same time to be present at the festive occasion in person, accompanied by the royal family. The presence of the royal personages to honour the celebration lent a new zest to the wish of the committee to make the festival a success in every respect. The programme for the festivities, as is given below was accepted by the King and by the royal ministry of finance.

---

* *The discovery of china and the events which preceeded its foundation have been particularly treated in the introduction of the history of the royal factory.*

PROGRAMME FOR THE CELEBRATION OF THE 200ᵀᴴ ANNIVERSARY
OF ROYAL CHINA FACTORY IN MEISSEN
ON MONDAY JUNE 6ᵀᴴ 1910.

1. 10.30 to 11.30 a. m. convocation of all the people connected with the factory. Distribution of royal marks of distinction in the large courtyard of the royal china factory.
2. Midday to 1 p. m. divine service in the town church.
3. 1.30 to 3.30 p. m. banquet of the employées in the Albrechtsburg and in the restaurant of the Bourg.
4. 3.30 p. m. social.
5. 4.30 to 5.30 p. m. presence of His Majesty the King and suite on the site of festivity, welcoming His Majesty, introduction of the persons honoured with royal marks of distinction; musical performance and other entertainments.
6. 5.30 to 11 p. m. social, concert, vocal performance, dance.

The following rather important part of the arrangements made for the celebration, may precede the description of the festivities themselves. The government and the houses of parliament decided that the following sums should be subscribed out of the funds of the royal porcelain factory:—

to the pensioneers fund of the royal porcelain factory { 30000 marks as a contribution for the support of the reserve fund, 6000 marks yearly to be paid in addition to the 29000 marks paid to that time altogether 35000 marks.

9000 marks were granted by the government in relation to chapter 8 state account to cover the expenditure incurred by the royal china factory in hospitability to its employées and guests of honour.

The royal ministry of finance agreed that:—

the employées, as guests of honour, should receive their pay for the day of the festival and that the following mementoes of the 200ᵗʰ anniversary should be issued:—

a) the festival work lying before should be written and issued;
b) the participators of the feast were to receive a small arched china shield showing the blue electoral swords, surrounded by a wreath of laurel;
c) mementoes to be produced for sale:—

a souvenir dish with electoral swords surrounded by a wreath of laurel leaves among which the electoral and royal Saxon coats of arms, as well as the coats of arms of Meissen are placed — under the wreath the figures 1710—1910 are painted in blue under glazing, the centre showing to number 200,

further — a wine jug, ornamented with the electoral swords, the electoral and town coats of arms the dates 1710—1910 and laurel boughs painted in cobalt blue under glazing, and, after the celebration,

a large assortment of the best plastic and decorative productions of the royal porcelain factory of artistic and practical nature were marked with

1710 ⚔ 1910

for a year dating from June 6ᵗʰ 1910.

In order to give the celebration a peculiar character, entirely characteristic of the royal porcelain factory, the employées, encouraged by the artistic managers decided to produce a series of tableaux which were to be true to life and were to represent the best plastic work of the classic period of the royal china factory and some of the creations of modern times. These artistic productions were to be represented by the employées of the royal china factory dressed in historical costumes which were to be correct in every detail. The characters were not to be placed in stiff poses as in ordinary tableaux but were to move in accordance with an original composition to recite a text in poetical form which had been composed by persons connected with the factory. As the materials with the Rococo-pattern, so much in vogue in the 18ᵗʰ century were nowhere to be obtained, the painters of the factory painted the designs on the materials themselves. These preparations as well as the rehearsals required much time and trouble which were fully repaid by the success of the undertaking.

Illustration 372. COURTYARD OF THE ALBRECHTSBURG.

About 50 persons took part in the artistic performance. The cost of the same, without reckoning the time and labour spent on it, amounted to several thousand marks and was subscribed by the employées. For months before the feast and during the time it lasted economical, decorative, erection and hospitality committees were at work. The town of Meissen presented a barrel containing 500 liter of excellent wine to celebrate the occasion; for this presentation here once more thanks are rendered. Order was kept by the members of the festive committee consisting of employées of the factory with the assistance of the town police and a column of the red cross. The fire brigade was present so at as to be on the spot in case of necessity. A red cross ambulance was in attendance in one of the halls of the castle. A copious program of musical entertainment was offered by the singing clubs of the royal china factory, the Hippokrene and the Wettin as well as the town band whose members for the occasion numbered 36, under the approved direction of the royal musical director Stahl. The assembly was catered for by the tenant of the royal castle restaurant, he was allowed to make use of the court kitchen in the castle, in addition to his own premises, and 30 cooks and 100 waiters were told off to assist him, as the number of people that had to be catered for was very great. Decorations on a very extensive scale were planned and executed under the supervision of the leading artists of the royal factory (the professors Hoesel and Achtenhagen, the artist Grust) and justified all the expectations that had been set upon them. Before the principal entrance of the royal porcelain factory in the valley of the Triebisch an arch was built, it consisted of decorated flag-staffs connected by green garlands, the large courtyard as well as the pavilion built on it was copiously ornamented with flags. The lawn before the Albrechtsburg which was to be used for the festivities is surrounded by a round green hedge in Rococo-style, within this circle the royal pavilion is placed, behind the pavilion the stage and the large pavilion to hold 700 people are erected. Rows of green trees cut in the shape of pyramids and bearing golden fruit encircle the castle grounds, cupids and figures from Kaendlers time enliven the gardens all through to the

Illustration 373. COURTYARD OF THE ALBRECHTSBURG.

bastion. In the border beds the monumental busts of King Friedrich August, King August the Strong and of Boettger find a place; about the castle yard are beautified, large and lovely china vases executed in the most famous patterns of the 18th century. The walls of the large subterranean halls of the castle are decorated in a highly artistic manner by the most able artists of the factory. They, as well as the garden, are copiously ornamented with green garlands and Saxon and German flags. The royal depôts in Dresden and Leipsic receive decorations to celebrate the festive occasion. On Boettger's monument in the "Neugasse" a large laurel wreath dedicated to his memory and ornamented with green and white ribbon is placed. The following were especially erected for the occasion, a large pavilion with a podium, a rotunda, a royal pavilion and a terrace for the orchestra, as well as arches in the cornhouse and numerous arrangements for electric lighting. The government gave permission for the entrance into the Albrechtsburg, the cellar, the garden and grounds of the castle to be closed to the general public, during the time the festivities lasted. The following invitations were to be sent according to the decision of the royal ministry of finance:—

To His Majesty the King and all the royal family with their suites.

To their excellencies the ministers of state and of the royal house.

To the directors of the ministry and some of the higher counsellors divisions I and III of the ministry of finance.

To the presidents, the secretaries and several members of the houses of parliament.

Illustration 374. FESTIVE ASSEMBLY IN THE LARGE COURTYARD OF THE WORKS.

To the members and the secretary of the academic council.

To the heads of the royal and town authorities and of the high schools in Meissen.

To prominent representatives of art, commerce (especially those connected in business with the royal china factory) and the press.

The following members of the royal ministry of finance, so to speak, the authorities for the royal china factory may be particularly mentioned as having participated in the celebration:—

His excellency the minister of state DD^{r.} von Rueger,

Director of the ministry Privy counsellor D^{r.} jur. Wahle,

Privy counsellor of mines Fischer and

Privy counsellor of finance Dr. Kretzschmar.

Owing to limited space the invitations could not be sent out as widely as might have been desired. In order not to lay a restraint upon the guests with regard to want of room it was necessary not to let the number of participants exceed 2000. As the army of employées with their wives and the pensioneers numbered 1525, it was quite impossible to extend invitations to various classes of society, as accorded with the mutual wish of the management and the public and with the numerous business connections of old standing of the factory.

In order to keep to the program with regard to time it was necessary to take certain precautions and to acquaint each participator with his place at table. The following rooms were put at the disposal of the festival committee:—

in the Albrechtsburg:—

the church hall and the electoral chambers I and II for the guests of
  honour, the administration and the upper officials and part of the
  employées room for . . . . 300 people
the armour passage for. 100   ,,
the cornhouse 150   ,,
the large pavilion 650   ,,
the subterranean halls 310   ,,

1510 people

For all these places coloured menus of a differents shade in every case were given to the participators at the banquet, each menu bearing the number of the table and of the seat. For each place of assembly a speaker of the toast "the King" as well as several committee-members to keep order were told off. The meal, consisting of soup, two courses (salmon and roast beef) and dessert and two sorts of wine, had to be punctually served so as to enable the guests to rise from the table at a given signal exactly at 3.30 p. m.

Thus having given notes on the disposition now follows the description of the feast itself.

On June 6th 1910 at 10.30 a. m. the gentlemen of the royal ministry of finance (director of the ministry Privy counsellor Dr. jur. Wahle, Privy counsellor of mines Fischer, Privy counsellor of finance Dr. Kretzschmar), the guests of honour headed by the high constable of the district Freiherr von Oer and the mayor Dr. Ay as well as the administrative board with the head officials assembled in the beautifully decorated pavilion in the courtyard of the royal porcelain factory, while the employées and the band gathered outside it. The singing club of the factory Hippokrene accompanied by the orchestra under the leadership of the musical director Stahl, fittingly introduced the festival by performing the Schiller ode "to the artists", by Mendelssohn-Bartholdy. The director of the royal factory Privy counsellor of commerce Gesell stepped on the daïs and addressed the assembly as follows:—

Gentlemen!

It is an extraordinary rare, important and highly joyons occasion which causes us to assemble here this day. It is the 200th anniversary of the great day when the royal china factory was founded in the Albrechtsburg in Meissen, by order of His Majesty August the Strong, Elector of Saxony and King of Poland. Its foundation opened a new source of income and prosperity to the Saxon land. By a rescript of May 6th 1710 Friedrich August, by the grace of God, King of Poland, Elector of Saxony, ordered by royal commission that the Albrechtsburg in Meissen should on June 6th 1710 be given over to the Boettger manufactories as the site of its works. Therefore June 6th 1710 is to be considered as the day on which the royal china factory was founded and to-day we celebrate the 200th anniversary of that great and important date in the life of the factory.

Two hundred years! Only a drop in the ocean of Eternity! But what an enormous space of time do they represent when we measure by them the work and the success of human life, the coming and passing away of generations, the foundation and decay of so many undertakings on a large scale, ay even of states which seem to have been founded on firm bases and yet have sunk into the river of Letha during two centuries.

The royal china factory has victoriously overcome the storms of these two centuries. It has maintained the first and leading place as the pioneer of all the china factories in Europe; standing on the rock of brilliant tradition, it has obtained by strife and endeavour the foremost place in following the new artistic tendencies and has kept the escutcheon of its honour and respect bright before the judgement of the world.

The royal porcelain factory, already in the first century of its existence began to run a victorious course through the whole world and even to day its artistic productions are in great demand. They are highly valued by modern civilization at the Rhine as at the Newa, at the Seine as at the Mississippi, at the Thames as at the La Plata. The otherwise forgotten existence of the kingdom of Saxony is often vividly put before the minds' eye of educated people in distant lands by a view of the crossed electoral swords, that ancient trademark of the royal china factory.

A universal feeling of joy fills us, who are heirs to the labour of a number of generations who have worked in the royal china factory before us and we offer thanks to a kind fate which gives us the possibility of celebrating to-day's festival. These sentiments are connected with feelings of the deepest thankfulness to the Almighty Disposer of all things Who led the apothecary and adept Johann Friedrich Boettger to Saxony, against his own will and Who has so faithfully protected the work begun by him during the two centuries of the existence of the royal china factory. We think with feelings of profound gratitude of the founder of the royal factory King August the Strong and the long row of his august successors on the Saxon throne, especially of our beloved King, His Majesty Friedrich August whose generous monarchial care has made itself felt in his solicitude for the wellfare of his lowly subjects the workmen in general and the employées of the royal china factory in particular, as well as in the interest shown by him in word and deed for the general wellfare of the royal china factory. Besides we gratefully think of all those men who, in the course of centuries have by successful works founded the fame of the factory all over the world and have conscientiously and dilligently furthered its artistic, technical and commercial development. They have at the end of 200 years delivered it to us in such a state as to allow us to step over the threshold of the third century of its existence with confident trust and joyful hopes.

At the turning of two centuries we bear the two faced head of the god Janus, one face is turned towards the past, the other looks into the future. It behoves us first to cast a look into the past and let the principal events in the historical development of the royal china factory to pass in review before us. Porcelain, according to the assertion of some chroniclers was produced in China already between 185 and 80 B. C. while others declare it to have been first made in the sixth century. The Portuguese when they settled in Macao in 1518 introduced it into western lands. All attempts to imitate the porcelain — which had been made in Europe for over a century by the elect-were unsuccessful. The apothecary's assistant Johann Friedrich Boettger — born in Schleiz — was the man fated to lift the veil from the east asiatic secret of producing china. His discovery created a great sensation in all Europe and the foundation of the royal china factory in Saxony excited the envy of all the high and mighty people of the time. In the same way as Prometheus stole fire from Olympus to bring it down to man on earth, Boettger took the secret of china production from China the self-styled empire of heaven, based it on his own discovery and laid it at the feet of August the Strong and his country. In the same way as Prometheus had been fettered to the Scytic rock by the angry Zeus, Boettger was kept a captive — although in a golden cage and under brilliant conditions of life — still a captive to the end of his existence. Boettger between 1708 and 1709 discovered the production of china, real east asiatic china which at this time was valued at its weight in gold in Europe. He did not discover it by chance; his discovery was based an systematic and logical experiments which so unfavourably influenced his health as to cause an untimely death. Whether he betrayed the trust of his royal master with regard to alchemistry — goldmaking — or not can not form the object of our discussion to-day. Boettger's biography published by Engelhardt in 1837 allows doubts as to the truth of the verdict with regard to Boettger's character to arise through the very animosity of its statements. We have every reason to pay a full meed of tribute and out heartiest thanks to the Manes of the discoverer of china and the first administrator of the royal china factory. As soon as Boettger discovered china the King decided to found the factory. Therefore the royal china factory was the pioneer of all the china factories in Europe. Before the royal porcelain factory was put into a working state tremendous difficulties had to be overcome; we can only imagine their greatness by recollecting the fact that the administrator Boettger in performing his great work had no predecessors whose experience he could have profited by. All that was necessary for the production of porcelain, as well as the china itself had to be invented and made by Boettger. We must admire to this day the greatness of his creative powers, as well as his bodily strength, notwithstanding the fact that the royal china factory did not, during his life time, bear the golden fruits which had been so longingly and impatiently expected by the discoverer, as well as by his royal protector. Out of the seed planted by Boettger's discovery in the soil of the old margravic town of Meissen in 1710, at first only a small twig sprang up which was carefully fostered by Boettger until his death in 1719. No one could at that time have imagined that this small weak plant would grow into a tree whose trunk endeavours to reach the skies and whose branches, reaching over land and sea, fill the world with precious fruit. For the first time the affairs of the royal china factory were brought to a flourishing state by the painter Hoeroldt who introduced the art of brilliantly decorating the already valuable china with the charm of colours and opened new vistas for artistic painting. The height of artistic and economical prosperity was attained by the royal china factory, when Kaendler was engaged. His ingenuity and assiduity as a sculptor stand unequalled in ceramic art up to the present and, even to this day, meet with the admiration of all connoisseurs of art. But the years of the second Silesian and the seven years' war fell like deadly hoar-frost upon the flowers called forth by Hoeroldt and Kaendler on the tree of the royal china factory. After the Peace of Hubertusburg concluded the seven years' war in 1763 the factory sank again from its proud height and could not regain what it had lost either through a return to the classic style, or through the Empire-style fostered by Count Marcolini till 1814 in place of the Rococo-style which had reached a point of brilliant success during the flourishing times of the factory. The second century of its existence was ushered in under sad circumstances and with dark prospects in view. After the battle of Jena Germany lay conquered by Napoleon. The royal china factory as well had to suffer the hardships of war. In 1813 its working had to be altogether discontinued for months and it would have entirely ceased to exist had not its royal owner and protector, King Friedrich August I, afforded it material support, a thing not easily done under the circumstances of the time. In 1814 Count Marcolini laid down the directorship of the royal china factory. In the same year the reformation of the royal factory was begun by inspector Kuehn — who for long years afterwards filled the post of director —. He regulated the technical and economical affairs of the works and did away with the "secret" of the arcanum which now only hampered the progress and growth of the factory. Besides the debt of gratitude owed him for his powers of organisation the royal porcelain factory has to thank him for the discovery of lustre-gold in 1827. The business use made of this discovery assured the financial prosperity of the factory for decades. Under his direction inspector Koettig discovered artificial ultramarine in 1828; works for producing it were attached to the factory and formed a source of income for half a century. An important event in the life of the factory happened in the second century of its existence in 1831 when, through the Saxon constitution, it ceased to belong to His Majesty the King and went over into the possession and management of the royal Saxon government treasury. Great improvement in the financial affairs of the factory was caused by the foundation of the German customs union in 1834. Through having harboured the factory for 150 years, the Albrechtsburg, that proud castle of Albrecht the Courageous was threatened by gradual destruction trough constant use. Through this and the small financial success of the undertaking, it was feared that the royal china factory would cease to exist. It is owing to the enormous influence of his late Majesty King John that the house of lords in a meeting of parliament of 1857—58 decided to move the royal china factory out of the Albrechtsburg into another place. This decision was due to the newly awakened historical sentiments for the necessity of protecting the castle of Albrechtsburg as well as the royal china factory. A new building was therefore erected in the valley of the Triebisch and moved into in 1863. The acme of financial success of the factory was reached after the great war and the political union of Germany in 1870, from 1890—1900 a gradual retrogression may be noticed. From 1900 to this day, year by year, an increasing improvement in all respects, artistic, technical and commercial has taken place in the affairs of the factory; this was partly due to the lessons learned at the Paris Worlds exhibition of 1900. The royal porcelain factory has not only created lasting ideal works, depopulating Olympus in order to reconcile men with the rough realities of life, it has not only written a full and rich page in the history of art, it has not only spread the fame of Saxon art and industry all the world over and has been the pioneer of Saxon industry in general; it has, besides all this, been of material use to its country and has brought a profit of about 14 millions to the chief royal treasury, from 1863 to 1909 i. e. since its removal to its present place of working. From this brief historical sketch it may be gathered that the destiny of the royal china factory has not flowed quietly and evenly down the river of the centuries. The diagram drawn by its artistic and mercantile movements, during the two hundred years of its existence, shows great curves, it is now raised on a high mountain wave now hurled into the depths of the river; a constant change reigns over the whole time of its existence. Only in one point does its history show constancy, in the wise and benevolent care which the august wearers of the Saxon royal crown and the government since the constitution, especially the royal ministry of finance as head of the management have dedicated, often under difficulties and in connection with sacrifices, to the weal and progress of the factory; but their faith as to the strength living in the royal china factory itself has stood firm at all times. Therefore gentlemen, and especially my beloved co-workers at the weal of the royal china factory, we are to day filled with deep and heartfelt gratitude towards our Saxon reigning dinasty and King Friedrich August and towards the government. In order to give voice to this gratitude we vow faithful love and devotion to His Majesty Friedrich August our beloved sovereign and promise to continue, as the employées of the royal china factory have always done before us, to form a firm bulwark against the dark powers of destruction which — out of the depth of the soul of a deluded nation — threaten the throne, the altar and the peace in the home and family and in the political community of our native country.

Gentlemen, and especially my beloved co-workers, who at present represent the active element of the royal china factory, we can step over the threshold of the third century of the existence of the royal china factory with joy, courage and trust, for we are the heirs of the long and blessed work of generations of our ancestors. It is now our duty, mindful of Goethe's words "What thou hast inherited from thy fathers, thou oughtest earn in order to possess it", to exert ourselves and to use our full power and ability to one end:—Our aim in view should be to further the development of the royal china factory, to have at heart its artistic, technical and financial interests and to safeguard its wellbeing in such a manner as to show ourselves in the new century worthy of the grace of His Majesty the King and the trust of the government. We should act so as to cause coming generations to think of us with the same joy and pride as we feel in recollecting the generations that have gone before us and that the future of the royal china factory in its cultural and socio-political sense should ever be progressive, blessed and happy! May God grant it!

Now the Privy counsellor Dr. jur. Wahle stepped on the dais in the name of the royal department of finance and made the following speech:—

Gentlemen!

Our native country in a narrow sense of the term has for centuries taken an important part among civilized countries and has kept it to this day although, or perhaps, because, it carries so dense a population in a narrow space and partly on unfertile soil. The intelligence of this dense population which at an early time led to an economy based on science, especially developed in two directions that of industry and of art. A combination of both is offered in the Saxon artistic industry which can well bear comparison with any other industry of the same description. This is true not in the last instance with regard to ceramics and, last but not least, in the production of hard china.

The ancient house of our rulers, the illustrious royal family of Wettin, has enormously furthered this industry through its love of the art combined with it and has, in acting according to its ideals, created a lasting and profitable source of income for its country. That lover of luxury and art Elector Friedrich August (as King of Poland August II) inspired by the wish of raising the means for obtaining the favourite and unattainable china by having gold produced in his own country he secured the services of the capable adept Johann Friedrich Boettger who, through the encouragement of the man of science Tschirnhaus and with the assistance of the Freiberg miners, discovered the china which had been vainly sought by Italians and Hollanders.

The full use made of this arcanum has not only developed into an inexhaustible source of income, but has formed an artistic institution which has played a leading part with regard to development of taste. Technique, art and commerce have combined in its working which became a model for the whole artistic and civilized world. The artistic productions arising from it which made the rococo the classic style for china have obtained worldly renown as "Vieux Saxe" and have not only become the hobby of art connoisseurs and the darling of collectors of china, but have remained an object of mutual love for the ruler and his people:—Under the evergreen rue with the sign of the electoral swords, fostered by the ruler and cared for by his subjects.

In the course of the past two centuries sister-institutions in other countries have begun to compete with our royal china factory and so successfully that it has often been difficult for it to keep its wonted leading place. It has only been possible to keep its worldly renown by faithfully keeping to old and approved traditions in delivering always what was best and most beautiful in all the three branches of its working (pastemaking, modelling and painting) and in trading on strictly honest business principles. It will, with God's help, keep up its prestige in future as it has in the past. When we consider the constant change of taste and the rapid progress in technique and commerce we shall see that this will require no small exertions on the part of the factory. But:—"No gains without pains!"

A particular encouragement will be offered to the employées of the factory (officials, artists and workmen) by the general trust put in them by the whole Saxon people. To work in an institution which forms the pride of a whole country will be felt as an honour by everybody concerned, from the first director to the last workman, and they will ever seek to prove themselves worthy of the trust put in them.

Notwithstanding many inimical attacks of criticism I must assert that the china paste has improved in purity, the palette of colours in richness, the sale has grown and in many meetings of parliament — not excluding the last — the chosen representatives of the people have paid us, the workers of the factory, a full and warm tribute of recognition for the services rendered. But above all else we value the strong and generous protection which our royal house has offered to its factory and its employées.

His Majesty our most illustrious and beloved King Friedrich August who will consecrate this festival by his own presence and that of his royal house wishes to offer you his best wishes in person. He has had the grace to sign the bill of parliament by which a sum of 30 000 marks besides a supplement of 10 000 marks yearly have been voted to your pensioneer's fund in commemoration of this joyous day. Besides, a number of royal marks of favour has been conferred on the old deserved officials and workmen. I shall now, having been deputed by his excellency the minister of finance Dr. von Rueger, read them out.

Here the names of officials and workmen who had been honoured with marks of royal favour in honour of the rare and festive occasion were read out by the Counsellor of mines Fischer, while the decorations and decrees were being handed out by the Privy counsellor Dr. Wahle and the Privy counsellor of finance Dr. Kretzschmar. This was followed by the end of the speech of the Privy counsellor Dr. Wahle:—

In the name of the royal government, I heartily congratulate all those who have received marks of royal favour, thereby bringing to a close what I have been deputed to perform.

Gentlemen, you will all see in the proofs of royal grace and favour accorded you, not only a grateful acknowledgement of the work of the whole factory, but a request to all the employées to further follow the path of hard work, earnestly and faithfully trodden in the past. For the present I believe to be acting according to your wishes, when I request you as a sign of your gratitude and in expression of loyalty to the royal house and its illustrious head to exclaim:—Long live His Majesty the King, the protector, patron and promoter of these works and everybody connected with them.

The cheers which follow are loudly and heartily joined in by the assembly.

By grace of His Majesty the King the following marks of royal favour were conferred:—
the cross of an officer of the order of King Albrecht:—
on Privy counsellor of commerce Gesell, director,
Counsellor superior of mines Dr. ph. Heintze, director of the working;
the crown to the cross of the order of the knight I of the order of Albrecht:—
on Counsellor of mines Dr. ph. Foerster, inspector of the working;
the cross of the knight I of the order of Albrecht:—
on Professor Hoesel, manager of the modelling department;
the title of professor:—
the manager of the painting branch Achtenhagen;

the cross of the knight II of the order of Albrecht:—
  on manager Teitge of the royal depôt in Dresden,
    manager Wuerfel, chief depôt in Meissen,
    cashier Guennel;
the cross of the order of merit:—
  on the oldest figure painter of the royal china factory Nemmert (60 years of service);
the cross of Albrecht:—
  on two officials and six artists;
the cross of honour:—
  on six officials and workmen;
the Friedrich August medal in silver:—
  on two officials and thirteen workmen;
the Friedrich August medal in bronze:—
  on twelve workmen;
the mark of honour for faithful work:—
  on four workmen;
altogether 16 decorations were conferred on officials 38 on artists and workmen.

After those who had received marks of royal favour had been congratulated and had offered thanks to the representative of the government, the mayor Dr· Ay made the following speech:—

The royal china factory has not chosen for its official anniversary the day on which china was invented, or the day on which it was first produced, but the day on which it was removed to our town. It therefore reckons its foundation from the day it became connected with Meissen and greatly values its connection with this town. The town of Meissen itself values this connection equally greatly. The removal of the royal factory into our town has proved a piece of luck for Meissen. The manufacture has for centuries pressed its stamp upon the character of the town and the artists working in it have raised its intellectual level, and art school gave children of the town artistic education, while the economical prosperity of the factory and everybody connected with it exercised a benign influence upon the well-being of the town. Closer and closer yet did the town and the factory grow together. Many an able citizen who has proved a worthy town counsellor has been given to the town by the factory and many general plans for the artistic development of the town have been raised and fostered by officials of the factory. It is to-day two hundred years since the factory and the town of Meissen have been connected, many happy days and many sad and difficult weeks and months have they spent together and they have always faithfully clung to and supported each other. It follows as a matter of course that the town council of Meissen could not leave unnoticed the day of rejoicing of the factory and through me offers the royal china factory its sincerest and heartiest congratulations on this auspicious occasion. We shall not limit ourselves to this, but shall follow the example of our fathers. As they a hundred years ago, at the celebration of the first centenary of the existence of the factory offered a present of wine, so the town council of to-day has put a barrel of this noble beverage at the disposal of the factory. May the factory go on prospering and flourishing within our walls and further its own well-being and that of the town, and may the good terms between the factory and the town exist to their mutual satisfaction from century to century!

The orchestra began to play and the assembly numbering about 800 people formed a procession to the town church for divine service. In the church the organ played a festive hymn to usher in the assembly. The Hippokrene performed the hymn out of psalm 23, music by Schnabel, "O Lord our God how great Thou art" after "Praised be the Lord" had been sung by it and the public. Then the Counsellor of the church, superintendent Grieshammer preached the jubilee sermon. The worthy minister spoke in his eloquent and heartfelt manner of the history of the royal china factory in connection with the inscriptions of the two large church bells which had been offered to the town church, partly by subscription of the factory employées in 1827. He spoke of the signification of true art and of the necessity of united work and mutual union of the workers, he said that the head could do nothing without the members — the members nothing without the head. Then he spoke of the blessedness of work which had here sprung up out of the union of art and science and which was to be offered to the glory of the Lord, of the merits of the factory with regard to its native country and its town which had been developed in seeking after the beautiful and in scientific research and in well ordered management. The edifying sermon closed with the singing of psalm 128, 1. 2 and psalm 90, 17. The prayer of thanksgiving by Kremser, its text of D^{r.} med. von Keller of Meissen closed the service. The assembly again stood to order and proceeded out of the church across the market square, through the Burg-gasse and the Hohlweg to the Albrechtsburg. On arrival at the site of the festival, the employées of the factory joined their wives and the pensioneers and widows of former employées, in order to take their seats at the tables laid in the Albrechtsburg, the pavilions and "Bourgkeller". The guests of honour, the administrative board, the higher officials and the committee of the employées as well as the members of the artistic branch, chosen by the employées themselves, found their places in the church hall and in the adjoining electoral chambers. The tables in the church hall were laid with the choicest artistic china of the classic Meissen period, the tables in all the festive rooms bore the especially-made, porcelain jubilee wine jugs copiously decorated with flowers. The table utensils had been borrowed from the factory. At all the tables, where in seven different places about 1500 persons were served at the same time, speakers were told off who were to pronounce the first toast of His Majesty the King, the illustrious protector of the factory. At the principal table the following speeches were made. In honour of:—

HIS MAJESTY THE KING
(by Counsellor superior of mines D^{r.} ph. Heintze):—

Ladies and gentlemen!

A festival day like the present, — the celebration of the 200th anniversary of June 6th 1710, the day of the foundation of the royal china factory, demands an involuntary retrospect into its history.

Here we see how the King — Elector Friedrich August I — had the new factories founded on Boettger's chemico-technical discoveries in the royal castle of Albrechtsburg at his own expense, on this day. The most noble and important of these factories was fated to produce the white transparent porcelain. It became the first china factory in Europe!

The King could look upon this as his own personal merit, as Boettger's successful experiments had been made partly at his initiative. Therefore the King, when dividing the ordinary offices, retained the chief management of the works to himself. This was in force under his successors all through the 18th century and notwithstanding many difficulties in the way of the development of the factory, Meissen china has obtained world wide renown and has become a model to be copied by all countries.

In the 19th century the factory ceased to be a crown institution and was given into the hands of the state. Although the King ceded the chief management to the privy chamber of finance, still the factory retained the protection and grace of the illustrious ruler of Saxony.

His Majesty King Friedrich August, our King and Ruler, like his ancestors has been particularly gracious to the factory. To-day His Majesty has emptied the horn of plenty of his generosity over the employées of the factory.

In the same way as the rulers of Saxony have furthered the welfare of the factory by word and deed, so we vow fidelity to our King. We shall be ever mindful of the honour and protection shown us and keep up the prestige of the royal china factory.

Raise your glasses with me and let us all join in the heartfelt exclamation:—

Long life to His Majesty the King!

THE ROYAL MINISTRY OF FINANCE
(by Professor Hoesel):—

Notwithstanding all the fortunate circumstances, connected with the foundation of the royal china factory, which led it already during the first decades of its existence to unexpected heights, it has not always been so greatly favoured by fortune. Its past, now stretching over 200 years, can, in this respect, be considered as very changeable. Times of prosperity have alternated with times when it was on the verge of ruin. More than once its existence was seriously endangered. That this institution which is so important for our native land of Saxony, still grew stronger in its growth, that it has victoriously overcome all difficulties is owing, besides the power of its own value, to the care for its wellfare ever exercised by the Prince and the government. A certain steadiness in its development since the kingdom of Saxony possesses a constitutional government is undeniable. Although during these eighty years, favourable circumstances, comparatively speaking have accompanied us, still much merit in the well-being of the factory may be ascribed to the royal department of finance our ruler and shelter. Furthered by an understanding of our aims and problems, buoyed up by the consideration shown for our wishes and our claims, we may look back with satisfaction at a series of successful years. We do so with feelings of especial gratitude towards our superior management. It gives us pleasure and does us honour to see its representative among us on to-day's joyous occasion.

Long live the Royal Department of finance!

THE ROYAL CHINA FACTORY
(by the Privy counsellor Dr. jur. Wahle):—

Ladies and gentlemen!

You will permit me to offer thanks of the royal government and especially of the ministry of finance and to express them by cheering the royal china factory. Although I, already this morning, had the honour to mention many a fact conducing to the renown of the institution whose 200th anniversary we are celebrating to-day, you need fear no repetition. This topic is inexhaustible, as I have found out during the many years I have been connected with the factory. I can therefore here again discuss of a few points.

The historical renown of the royal china factory of Meissen is undisputed and incontestible. The attacks which it experiences from artists, art critics and merchants can be sumned up in one question:— Has the factory retained its foremost place, from an artistic and mercantile point of view, it is still the first and first class art and model institution of ceramics? This question is a difficult one to answer. The financial success would cause it to be answered in the affirmative, but this can not serve as proof positive of the factory having kept its prestige. At any rate, we can only say that the endeavour to keep the factory in its eminent position among institutions of the kind is to be clearly perceived in everybody connected with the works and, to quote Propercius "in magnis et voluisse sat est". But each person who understands these matters will clearly see that it is a great thing to retain a foremost position in the sharp competition which is now rife.

The words of the quotation mentioned by the Privy counsellor Gesell this morning are easily said:—"What thou hast inherited from thy fathers, thou oughtest earn in order to possess it", but its execution, especially here, is met with difficulties. Taste changes now more rapidly than ever. The happy time of the Rococo-style are long since past and gone, and a Kaendler can at best fall from the skies but once in a century. The number of competitors continually increases and the mercantile spirit haunts all the corners like a wandering ghost. To all this other difficulties must be added. The historical renown is — paradoxical as it may sound — in some respects, really disadvantageous to the factory. Just think, for instance, of dishonest competition, of imitations of goods and of trade-marks and other unpleasantnesses. At times best friends can act so as to disturb rather than to help us. It is not always easy to be everybody's favourite. However willingly and thankfully all the good advices and suggestions may be accepted and followed, often the administrative board is tempted to exclaim:—"May God preserve us from our friends!"

Briefly speaking there can be no question of resting on laurels, it is now, more than ever, necessary without resting to fight, to strive, to work and never to get weary. May the factory ever be led and worked — as it is at present, in a like spirit —. For this it is, above all things, required that everybody connected with the factory:—the administrative board, the officials, the artists and the workmen should work hand in hand, having one common aim in view — the wellfare of the factory. The whole country takes a sympathetic interest in your joyous festival and looks with rightful pride upon its royal factory. The royal government felicitates you to this, trusting that the china factory in Meissen will always stand firm as the first ceramic artistic and model institution, that it will keep to the great old traditions of its past and remember its high problem in the future. Now ladies and gentlemen, in this meaning I request you to exclaim with me:—

Long life and many years of future success to the Royal China Factory in Meissen!

THE GUESTS OF HONOUR

(by Counsellor of mines Dr. ph. Foerster):—

Ladies and gentlemen!

A great silence and quietness rests over the workrooms of our royal china factory to-day. The din of machinery is stilled, the modelling wood, the brush and the palette are put aside, the account books are closed, for the joyous band of workers has moved in a festive procession out of its decorated portal, up to the old and time honoured castle of Albrechtsburg. For to-day in the beautiful halls, filled with Boettger's spirit, a rare festival is to be joyously celebrated, it is the 200th birthday of the Meissen china. The good fairies who stood at its cradle and have endowed it with grace, daintiness, everlasting youth, have invested it with the power of making itself generally popular and beloved. They have protected its tender existence which untoward circumstances and the storms of life threatened to put to an untimely end. Through their care, the child born in Boettger's fertile mind, was able to grow big and strong and beautifully developed. That our Meissen china can still boast of possessing widely-spread sympathy, is proved by the fact that so many noble guests have done it and us the honour and pleasure of giving us the opportunity of welcoming them to our festival and who so joyously and with such good-will gratify our festival disposition by their appearance. The first place among the guests must he afforded to the royal ministry of finance, under whose protection we dare to strive to reach great heights as far as art and science are concerned. We further perceive the heads of royal, town and other authorities, coryphees of art and science, representatives of an influential and generally respected press, many friends and protectors of our factory. To one and all of these our honoured guests we offer a hearty welcome and express deep and sincere thanks to them for the good-will and interest they have so fully shown by appearing among us to-day. May you retain this interest and good-will for our factory for long years to come! We ask you to take with you a friendly remembrance of this place and the day when you have shared our joy with us and have redoubled it value in by your presence. For us this is a never to be forgotten day and its memory will live in us from year to year from generation to generation, until our successors will D. V. live to see the happy day when the royal factory will celebrate its 250th anniversary.

Ladies and gentlemen! I request you to express our thanks for the presence of these our most honoured guests at our feast, by raising your glasses with me and drinking their health.

Cheering of guests.

THE EMPLOYÉES OF THE FACTORY

(by Privy counsellor of mines Fischer):—

Ladies and gentlemen!

To-day's festival is a day of rest from the daily work and the constant development of the royal china factory. It is a day of settling accounts of the present with regard to the past, a day on which we seek to look into the future. For centuries it had been sought to produce chinese hard porcelain in Europe, out of materials to be locally found, until at last the clever discoverer Boettger succeeded in finding in systematical operation what had been so long and vainly sought for. At first Boettger discovered red china, the so-called Boettger china, then a white frit which received the mystical and phantastic name of Semidiaphanum tremuli Narcissuli ideam lacteam, i. e. partly transparent and of the milky whiteness of the narcissus. The final result of the Boettger experiments was real hard porcelain. When Boettger, the alchemist made his experiments, according to the opinion of the chemists of the time all bodies could be divided into three elements, viz. salt as a fire-proof residue, mercury as the body which evaporated by heat and sulphur as burning principle. Although these ideas are of no value at present, still three ingredients are necessary for the production of china, as it is sold by the Meissen factory; these bodies are the porcelain paste, the glazing and the fire-proof colours. In the factory itself the three principal elements into which, according to former ideas, all bodies were divisible, find a place. The burning principle is represented by the moulders, turners and bakers, i. e. all the technical employées, or as it was formerly called, "the white brigade". The mercury that lively, brilliant body which is evaporated by heat is represented by the artists, or as it was formerly called the "painter brigade". The salt, that fire-proof residue, is the administrative board which, while keeping up the artistic prestige of the factory, has to see to its financial success and to deliver a fire-proof sediment to the government treasury. If the factory be to exist in the future to the honour and glory of our native country, the three above-mentioned bodies should combine so as to act and feel as one; for unity is strength.

May the unanimous and cheerful co-operation of all the employées of the royal china factory go on in the future as it has done in the past.

Then the factory will be able to look the future victoriously in the face, notwithstanding the difficulty connected with harbouring art and business under one roof.

In gratitude for the good work done in the past and as a pledge of the same in the future, let us cheer the employées of the royal china factory. Three cheers for the employées!

THE TOWN OF MEISSEN

(by the Privy counsellor of commerce Gesell):—

Like Rome, the eternal city, Meissen is built on vinewreathed hills from which more than a thousand years look down upon the town, at whose foot a proud stream flows. Its youth belongs to the grey time of Germany, filled with danger and strife in hard work. A character of steel has remained peculiar to its citizens up to the present; in them fidelity and uprightness unite with a daring which grasps at all that is progressive. During the thousand years of its existence the town has many a time healed the wounds it had sustained through war and through the unfettered element, out of all its misfortunes it has risen unharmed and strengthened and now harbours the progressive gracious and cheerful community which it is an honour to belong to. For 200 years the royal china factory and its employées have shared joy and sorrow with the town of Meissen; the town council and the royal china factory have honestly supported each other in their common interests. In many instances the flowers and the fruits of these interests have remained to be used and enjoyed by both I request you, ladies and gentlemen, to unite with me in the wish:—

May God bless Meissen in its further growth and development!

Three cheers for Meissen, its mayor, the town council and the citizens!

THE ADMINISTRATIVE COUNCIL AND THE FACTORY

(by the mayor Dr. Ay):—

In the name of this town and its council, I thank the Privy counsellor Herr Gesell for his kind words about the town of Meissen and its town council and you, ladies and gentlemen, for the joyous echo which his sentiments have found in your breasts.

Meissen was at one time thought worthy of giving its name to our native country, in a limited sense of the term. But after Frederick the Bellicose had obtained the Electorship of Saxony in 1422 and after in 1547 the electory of Saxony had again been united to the margravy of Meissen, gradually the name of Saxony began to be used for all the lands of the Wettins and the margravy of Meissen began to be more and more forgotten. Only at the beginning of the 18th century was the name Meissen again carried out into the world and has since that time been better known to all the civilized peoples of Europe than any other town of its size. For this renown Meissen has to thank the artistic institution whose jubilee we are to-day celebrating. It is not less grateful to the royal administrative board which has always kept up the best understanding with the town council. May the royal china factory go on growing and developing in the future as it has done in the past, especially under the administrative board acting at present and may the mutual understanding and good will existing between the factory and the town, between the administration and the town council never cease to be. With this wish I raise and empty my glass. Long life to the royal china factory and its administration!

THE ADMINISTRATIVE BOARD

(by the chairman of the workmen's committee embosser Taggeselle):—

Here, at the cradle of the royal Saxon china factory, ay at the cradle of european porcelain, on the 200th anniversary of the foundation of the works, many an excellent retrospect has been sketched. But I shall cast no look backward at the work of our old masters and of our ancestors in the art of manufacturing and decorating china. I think of the years lately past and of the present, of the extensive preparations made for us on to-day's festive occasion and of the benevolent care which has been shown for the employées of the factory during the last year. All this is connected with the noble sentiments of the administrative board has shown towards the employées of the factory taking at the same time due care of its live interests. It is my pleasant duty to express our recognition of this fact and to give voice to the feelings of gratitude of the employées. I can further joyfully state that the tone of intercourse between the administration and the employées is of the most harmonious nature imaginable. This is due to the goodwill which the administration exercises towards its employées in business and in personal matters. I should like to mention that these good relations rest upon old traditions and have been always kept up. They have done much towards the success of the factory as through them the administration and the employées were always united in their work. I am convinced that these good terms will continue to exist owing to the noble sentiments of the administration and that the royal china manufactory will develop freely and will live to see many new and successful works in centuries to come. Now I shall ask you to join me in cheering the administration of the royal china factory. Three cheers for the administrative board, the Privy counsellor Gesell, the Superior counsellor of mines Dr. Heintze and Professor Hoesel!

THE EMPLOYÉES OF THE FACTORY

(by Privy counsellor of commerce Gesell):—

In the name of the administrative board I give thanks to all the employées of the royal china factory for the sentiments so eloquently expressed by their representative. The administrative board has to fulfil a double duty, towards the royal exchequer and towards the employées of the factory. In exercising its strength and powers of observation, its good will and its knowledge in this direction, it has done nothing but its duty. The imperfection peculiar to all human actions adheres to the fullfilment of this duty as well. If our beloved co-workers of the royal china factory express their approval of our doings, we shall express our heartily thanks for it by seeing in these well meant words an incitement to fulfilling our duty towards them as is compatible with the interests of the royal exchequer. We have at all times found the greatest support in the employées of the royal china factory. Care of the classic art in the factory, conscientiousness, faithfulness in service towards the state, their superiors and their fellow-workmen, these are the foundation stones on which the success of the royal china factory has been built. In all these respects the employées of the royal china factory have always been a model for all artistic and industrial undertakings; it stands alone in the world with regard to unity among its workmen based on mutual understanding, assistance and good-fellowship. Goethe's words "Man should be noble, helpful and good" can nowhere be more justly applied than here with regard to the employées of the royal china factory as a whole. It is a matter of pride for the administrative board to be the head of this élite of workmen. In the name of the administrative board and as director of the royal china factory, I sincerely pray that God may protect and keep the employées of the factory and that their corporation may grow and develop to the pride and honour of our Saxon land! Cheers for the employées!

THE LADIES

(by manager Wuerfel):—

Like a great-grandmother who celebrates her birthday among quite innumerable relations and friends, our dear old institution has called us together to this festival in the old beautiful halls of our royal castle — the halls where it has spent its youth. We have left the place of our daily labours below in the valley and have come up to these airy heights to this joyous feast in faithful remembrance of great old times.

Our factory could not be imagined without women — at present they profitably work in nearly all the branches of our institution, while our wives are among the most enthusiastic and faithful admirers of Meissen china — and we could not celebrate this festive day without having them with us in good, old German style.

They have, certainly, not taken immediate part in the work of the factory, but who would deny the part they have indirectly taken in its weal and woe, in its progress and development by performing their housewifely duties and by offering their husbands rest and home comforts after the exertions and vexations of a long day's work?

Therefore I utter a toast on our wives:—in our youth they are the object of our enthusiastic adoration, as our wives they, to quote the poet's words, wreathe heavenly roses into our terrestial life and in our old age, when we have grow tired and lonely, they beautify the evening of our life by true love and faithful care. In their honour I have made my speech.

I beg you, gentlemen, to join with me in three cheers for our ladies!

Table music was excellently executed by the town band which had divided itself into the various rooms.

The participators of the feast rose from the table at 3.30, after having partaken of an excellent neal which brought to much praise to the caterer Koempel. The guests dispersed in groups to drink coffee or to admire the beautiful decorations from various points of view.

The raising of the royal standart announced the arrival of His Majesty the King who came by extra train at about 4.30. Accompanied by joyous cheers of the multitude the royal guests arrived in a number of royal carriages and ten landaus. His Majesty the King, their royal highnesses Prince and Princess Johann Georg and the Princess Mathilde were accompanied by his Excellency von Haugk, chief of

Illustration 375.
HIS MAJESTY THE KING BETAKES HIMSELF TO THE FESTIVE PERFORMANCE.

equerry, adjutant, major Baron von Koenneritz, Court marshal von Mangoldt-Reibold and the maids of honour Excellency Baroness von Finck and Baroness von Gaertner, their excellencies the ministers of state, as well as a large number of guests of honour from Dresden. At the place of the celebration His Majesty the King was, under loud cheers, respectfully conducted by the Privy counsellor of commerce Gesell before the monument of Albrecht the Daring and was escorted over the large turning staircase through the church-hall into the large banqueting room. In this room the employées of the royal china factory distinguished by royal favours of the day and the guests of honour were already assembled. The Privy counsellor of commerce Gesell addressed His Majesty as follows:—

Will your most gracious Majesty deign to accept my respectful words of welcome in the name of the employées of the royal china factory, on the place where Your Majesty's illustrious ancestor King August the Strong founded the royal china factory two hundred years ago. All the employées and the festive assembly are filled with feelings of joy and awe at Your Majesty's presence leading to the highest consecration of these festivals. The employées of the factory wish through me to express sentiments of humble gratitude for the care shown and the benefits showered upon them by Your Majesty and all Your Majesty's royal ancestors for centuries. The royal china factory owes not only its foundation, but its existence up to the present to the illustrious rulers on the Saxon throne, and being conscious of this fact, is faithful to its Kings with all its heart.

Those honoured by marks of Your Majesty's royal favour have taken the liberty of presenting themselves here. Will Your Majesty deign to accept amongst them my especial, respectful thanks for the mark of royal favour shown me?

The Superior counsellor of mines Dr. Heintze thanked His Majesty in the name of all those who had received marks of royal favour and proposed three cheers for His Majesty, in which all those present heartily joined.

His Majesty then deigned to wish the royal factory luck to its jubilee and to have those who had received marks of royal favour introduced to him and honoured some of them and of the guests of honour by addressing them. His Majesty deigned to express the hope that the royal factory would in future as well attain a great measure of success at home and abroad. His Majesty with the royal highnesses and suite as well as their excellencies the ministers of state and a number of especially invited guests of honour among the last-mentioned the wives of the chief officials of the royal china factory, betook himself into the small banqueting hall where tea was served out of the royal household. After tea, His Majesty was escorted by the Privy counsellor Gesell across the courtyard and into the royal pavilion, before which the stage for

Illustration 376. ROCOCO.

the artistic performance was placed. In going through the church hall His Majesty was welcomed by the song "Take thy most beautiful melodies", by Abt executed by the Hippokrene. It sounded particularly effective owing to the excellent accoustics of the hall. On the way across the courtyard, His Majesty honoured some of the workmen who had formed an espalier at its sides by addressing a few affable words to them. As soon as His Majesty and their royal highnesses had taken their seats in the royal pavilion, the performance began. As has already been above mentioned, the most notable plastic works of the royal china factory of old times and of the present were to be represented in original costumes and actions by artists of the royal china factory.

The performance consisted of the following pictures:—
1. Rococo:—A hunting company returning to the castle, in their midst are King August the Strong and his spouse (motives etc. after groups 550, 518, 398, 2261, 2265, 2294, 2319, 2280, 2283).
2. Dance of the shepherds:—Four gardner's and shepherd's couples executed a circular dance (motives etc. according to groups 35—38, 2127).
3. Italian comedy:—Italian carnaval scenes (motives etc. after figures 523, 538, 577, S 121, S 125, D 39, 42, 941, 897, 118, 1596, 1597).
4. Vine gatherers life:—Circular dance of gardner's children (according to figures G 1—12).
5. Dances of the horae (according to group L 15).
6. Modern creations (player of bowls [woman] Q 180, children by Hentschel:—W 117—124, Koenig:—X 101—102, Hoesel:—V 124).
7. Group of all the actors of the performance.

Carl Stein an embosser employed at the royal china factory had composed a poetical prologue and a text connecting the actions on the stage. They were spoken by Professor Dr. Pollack of the royal Landesschule in accomplished manner.

Owing to the limited time of the royal visit only the numbers 1, 2, 3, 4 and 7 could be acted before His Majesty. The performance which was accompanied by the town orchestra met with the full approval of His Majesty, their royal highnesses and the guests of honour as well as of everyone assembled. Really such a performance could only have been perfectly and stylefully executed by the artists of the royal china factory whose education and artistic work is saturated with the spirit of the time of the Rococo-style.

After the festive performance, His Majesty with the members of the royal house and their suite was escorted through the castle garden into the large artistically decorated subterranean halls, where twelve young ladies employed at the factory dressed in Rococo-style served champagne. During this time the Hippokrene sang German songs on the castle bastion. In returning to the courtyard, His Majesty deigned to express his satisfaction at the beautiful festival and successful performance and took his leave after affably shaking hands with its leaders.

His Majesty the King and the members of the royal house returned with a number of the guests of honour to Dresden by extra train at 5.30.

In the course of the festival to which after 5.30 about 400 invitations had been extended the whole program of the artistic performance was again gone through. It met with gigantic success and had to be repeatedly again performed, as an undertaking of the employées of the royal china factory. The singing clubs Hippokrene and Wettin, as well as the town band offered musical entertainment and the young folks were not in vain lured by Terpsichore to a dance. Groups of participators of the feast spent their time in the beautifully lighted halls of the castle of Albrechtsburg, in the castle garden with its poetical outlook from cosy places under the roof of leaves of ancient trees, in the subterranean halls of the castle and in the castle restaurant. Nothing broke the harmony of the festival and its participators. What the caterer could offer in the shape of good cheer did much to conduce towards the joyousness of the feast. Exactly at 11 p. m. the celebrations were officially closed. Excellent weather had accompanied the festivities all the time they had lasted. Although the sun which had made such brilliant promises in the morning, had been gradually hidden by clouds, the threatening storm did not break out.

The festive day is over, the sound of speech and song is stilled and silence again reigns supreme in the halls of the royal castle, the high billows on the sea of festive enthusiasm have again subsided.

Illustration 377. ITALIAN COMEDY.

Only the memory of the festival lives in the hearts of all those connected with the factory, because this celebration of historical signification has been an important event in their professional life. A feeling of gratitude pervades them at the very thought of it.

Out of the depths of our heart, we, first of all, thank the Almighty Who has so wonderfully led the fortunes of the factory over the hills and depths of the two centuries of its existence, through the darkness of many dangers to the light of its jubilee on the threshold of its third century under the sign of the luckiest promises, Who has taken it under His protection and Who has given it, as a special sign of His grace and favour, so beautiful a day for the celebration of its anniversary.

We offer respectful thanks to His Majesty the King and all the royal house for the gracious favours extended to the employées and for the royal beneficence to which the royal factory owes its foundation, its existence and support in many a dark hour when it was on the verge of ruin.

We thank the government and both houses of parliament under whose wise and kind management and advice the royal china factory has arrived at its present flourishing state and has been put in a position to celebrate its 200th anniversary so brilliantly.

Thanks to all those who by being present in great numbers have granted to our festival so prominent a feature and to all those who by their assistance and support in the preparation of the feast have furthered its joyous success!   GESELL.

NOTES.

1. *For details see P. 117.*

2. *A biography of Boettger written by Engelhardt in 1837 allows one to draw false conclusions and throws a false light upon his character. In opposition to Engelhardt I wrote already 1900 in "the Meissen china": — As far as morality is concerned he does not stand very high in my opinion either. He was conceited, pleasure loving and frivolous to a high degree, still these faults might have been the direct result of the peculiar circumstances under which he spent his life. I should particularly wish to mention that I do not think so little of this knowledge of chemistry as Engelhardt does. Although he had an excellent professional adviser in the person of Tschirnhaus, still the discovery of red stoneware and china which is due to Boettger can not have been purely a matter of chance. On the contrary, much real and earnest work was required before the right pastes and mixtures could be discovered. Having discovered these Boettger managed to give his productions that artistic appearance which allows them to enjoy praise and recognition to this day. In the meantime documents have been found in the Meissen factory by the Counsellor superior of mines Heintze and in the Dresden china collection by Prof. Zimmermann, documents which not only fully confirmed my assertions but even extended them. Full tribute was here paid to Boettger by a recognition of the great difficulties he had to overcome owing to the complete ignorance of ceramics at that time. This labour of his is and may be considered a work of genius. The combination and mixing of the pastes and glazings, the moulding of the vessels, the construction of kilns suitable to the purpose and the baking itself which was connected with so many difficulties — all this required great and varied knowledge which Boettger had to become possessed of in on experimental manner. Credit is due to the Counsellor superior of mines Heintze for having repeatedly drawn attention to these facts in various reports and for having thereby caused a change in the estimation of Boettger in many minds.*

3. *In the documents of the Dresden principal state archives, Loc. 1340, Vol. I, "Remarks regarding Boettger" 1701, Page 30 we find a note that Lascaris presented Boettger with a highly valued manuscript and a powder, remarking that "with its assistance he would certainly be able to make 8 ozs. of lead into gold".*

4. *Loc. 1339, Vol. I, Page 58 f. Copied word for word from "New Archive for Saxon History" by von Seidlitz, IX, P. 118f.*

5. *Loc. 1339, Vol. I, p. 80 f.*

6. *Archive for the history of physics and technique, 1810. Page 183 ff.*

7. *Peter Geitner, Joh. Georg Krumbholz and Gottfr. Lohse are probably here concerned. Besides the three workers in the smelting houses (mentioned Page 2) who had followed Boettger from Meissen to Koenigstein and Dresden, he had Balth. Sorbig-Tschirnhaus, Sam. Kempfe and Chr. Wieden in the laboratory as well.*

8. *In this "institution for baking stoneware", as it was then called, erected in Dresden Neustadt in 1708 flag stones and vessels in Delft style were to be produced. It was let to Eggebrecht in 1712 and sold in 1718.*

9. *Dr. Bartholomaii and Dr. W. H. Nehmitz were the arcanists proper, i. e. the men who besides Boettger knew the combination of the pastes and glazings. The first mentioned supervised the paste makers while the latter saw to the baking and glazing.*

10. *Besides Geitner, Krumbholz and Lohse mentioned above, there were Georg and Joh. Kittel, Wildenstein, Fritsch and Guemlich.*

11. *The varnisher Martin Schnell, the painter Joh. Schaeffler, the goldsmith Joh. Carl Baehr and the workers in filigree Stefky were engaged in executing these improvements.*

12. *The forms and decorations of this stoneware are treated in detail by E. Zimmermann, "the discovery and the early days of the existence of Meissen china", P. 122 ff., founded, on the contents of the Dresden china royal collection.*

13. *Archive for the history of physics and technique 1910. P. 187 ff.*

14. *Heintze declares P. 187 a. a. O. that silicious earth was added so that the china should bake pure white, The china had not always been a good colour owing to the admixture of sesquioxyd of iron and titan in Colditz clay.*

15. *The conductor Blumenthal was employed as artistic manager of the painting branch, while Goldschmied Funke, Jonathan Pappelbaum, Joh. Dav. Stechmann and Anselm Bader were engaged in painting as well. The two last-mentioned are in 1717 explicitly spoken of as "painters of the good china ware".*

16. *Judging by what was known to me about china callot figures I believed them to have originated exclusively in Vienna (Meissen china P. 44). Judging by what has since come to light about them (see Bruening, European china P. XXII) it must be assumed that they were made in Meissen during the early times of its existence as well. It is even possible that they were produced in Boettger's time. It is true that up to the present no trace of them has been found either in the registers or in the forms. Probably they were freely modelled, or else the forms were first trials which have not been preserved.*

17. *See note 12.*

18. *These were the privy counsellors von Seebach and von Alemann as well as the counsellor of the chamber von Lesgewang. Alemann was soon followed by the vice director of mines von Ponikau.*

19. *These were the counsellors of the chamber and of mines Wichmannshausen and von Pflugk and the Meissen Kreisamtmann Fleutner.*

20. *At first this was done at discretion. In 1740 on order was issued by which the three sorts had to be strictly differentiated. The medium goods were to be sold at a price fixed at 5%*

lower than the perfect goods, the garbage was not to come on the market at all. The last-mentioned goods were to be given for their own use to the employées of the factory, later to their relations and other people who were sure not to sell them.

21. *Loc. 1339, Vol. II, closed with seals 1719—20 leaves 189, 295 and 321.*

22. *Samuel Kempfe is supposed to have caused the foundation of the factory in Plauen on the H., where red stone ware was imitated from 1713. Samuel Kempfe was engaged in Tschirnhaus' laboratory and afterwards worked for a short time with Boettger.*

23. *Loc. 1341, Vol. IV, P. 109 ff. and Vol. V, P. 462ᵇ; von Seidlitz, "New Archive for Saxon History", X, P. 65 f. Hunger's further history is written about by Pazaureck in his Information from the Northbohemian museum of industry 1903, P. 1 ff.*

24. *Loc. 1341, Vol. IV, P. 1.*

25. *It seems that the use of the mother of pearl colour was well known. It was a peculiar variegating reddish brown colour with a metallic lustre which appears in many cases in quite early pieces and is generally called "reflet metallique". It was probably a solution of gold with ammonia, the so called fulminating gold the use of which was soon given up owing to danger of explosion.*

26. *Loc. 1341, Vol. V, P. 267.*

27. *Loc. 1339, Vol. II, P. 312 and 321.*

28. *Loc. 1341, Vol. V; 1731, P. 284 f.*

29. *According to a communication of the parsonage Archive in Jena. The spelling of the name Herold made use of in the church register may often be come across in the documents and was at first used by me as well. I now agree with the gentlemen of the administration in writing Hoerold, as this is the spelling he himself made use of in signing the Meissen reports.*

30. *Loc. 1341, Vol. IV, P. 165 and 230 f.*

31. *Loc. 1341, Vol. VI, P. 160.*

32. *Loc. 1341, Vol. VI, P. 114 f.*

33. *Loc. 1341, Various matter concerning the china factory (without a date).*

34. *Loc. 1342, Vol. VIII, P. 1.*

35. *Loc. 1342, Vol. VII, P. 103.*

36. *Loc. 1341, Vol. VI, P. 312.*

37. *Loc. 1342, Vol. VIII, P. 4 and 32.*

38. *Loc. 1341, Vol. V, P. 464ᵇ.*

39. *Loc. 1341, Vol. VI, P. 198.*

40. *Loc. 1341, Vol. V, P. 463ᵇ.*

41. *Ibid. P. 331.*

42. *Ibid. P. 328 and 369.*

43. *Loc. 1341, Vol. VI, P. 85 f.*

44. *Loc. 1342, Vol. VIII, P. 98ᵇ.*

45. *Ibid. P. 101 and 104.*

46. *Ibid. P. 231.*

47. *Loc. 1341, Vol. IV, P. 1 and Vol. V, P. 285; Loc. 1342, Vol. VIII, P. 129 and the documents in the possession of the Meissen factory which I shall abbreviate M. A.*

48. *The figures and letters placed after the numbers of the table or figure refer to the descriptions of the forms made use of to this day. For instance the vase illustrated on table 2 has the description of form H. 128.*

49. *The figure here shown probably originated at on earlier date but was made over again by Kaendler.*

50. *Loc. 1341, Vol. V, P. 360 and M. A.*

51. *Vol. IV, P. 131 and M. A.*

52. *Ibid., ibid. For further information about Luecke especially about his adventurous life see Scherer "Studies of ivory plastique of the Barock time", P. 74 f.*

53. *Ibid., ibid. Up to the present this has not yet been found. The model books existing to this day into which the old models were partly entered originated only in the years between 1760 and 1770; being only registers they contain no drawings.*

54. *Loc. 1342, Vol. VII, P. 126 f. and 186 and M. A.*

55. *Loc. 1341, Vol. V, P. 457.*

56. *Loc. 1342, Vol. VII, P. 95ᵇ and 134.*

57. *Loc. 1341, Vol. VI, P. 203.*

58. *Cabinet pieces of Meissen china P. 67 ff.*

59. *Meissen china P. 44.*

60. *Kirchner has in February 1733 created "a wagtail on a tree". (M. A.)*

61. *This clockcase crowned with a different figure is illustrated in "Meissen china" Fig. 160.*

62. *I believe to be able to assume that these three works are identical with those found in the Dresden collection of china, illustrated in Sponsel P. 116—117, it is possible that the Virgin (Fig. 5, 136) and the genius near St. Anthony are the work of Kaendler.*

63. *The fact that these vases as well as the large animals were in the oldest time painted not with muffle but with drop colour is probably due to the imperfect technique of baking. At that time such pieces came out of the final baking in a very cracked state and it would have risked spoiling them altogether to submit them to a second baking process.*

64. *"The Museum" by W. Spemann, I, P. 47. Illustrated in Meissen china, Fig. 1.*

65. *Seven complete and 4—5 incomplete forms are extant in Meissen to the present. Probably 12 variations are alluded to here. Most of them have been made by Eberlein.*

66. *" . . . a fairly large bird, namely, a gackedu has a peculiar growth shaped like a cap on its head, therefore it is pretty to look at. The bird rests on a pedestal overgrown with branches and leaves." (M. A.)*

67. *Loc. 1341, Vol. VI, P. 323.*

68. *Illustrated Sponsel a. a. O., P. 83, 84, 87, behind 96.*

69. *Loc. 1341, Vol. VI, P. 125.*

70. *Illustrated in Sponsel's book a. a. O. P. 176, but not ascribed to Kaendler.*

71. *Epargne is synonymous with Platmenage and with "centre piece for sweets and cakes" as it served in "surtout de table" for the arrangement of the desert. (Compare O'Byrn, a. a. O., P. 105, Note 1.) The use of china for table decoration see Bruening art and artistic handicraft 1904, P. 130 f.*

72. *Loc. 1341, Vol. V, P. 267 f. and 375 f.*

73. *Brown was not properly speaking a colour for painting under glaze. It was mixed with the glaze and then applied. Brown glaze was invented by Stöltzel or first used by him in Meissen. It was used for the so called brown china all through the 18ᵗʰ century.*

74. *Ibid. P. 205 f. and P. 375 f.*

75. *Loc. 1342, Vol. VIII, P. 28. Black glazing had been used as well. In the inventory of 1731 (M. A.) it says: "black glazed services are not being made any more."*

76. *Loc. 1342, Vol. VIII, P. 129.*

77. *J. Pichon, Vie de Ch. H. Comte de Hoym, P. 99 f.*

78. *In 1725 a tea service and chocolate goblets ornamented with sardinian coats of arms were made for the king (M. A.).*

79. *Loc. 1341, Vol. V, P. 248 and 280ᵇ.*

80. *Ibid. P. 252.*

81. *Loc. 1341, Vol. VI, P. 5 and 29 f.*

82. *Loc. 1341, Vol. V, P. 464.*

83. *Pazaurek in Thieme-Becker, General Lexikon of educational arts.*

84. *Brinckmann, The Hamburg Museum, P. 455.*

85. *Loc. 1342, Vol. IX, P. 51.*

86. *Minister of the conference and Privy Counsellor Johann Christian von Hennicke. Loc. 1342, Vol. X, P. 263 and 292.*

87. *In 1737 the king ordered all the china "which had up to that time and should in future be received to be given over to him without pay and presented as a particular flower". This order was used by Brühl to its fullest extent and was again repeated on Jan. 30ᵗʰ 1740.*

88. *Ibid. Vol. IX, P. 310, 336 f.*

89. *Ibid. Vol. X, P. 456.*

90. *Ibid. Vol. XI, P. 88.*

91. *Nimpsch became a member of the commission after Pflugk's death. Ibid. Vol. XII, P. 115.*

92. *On March 3ⁿᵈ 1741.*

93. *Loc. 1343, Vol. XVᵃ, P. 124 f.*

94. *Ibid. Vol. XIII, P. 69.*

95. *Ibid. Vol. XVᵇ, P. 455.*

96. *Ibid. Vol. XVᵃ, P. 58.*

97. *Loc. 1342, Vol. XI, P. 9 and Vol. XII, P. 171. In 1750 for instance 12140 talers worth of medium china was sold. Loc. 1343, Vol. XVᵇ, P. 249.*

98. *Ibid. P. 274.*

99. *Loc. 1342, Vol. XII, P. 309 and Loc. 1343, Vol. XVᵃ, P. 243.*

100. *Ibid. Vol. XIII, P. 414; Vol. XIV, P. 297ᵇ; Vol. XVᵇ, P. 200 f.; Vol. XVI, P. 253.*

101. *Loc. 1342, Vol. XII, P. 387; Loc. 1343, Vol. XIII, P. 424; ibid. Vol. XVᵇ, P. 471; ibid. Vol. XVI, P. 130.*

102. *Ibid. Vol. XVI, P. 195.*

103. *Ibid. Vol. XVᵇ, P. 155.*

104. *Ibid. P. 349.*

105. *Loc. 1342, Vol. IX, P. 49.*

106. *The factory in Meissen took three brothers Loewenfinck into its employment out of compassion. The eldest remained there till 1734 and then joined the army. Adam Friedrich, born in 1714, come to the factory in 1727. Karl Heinrich, born 1718, was employed as a painter in the factory in 1730. The former painted coloured flowers, the latter worked exclusively at blue painting. In reference to the work done by the two men last mentioned see Zais. "The Mainz electoral china factory" in Hoechst, see 2 f., the work of the first mentioned brother in Strassburg will be found described by Polaczek in Cicerone, 1910, P. 388 f.*

107. *Loc. 1342, Vol. XII, P. 246.*

108. *Bengraf, who afterwards played apart in the Hoechst factory (Zais, a. a. O.; see 12 f.), pretended to have fled from Meissen. I have not to the present found any mention of his name.*

109. *Loc. 1342, Vol. XII, P. 465 f.*

110. *About these see Folnesics and Braun, History of the Vienna china factory, P. 47 and 178.*

111. *This chinaware which was packed in 52 cases consisted of 120 most complete table services which were decorated in most varied fashion, 74 breakfast sets, 61 birds, 9 other animals, vases, tabacco-pipes, boxes, tops of walking sticks writing materials and a great number of figures and groups. A detailed list of these spoils of war in extant. Loc. 1343, Vol. XIII, P. 388; Vol. XIV, P. 53 f.*

112. *Sponsel, Cabinet pieces of Meissen china, P. 6.*

113. *A. a. O., P. 3 f.*

114. *Loc. 1342, Vol. VIII, P. 51.*

115. *Concerning Kaendler's birth see "Meissen china" as well. Note 187.*

116. *Born 1682 near Dresden, died 1751 in Dresden. G. O. Mueller, "Forgotten Dresden artists", P. 40 f.*

117. *Obituary in the "New library of the fine arts" 1775, P. 206 f.*

118. *Loc. 1342, Vol. X, P. 95 f., 187 f. and 480.*

119. *Loc. 1343, Vol. XVᵃ, P. 252.*

120. *Ibid. P. 131.*

121. *Kaendler married a daughter of Eggebrecht's shortly after 1737. Loc. 1342, Vol. VIII, P. 54 and 234; ibid. Vol. IX, P. 336.*

122. *Loc. 1343, Vol. XIV, P. 333, Vol. XVI, P. 273, 145 and 190; Loc. 1342, Vol. XI, P. 170 and 178.*

123. *Ibid. Vol. VIII, P. 264; Loc. 1343, Vol. XVᵃ, P. 252.*

124. *Loc. 1342, Vol. VIII, P. 264 and Vol. IX, P. 2.*

125. *These animals are each of them separately treated in "Meissen china" appendix.*

126. *Loc. 1342, Vol. VII, P. 15, 25, 30.*

127. *Ibid. Vol IX, P. 35.*

128. *Ibid. Vol. VII, P. 15, 30, 129, 133.*

129. *Ibid. Vol. X, P. 486.*

130. *Ibid. Vol. IX, P. 243ᵇ and Vol. X, P. 29ᵇ. Here it says — "excepting the set of bells most parts of which have already been delivered". This set of bells was later delivered for the palace. Sponsel, a. a. O., P. 59.*

131. *Loc. 1342, Vol. X, P. 192 and 484.*

132. *Ibid. P. 106.*

133. *The model of the vase R, 145 has at the end of the 19ᵗʰ century been greatly altered. Here as well as on table 3 the difference between the application introduced by Kaendler and the old application, as shown in table 2, 107* and 51, may be seen.*

134. *Godronirt is in Meissen understood to apply to a certain cut of the edge in which two flat arcs alternate with a point. Each point has a slightly marked ridge, between the two arcs there is on indentation which runs outwardly and downwards.*

135. *Loc. 1342, Vol. XI, P. 191 f. and Vol. XII, P. 423 f.*

136. *Loc. 1346, Vol. III, 1766, P. 98.*

137. *He probably had this made in 1797 for the wedding of his daughter Christine with Prince Charles of Savoy which took place in that year. She got married for the second time to the Duke of Montleart who returned the service to the Saxon court after her death in Paris in 1851 (O'Byrn, a. a. O., P. 150 and A. Fiedler, The history of the Courland palace, P. 14).*

138. *"Besides a few pieces namely enamelled chocolate goblets and saucers with the Sardinian coat of arms made by the court painter Herr Hoeroldt which were a few days ago sent for his Majesty to the depôt to Dresden and turned out so well as to be exceedingly beautiful to look upon" (M. A. of March 31ˢᵗ 1725). — On June 28ᵗʰ the tea service which had been ordered to be decorated with the Sardinian coats of arms was sent to Dresden as well. (M. A. of June 30ᵗʰ 1725).*

139. *J. Lessing has proved (Periodical for artistic industry 1888, P. 43 f.) that the form of this tureen which was ornamented with a lion is copied from a silver tureen made by Joh. Biller in Augsburg and to be found in the court plate chamber in Dresden. The tureen and candlesticks with figures are illustrated a. a. O., the saucière in Brinckmann's "Guide through the Hamburg Museum" P. 391, the "flower table" in "Meissen china" Tab. XVII. The last mentioned now has a place in the Feist collection.*

140. *At the end of the eighties of the last century parts of these services were put on the market from Dresden.*

141. *Baron von Zedwitz who has kindly advised me with regard to the coats of arms considers this fruit which looks like an apple to be misunderstood, he thinks that it greatly resembles a turnip Colonel von Kretzschmar kindly informed me that he considers the coat of arms to be Paris de Dagonoille, compte de Sampigny.*

142. *Loc. 1342, Vol. X, P. 70 f.*

143. *Parts of this service, namely a large jardinière copiously ornamented with bunches of flowers, double fluted feet and half figures of women, a stand to match this jardinière, dishes, jugs, cups, candlesticks, oil and vinegar bottles were sold in 1903 from Dresden. One cup is owned by the Dresden museum of art and industry.*

144. *Loc. 1342, Vol. X, P. 44.*

145. *Parts of this service were on the Dresden market in 1909. A salt cellar came into the museum of art and industry there.*

146. *Loc. 1342, Vol. XI, P. 191 f.*

147. *Of this service as well single pieces came on the market from Dresden in 1901. One plate may be found among other things in the Dresden museum of art and industry, a medium tureen was sold on the Fischer auction sale (1906, Nr. 218), a coffee and a cream jug were disposed of on the Pannwitz sale (1905, Nr. 439 and 440).*

148. *A completion of a service delivered before is probably meant here. The Dresden museum of art and industry possesses a large dish with cut out edge relieved with brown. The centre is ornamented with a small circular medallion bearing a primitive landscape in chinese style besides a pattern of strewed flowers and corn ears, the border shows the coat of arms of Hennicke without any coronet. As Hennicke was raised to the Peerage in 1728, made a baron in 1741 and a count in 1745, it can with certainty be said that the service originated between 1728 and 1741.*

149. *Up to the present about 1400 pieces are kept in possession in the castle Pfoerten in Brandenburg, "Graeflich von Brühlschen Familienfideikommisses". Some parts have been lent to the museums of art and industry in Berlin and Dresden. Cups and plates are very seldom come across on the market*

150. *The Meissen archives read as follows: — "Tureen whose lid is ornamented with figures of the history of Galatea — the place of the handles is taken by mermaids". "A vinegar and oil jug formed in clay. It is shaped like a swan on which a triton babe is seated the babe is bare and its garment forms the handles. This belongs properly speaking to the epergne."*

151. *The name was probably first thought of by the gentleman of the chamber Friedr. Aug. von Brandenstein who was raised to the place of "Oberkuechenmeister" on August 21st 1739 and died on March 21st 1743 (O'Byrn, The court silver plate chamber and the court cellars in Dresden, P. 125, Note 1). It is impossible to make sure if a new table service had been ordered by him. Perhaps, owing to his office, he only influenced Meissen as far as a new design for a dinner service was concerned.*

152. *The name orginates from Joh. Ernst Gotzkowsky who was born in 1710 in Conitz. He was educated in Dresden 1715—24; he then began to learn the merchant's business in Berlin and was from 1730 working in the fancy dealers store of his brother (History of a patriotic merchant. Autobiography of Gotzkowsky of 1768. Reprinted in the papers for the society of the history of Berlin, Book VII, P. 1 f.). It can be proved that he gave large orders to Meissen in the years between 1740 and 1750. For instance in May 1743 Kaendler worked at a large epergne representing Parnassus for Gotzkowsky of Berlin (M. A.).*

153. *Probably this design was first produced to order by the mercantile house of Dulong, Godefroy and Dulong later Jean Dulong et fils in Amsterdam which had been in business connection with Meissen for many years. In June 1743, 2 plates 8 and 10 passigt were made for M. Dulong in gypsum so that a service could be ordered according to this sample. (M. A.)*

154. *The former probably got its name from the fact that in 1745|6 it was first ordered by the spanish ambassador. At that time an epergne, a large tureen, dishes, candlesticks etc. were made for a spanish ambassador after silver models sent for the purpose. The expression "spanish design" may be traced back as far as 1765. The prussian design is also mentioned in 1765, it seems to have originated at that time.*

155. *Loc. 1342, Vol. XI, P. 28.*

156. *Springer "Pictures from latter history of art", 2nd edition II, P. 238.*

157. *Loc. 1342, Vol. XII, P. 423 f.*

158. *The M. A. mentions in August 1748 the following of the works of Kaendler: "A very complicated holy water pot. It consists of a pretty shell among clouds which the water is poured into. The shell is borne by an angel, above it another angel holds the shell in his hand and pours water into it with a dainty little jug". — Another holy water pot of a different design "a pretty decorated shell resting in clouds is borne by 2 cherubim; above the shell clouds may be seen, among them there are an angel and a cherub and beautiful palm leaves flow out of them; all this is beautifully modelled."*

159. *In January 1740 Kaendler modelled "a cow in clay for the countess of Schellsack and made it most beautifully". Loc. 1342, Vol. XI, P. 191.*

160. *The description Loc. 1343, Vol. XVᵇ, P. 212 reads as follows: — "A flat ground 5 inches high long and 7 in wide on which a shepherd in an upright position is leaning against a tree, a dog is standing next to him, a little to the left of the shepherd there are 6 sheep. 2 are lying down, 2 are grazing and 2 are looking about them and not eating. The ground of the plate must represent a meadow.*

161. *An indian bird in the act of eating sugar out of its claws sitting on the bough of a cherry tree Loc. 1342, Vol. XII, P. 423 ff. and M. A. 1740 and 1741 Kaendler modelled no fewer than 38 animals.*

162. *As a counter-part he made one sitting upright 335.*

163. *Probably the Elector Friedr. Christian is here alluded to.*

164. *The collar is marked G(raf) H(einrich) V(on) B(rühl).*

165. *At the same time Kaendler modelled same size a deer striding along and one of the same size lying dead.*

166. *In 1741 Kaendler made the form of "a pantalon with a woman" again fit for use. Loc. 1342, Vol. XI, P. 423 f. — Braun (Art and artistic industry 1906, P. 429) has proved that models for most figures of the sort find a place in Riccoboni Historie du Théâtre italian which appeared in Paris in 1730.*

167. *Probably made by Kaendler in 1741. Vol. XI, P. 423 f.*

168. *As these 6 figures are of a more dainty type than usual it may be assumed that some other man had a hand in making them. Probably Reinicke.*

169. *Sponsel, a. a. O., P. 133. Krueger calls as engraver Comt de Caylus in his introduction to the catalogue of the Jourdan auction 1910. Of the craftsmen illustrated there the bakers man Fig. 1, P. 4, the peddlar Fig. 2, P. 4, the coppersmith Fig. 1, P. 3 and the hawker Fig. 12, P. 3 are similar to them. The first Nr. 877 was made by Reinicke.*

170. *This figure appears in the catalog of the Fischer auction sale Nr. 741; it has been ascribed to Kayser owing to a remark scratched at the bottom. There was no sculptor of that name employed in Meissen, only a moulder Kayser who was paid 6 talers monthly was engaged there, he must have been pretty unreliable as he was imprisoned and afterwards dismissed. For a joke or from a desire to play himself off as an important personage he might have put his name on a figure he had to mould. It is certain that this figure must have been modelled by Kaendler himself. This is doubtless not only because of the unmistakable style*

of the article, but is confirmed in the reports as well. According to them Kaendler is supposed to have modelled "an old man playing the bagpipes after a drawing" in July and August 1741. Loc. 1342, Vol. XII, P. 423 f. The M. A. says "an old man in strange clothing with peculiar bagpipes which he is playing."

171. A cuirassier in full uniform on horseback.

172. In 1741 Kaendler modelled a group which is described as follows:—"A man with a bird cage with a parrot in it, next to it a woman is standing who is giving the parrot cherries to eat and putting feathers on the man's head, while he presents her with a "maise!" Ibid. In the Meissen documents this man is called the country architect Knoefel.

173. "A small group, a cavalier with a star and a polish order on his breast and a snuff-box in his hand leading a nicely dressed lady by the hand."

174. "A group consisting of 4 figures. A shepherdess sitting on a meadow, next to her a nicely clad youth wishing to embrace her against her wish. On the youth's shoulder there is a Cupid who is pulling his hair and beating him with his bow, a harlequin is standing by railing at him." (M. A.)

175. A group of dainty size. "A lady with nicely dressed hair sitting on a lawn, she holds a music book in her left hand and sings while beating time with her right; next to her an "actor man" is sitting playing the lute and looking on at the music." (M. A.)

176. "A group of freemasons representing two freemasons one is measuring a globe while holding one hand in his month, the other is sitting by and thinking; both have their aprons and orders on." (M. A.)

177. "1 group, a polish lady in a fur coat is sitting on a lawn, a well dressed Pole comes towards her and kisses her hand." (M. A.)

178. September 1741. "Joseph Froehlich with a mouse trap in his hand and Mr. Schmiedel holding an owl standing opposite to each other." Vol. XII, P. 423 f.

179. April—May 1741. "A complete sleigh with horse harnessed to it, with a woman sitting in it. At the back Jos. Froehlich is sitting with his arm round the woman's waist, on the sleigh an ape and one owl are seated" (Ibid.)

180. "One little group representing a fox playing on a clavecin and a woman sitting on a chair listening to him." (M. A.)

181. Loc. 1341, Vol. VI, P. 323; Loc. 1342, Vol. IX, P. 35 and 243; Vol. X, P. 211.

182. "A picture of the Virgin was made of the same size as the apostles which had been ordered for the royal court as well. The statue is standing on a globe on which a dragon is lying on to which the Virgin is treading; on her left arm the Infant Jesus is sitting and pushing a spear into the dragon's month in order to kill it. (Later this spear became a cross.) The statue spoken of is garmented in the usual manner." (M. A.)

183. A figure representing St. John Nepomuc, $^3/_4$ yard high in such raiment as becomes him. He is standing on a pedestal and has a crucifix and palm branches in his left hand." (M. A.)

184. The Infant is standing on a pedestal. It is dressed, has a crown on its head and an imperial globe in its left hand. (M. A.)

185. Loc. 1342, Vol. X, P. 97, 101, 492. Illustrated Sponsel, a. a. O. 128, the upper part in "Meissen china" Fig. 109.

186. Up to the present it has only been possible with certainty to ascribe only one figure of Christ to Kaendler.

187. Cupids were at first made with or without wings. In 1860 they began all to be made with wings according to an order from France where they were used as prizes in the cotillion.

188. M. A. says about this:— "A very complicated vase 1 yd. 8 in high representing fire. It rests on a very dainty foot on to

which a slave is chained. Behind the slave there is a canon with a powder barrel, gun ladle and other ammunition. On the body of the vase a battle is represented in bas-relief, many men are fighting over a standard. Mars with trophies is standing by and flags, drums, standards etc. find a place as well. On the lid Jupiter is sitting or an eagle and throwing lightning with his right hand."

189. "Meissen china" appendix Nr. 5.

190. In November 1736 Kaendler "modelled his Majesty the King exactly to order of Count Sulkowsky i. e. $^3/_4$ yard high attired in Roman dress with a casque lying at his feet." He begain it already in August. Then it was to represent the King in german dress having a table next to him on which a crown, an imperial globe and a sceptre were to lie. As the Count in the meantime decided on roman attire, Kaendler had to alter the model. There is however another model resembling it, a copy of it marked G. K. is to be found in the Dresden china collection (illustrated in the auction catalog Fischer 1906, Nr. 740). This was probably modelled by Kirchner who must have made it to compete with Kaendler. This fact can not be ascertained from M. A. it only reports that G. Kirchner who was in Dresden at that time modelled two of these china figures himself "by verbal order of the King" in Meissen and received 30 talers for them. The size and general deportment are similar, the helmet is also there at his feet only in another place. The cloak is fastened on the right instead oft the left side, the left hand which holds the cloak is not placed so firmly on the hip. The whole is excented in a softer and weaker fashion.

191. A. a. O., P. 149.

192. "His Majesty in roman attire with sceptre on horseback (small size) beautifully executed. It was placed on the royal table on August 3rd". (M. A.)

193. May be now found in the china collection in Dresden.

194. A. a. O., P. 153 f.

195. This figure which I first thought to be Anna Iwanowna ("Meissen china", Fig. 108, P. 88), is referred to in my article in "Art and artistic handicraft" 1910, P. 162 f.

196. Maria Anna, daughter of August III, was married to the Elector of Bavaria Max Joseph — Maria Antonia Walpurgis of Bavaria was united to Friedrich Christian, son of August III. One of the cartouches is ornamented with a royal crown instead of the Electoral hat.

197. In November 1737 Kaendler "modelled the apostle Peter in clay after a drawing given for this purpose for her Majesty empress Amalia. It was of the same size as the statue formerly sent to Rome." (M. A.)

198. Most of the pieces here mentioned may be found in the court museum in Vienna. Bruening "European china", P. XIV f. — Loc. 1342, Vol. IX, P. 196.

199. Museum of Art and Industry Dresden, count Waldstein in Dux. See Braun in the "Cicerone" as well, 1910, P. 120 f.

200. Such a bust is to be found in the Dresden museum of Art and Industry.

201. M. A. says:— "Wentzel 15 inches high in his usual dress exactly resembling him in face and figure, beautifully moulded in clay."

202. "A Vase representing the flourishing state of France." (M. A.)

203. Loc. 1342, Vol. XI, P. 198 ^{b}.

204. It is described in M. A. as follows:" — It is of a shell like pattern having a very complicated handle shaped like a woman sitting on a swan, and a child in a mass of sea weeds, 4 dolphin's feet and a shield borne by 2 children."

205. It is possible that the figure here illustrated was made in 1747, as he at that time made it again.

206. "Gardner's wife with a poke-bonnet on her head and her apron full of fruit." (M. A.)

207. Loc. 1344, Vol. XIX, P. 25.

208. M. A. says that in 1744 Kaendler "invented and made Nepomuc completely fit for being finished by Reinicke."

209. A figure 10 inches high carrying a crate with bread representing a french baker's man. (M. A.)

210. "1 indian Bajodt, 1 indian woman dancing, 8 inches high, 1 indian Bajodt presenting a salver with two goblets. 1 Bajodt with bare head grasping a sword." (M. A.)

211. Loc. 1344, Vol. XVIII^a, P. 73. Helbig writes that Kaendler had "out of spite and professional jealousy done every possible thing to harm Meyer. He managed to spoil the models made by him either in cutting or casting, this happened, according to Meyer's trustworthy statements in the following manner:—A figure was cast so that some parts of it were fresh, while others were dried together so that when all the parts were combined in paste a disproportion met the eye, so that the heads of Meyer's models were mostly too small for the bodies." — Loc. 1344, Vol. XVII, P. 433.

212. Kolbe, "History of the Berlin china factory", P. 138, 140, 149 and 296.

213. Chladni and Rost.

214. It was probably Chr. Gottlieb Hentzschel. He worked by the piece till Jan. 1st 1744, then he was appointed overseer with fixed pay; in this situation he had to teach the painters ornamentation. — Loc. 1343, Vol. XIII, P. 56.

215. Loc. 1342, Vol. X, P. 364 and 367.

216. Ibid., P. 490 and Vol. XI, P. 61 f.

217. "Ponceau" is a mixture of scarlet and blood-red.

218. Joh. Georg Heintze, born in Dresden 1707, came to Hoeroldt as an apprentice in 1720. In 1745 he became ill owing to the dissolute life he had been leading, he therefore lost the situation of overseer. In 1748 his refractoriness caused his imprisonment in Koenigstein where he had to paint china to order of the factory. Joh. Gottlieb Mehlhorn who had ere this been confined on Waldheim was made his companion. In April 26th 1749 both fled from here. Ibid. Vol. XIV, P. 44, 165 and Vol. XV^a, P. 75, 83 and 111.

219. Ibid., Vol. XIII, P. 224.

220. No work could with certainty be ascribed to him until his Royal highness Prince Johann Georg was successful in 1906 in discovering his name behind the wooden back of his picture.

221. Loc. 1342, Vol. XI, P. 45, 141 and 166; Loc. 1343, Vol. XIV, P. 382; Vol. XV^a, P. 8; Vol. XV^b, P. 159 and 478.

222. Ibid., Vol. XV^b, P. 456; Loc. 1344, Vol. XX, P. 314.

223. Loc. 1343, Vol. XIII, P. 253; Vol. XV^a, P. 285; Vol. XV^b, P. 14; Vol. XVI, P. 136.

224. Ibid., Vol. XV^b, P. 433.

225. Loc. 1342, Vol. XII, P. 71 and Loc. 1343, Vol. XV^a, P. 54.

226. Rosy-red is rosy-purple.

227. Pompadour red is identical with the "ponceau" mentioned P. 49.

228. Finely ground slate containing silver and a little zinc and cobalt formed one of the ingredients of the glazing.

229. Loc. 1341, Vol. V, P. 281 f.; Loc. 1342, Vol. VII, P. 106; Vol. VIII, P. 28 and 129; Vol. IX, P. 35; Vol. XI, P. 33.

230. In 1739 Chladni and Rost complained that the blue colour had been very bad for some time past. Ibid. Vol. X, P. 364.

231. He is a son of the Peter Eggebrecht mentioned on P. 5 and 23 he was Kaendler's brother in law. Loc. 1343, Vol. XII, P. 45; Vol. XIII, P. 224.

232. Ibid. Vol. XV^b, P. 472.

233. Many of the early onion pattern plates show the letter K. besides the trade mark of swords under glaze. This according to my opinion must have been the initial of the man who originated the pattern. Among the painters in blue of the time whose name begins with the letter K. Kretzschmar is the only one who can here be considered. Kuehnel whom others have thought of can not, in my opinion, be considered. Two Kuehnels whom I found in the reports were employed at a later time and were not painters in blue. (Loc. 1344, Vol. XXI, P. 205) The overseer of the painters in blue Colmberger can not in my opinion be considered either, as he only gained importance later (see P. 83).

234. Regarding Schimmelmann see Wintzer in the papers of the society fo the history of Berlin, H. XXXV, P. 36.

235. Loc. 1343, Vol. XVI, P. 278 f. and 317 f.; Loc. 1344, Vol. XVIII, P. 256 and 259.

236. Loc. 1343, Vol. XVI, P. 360.

237. Helbig went in for other speculations as well. He took part in the delivery of food stuffs to the troops of the enemy and was in such relations with their leaders as to cause many of his actions to be misapprehended. The great dislike harboured by the Princess Maria Antonia against this man is often drawn attention to. She even went so far as to have called Helbig, in one of her letters, the greatest rascal in the world (written Oct. 25th 1750 Lippert, "The intercharge of letters between Maria Teresia and Maria Antonia", P. 48. Here the whole matter is dealt with under the heading "the Helbig affair". P. CCXIII f. At her inducement the Austrian Major General von Vela ordered a troop of hussars to plunder a wagon with several cases of china and 30—40000 talers belonging to Helbig and to pillage a vine-field in Oberloessnitz belonging to his wife. Bruehl, however, induced Maria Antonia to see to it that Helbig should again receive what he had lost. (Loc. 1344, Vol. XVII, P. 65 f.)

238. Iibd. P. 79, 143, 219, 223, 433; Vol. XVIII^a, P. 1, 8 and 15 f.

239. Loc. 1344, Vol. XVIII^b, P. 16; Vol. XVII, P. 235, 239, 245, 487, 497, 503, 237 and 239.

240. Ibd. Vol. XVI, P. 291, 303; Vol. XVII, P. 56.

241. Ibid. P. 60.

242. This is yellowish-red, or red 8.

243. Vol. XVIII, P. 60, 293, 382 and 519 f.

244. Ibd. P. 283 f., 296 and 334 and M. A.

245. Besides Apollo and Daphne there were: Pan and Syrinx (2921), Venus and Adonis (2890), Diana and Endymion (2891), Ariadne and Bacchus (2895), Kephalos and Aurora (2907), Hercules and Omphale (2932,27) and Jupiter and Semele (2996).

246. It is possible that these letters indicate the Paris merchant Huet to have been the one to order the articles. Perhaps he was the son or otherwise the successor of Jean Charles Huet who had for many years after 1730 been connected in business with Meissen.

247. One of these figures was before numbered 2392. This seems to point to the beginning of the seven years' war. It is however possible that 1753 was the year when they were ordered and that at that time the 40 figures began to be made. Afterwards they were numbered in a separate series 1—34.

248. Vol. XVIII^b, P. 28 f., 281 f. and M. A.

249. Kolbe, "History of the Berlin china factory", P. 139 and 149.

250. Loc. 1344, Vol. XIX, P. 399 f.

251. Vol. XVIII^a, P. 82.

252. Ibid. P. 141.

253. Ibid. P. 161. Dietrich or Dietricy, born 1712, died 1774. The school of painting in Dresden was in 1764 made an Academy of arts.

254. Vol. XIX, P. 163.

255. *Antiqua Heraclea and Stephani della Bella.*

256. *Ibid. P. 237.*

257. *Loc. 1344, Vol. XVIIIª, P. 391 and Vol. XIX, P. 176, 212, 228, 231 and 236.*

258. *Vol. XX, P. 20. These two painters were Grossmann and Wiedner. The former was employed as a painter in Meissen from 1750 and worked in Meissen in a satisfactory manner for some time after his return from Sèvres. After this, he fell out with his superiors, went to Ludwigsburg in 1768, in 1774 he reported himself in Meissen as a battle scene painter and was again engaged there on August 20ᵗʰ.*

259. *Vol. XVIIIª, P. 243. On this occasion Fletscher mentions that a thorough acquaintance with the following colours would he desirable in Meissen — "rose, flesh colour, royal blue and a pretty green."*

260. *Concerning royal blue see P. 83.*

261. *Loc. 1344, Vol. XVIIIª, P. 72 and M. A. Chr. H. Kaendler chied on Nov. 12ᵗʰ 1765.*

262. *"Meissen china", appendix, document Nr. 6.*

263. *Loc. 1344, Vol. XVIIIª, P. 72.*

264. *Ibid. Vol. XIX, P. 168.*

265. *"Firstly Time, impersonated in the figure of an old winged man holding an oval tablet in his hands is seen leaning against a naturally represented rock, opposite him the goddess Fortuna is flying on a winged globe with her flower wreathed sail, in one hand she holds forth a bunch of flowers to represent the future flourishing state of the country. Between the two figures an antique shield bearing the electoral hat and coat of arms in placed; next to the coats of arms a small genius holding a wreath in his right hand and a palm branch in his left is seated. Next to the coats of arms the Saxon rue is growing, further below it there is a little picture representing sculpture and a few painting instruments to mean and represent the art of painting. Next to Fortuna and the figure of Time beautiful palms are seen growing." (M. A.)*

266. *"One new pastoral group began: — "A beautiful shepherdess sitting on a meadow holding a dove in her lap" and "a young shepherd in roman dress presenting his beloved with a bunch of flowers; he has a dog and two sheep at his side" — "a pigeon with a letter is seen here as well."*

267. *A parrot "nearly a yard high". "It is sitting on a stick or branch surrounded by a rock. It is in the act of screaming, has slightly outstretched wrings and holds a little cherry branch with leaves and fruit on in his left claw. It its very naturally and beautifully executed." (M. A.)*

268. *March 1765. "A newly created group consisting of three figures. An ancient lady is sitting in an arm chair. Her face is covered with wrinkles which point to a high old age, her hollow checks and withered limbs confirm the fact, she is nicely dressed and has near her an open money box which is filled with gold and silver coins, several gold coins have fallen into her apron. A maître petit' in a most loving pose kissing her hand is standing near her. Behind the money box, Cupid in the shape of a satyr is sitting looking at the couple of lovers through a pair of opera glasses. He has a note in his hand on which legible satires may be written of desired." (M. A.)*

269. *Hercules and Dejanira, Neptune and Amphitrite, Bacchus and Bacchante, Apollo and Minerva, Monus blamer and blameress, Jupiter and Venus. (M. A.)*

270. *Here the measurements are not quite in proportion.*

271. *"An old man dressed in a dressing gown in sitting on a pretty chair, on his right side a young well dressed young woman is standing. She is pulling grey hair out of his head, on his left side another moman is standing in required posture and pulling the black hair out of his head." (M. A.)*

272. *"A genius with a bird and a bird cage and a pair of bellows in seen well seated on a nice pedestal." Fire, Water and Earth are marked C 97, C 98 and C 100 respectively. (M. A.)*

273. *"A gallant young lady in her night dress is lying propped up with pillows on a pretty little bed, at the head of the bed a breakfast tray with chocolate cups is standing on a table; the woman has a cup in her right hand and while drinking out of it holds a biscuit in her left. Next to her at the foot of the bed, her husband in a dressing gown and slippers and a cap with a feather in his head is seated. He has a newspaper in his hand. At his feet a Bologna spaniel is standing. It is barking in the direction of the space under the bed. The man moves the bed aside and finds a young dandy under it. He is represented in a dressing gown and breeches with slippers in his hand, as if he had been obliged to hide himself at the unexpected arrival of the husband." (M. A.)*

274. *"The portrait of the reigning russian Empress on horseback, modelled in small size. She is represented by order, in a hunting habit with a suitable hat on her head. The hat is ornamented with a feather bush and gold braid and green and white bows. She has a sword in her right hand and long hair tied by a ribbon. Her feet are clad in spurred boots. A russian order is hanging over her right shoulder to her left hip. The horse which bears a valuable gold-embroidered saddle as well as pistols and arms is in the act of galopping."*

275. *„Bishop Palafax with the Mother of God in clouds as she is supposed to have appeared to him during a time when he was absorbed in prayer. The Bishop is represented bending one knee in a pose of the greatest veneration and devotion before the Virgin and beating his breast with both bands. He is dressed in full biscopal robes and is resting on a high step which is covered with a carpet with golden fringes. Next to him many clouds are seen in which the Mother of God appears flying or sitting. She is dressed in the usual upper and nether garments, has a veil on her head and an expression of utmost sweetness on her face. At the foot of these two figures a Bishop's mitre and sceptre are lying on the clouds." Of the pedestal it says: — "It is well formed in classic style and decorated with beautiful architectural parts; it bears an antique tablet on which the description about the Bishop as was ordered may be seen." (M. A.)*

276. *"The foot is decorated with classie shell-like ornaments, while the body, neck and lid are ornamented with antique foliage and water leaves; on both sides 2 beautiful festoons of bay leaves are seen, they are tied together and hang forth from behind the handles which give the body a nice ornamentation." (M. A.)*

277. *My former supposition that here the work of the forties was dealt with has not proved correct. The Meissen archives 1772—74 with certainty mention the time when they were made. Katharine is here said to be the person who ordered them and not Elisabeth as I formerly supposed. The single groups are dealt with by me in "Meissen china" P. 103 after Loose a. a. O., P. 43 f.*

278. *"It is 1 yard in width and in height and consists of 11 various figures and pictures and 3 animals (2 dolphins and 1 tortoise). The pedestal consists of a classic socle with arched edges and dainty cornice. It is furnished with classic ornaments and can be combined of two parts which are covered with water in the shape of sea waves. On this sea there is 2. the main figure of Amphitrite sitting in a very heroic posture in a shell like chariot; on her head there is a crown, in one hand a sceptre, in the other a flying sail which goes over her head in the shape of an arc. 3. a beautiful sea nymph who accompanies her and shows her corals, she leads 4. the dolphins by a leading string which is connected with the harness. 5. riding on a Triton there is a baby Triton who at the same time acts as a postman blowing a horn and*

carrying a crowned shield in his hand an which the russian royal coat of arms was to be painted (this was afterwards altered) 6. on old Triton swimming next to the Dolphins and blowing his horn so that it sets the sea trembling. Besides there is 7. another servant of Amph. who is standing behind the chariot and holding in one hand a shell filled with pearls. 8. at the back follows Glaucus who was put among the gods as a protector of Amphitrite because of his fidelity. 9. a sea nymph with a festoon of sea shells in one hand is swimming beside the charriot while holding it with the other. 10. at the side of Amphitrite a Triton child is swimming, in its hand it is holding a map on which the turkish fleet in flames which the child is pointing to is represented. (The map is now missing.) Besides there are three beautiful sea children with water wings flying round Amphitrite above the sail and holding the name of the russian Empress 'Chatarina' besides festoons of flowers, a wreath and palm branches in their six hands, in sign of high honour." (M. A.)

279. After the description of the pedestal Kaendler further explains the group as follows:"—2 Mercury young and joyously formed is riding in his chariot, he has a small casque with wings and ornaments on his head, is suitably apparelled in clasic style, has wings on his feet. His l (?) hand holds his caduceum, while his left hand drives the two ravens which are harnessed to his chariot; in it is a money box on which he is seated. Next to the chariot there is 3. a genius which moves in the clouds with it, he holds the sign of Mercury in one hand and a money bag in the other. In front of Mercury's chariot there is 4. a rooster with outspread wings which is to represent liveliness and watchfulness." (M. A.)

280. "This Saturn, in very old manly form, is sitting in his chariot holding a scythe in his right hand. 2. the chariot on which he is seated, modelled with many ornaments and very complicated wheels. 3. a Genius modelled with the sign of Saturn in his hands. 4. a dragon of medium size which owing to its peculiar appearance and wings has caused much trouble in the making. 5. another similar dragon only in different form." (M. A.)

281. On the pedestal there is a rock on which 2. the Goddess Clotho is standing slightly uplifted. She is holding a spinning wheel whose rod is set with diamonds in her hand; on her right hand 3. the other Goddess Lachesis is sitting on a rock and spinning, she is modelled in gracious from and scantily clad. Further the third Parce i. e. 4. Atropos may be seen, she is holding shears in her hand with which to cut the thread of life. She is represented as an elderly woman dressed in classic style she is lying on the grouna, pulled down by her hair by 5. Saturn, representing Time. He is holding her hand with the shears, so as to prevent her from cutting the thread of life. This figure of time is very old, muscular, entirely dressed and winged. 6. a Genius is seen standing next to Clotho and bringing flax so that the life of the Szarina may be prolonged beyond the allotted span. (M. A.)

282. "2. is placed on a well-moulded pedestal (described under 1) in the shape of a naturally made rock on which a snake slain with many arrows still sticking in its body is lying outstretched. This creature was very difficult to make owing to the peculiar shape of its head, wings and claws. 3. the statue of the sun god Apollo who is standing sleightly raised and is made in most edifying and beautiful fashion. He is suitably clad in a talar, has a wreath of laurel leaves on his head he holds his right hand against his hip, while his left grasps his bow, next to him at his left side his quiver is hanging on a laurel tree. 4. further the goddess Minerva seated and modelled on a rock with the god Apollo at her right and her attributes, a lance and an owl. She is entirely dressed with a helmet on her head and a laurel branch in her hand which she hands to Apollo in recognition of his great deeds.

5. representation of Envy in the form of an old man, very well done. It is grovelling in the dust and is being trod on by Apollo; it is represented eating its own heath out great conquerors have ever been envied. 6. a small genius to represent Victory which flies behind Apollo and crowns him with a wreath and a palm bough." (M. A.)

283. Many men of the name Luecke, Lueck or Lieck have been employed in Meissen. Two have been already mentioned above (P. 12 f.) Johann Friedrich and Christian Gottlob were the sons of a Dresden sculptor whose name was Johann Friedrich as well. The elder brother was born in 1727, the younger in 1734. Both came as embosser's apprentices to Meissen, the elder in 1741. After having, in company with Reinicke, overcome the temptation of being enticed away from Meissen in 1749, he fled from Meissen afterwards — in 1757 with his brother to Frankenthal where neither seems to have played an important part. In 1764 they were again graciously received in Meissen where they remained till their death. Johann Friedrich became overseer of the moulders in 1794 and died in 1797, Christian Gottlob who was a better artist than his brother died in 1796 as a pensioneer of the factory. In 1743 a finisher Johann Georg L. is mentioned, in 1744 a moulder's apprentice Carl Gottlieb L. is spoken of. The latter is probably the one mentioned by Hoffmann "Old Bavarian china" P. 22f. who died in Frankenthal after having attained a position of importance there. Loc. 1343, Vol. XIV, P. 328 ff.

284. "A well-dressed girl with a table on which a bird cage with a parrot is standing, classic pedestal."

285. "Group of 2 figures; a peasant woman with fowls and eggs in a crate and a well-dressed woman taking 2 cupids out of the basket."

286. Loc. 1344, Vol. XIX, P. 221 and M. A.

287. Loc. 1346, Vol. III, P. 35 and M. A.

288. Loc. 1344, Vol. XVIIIᵃ, P. 336 and 341; Loc. 1346, Vol. II, P. 8. Prince Xaver decides on March 28ᵗʰ 1765:—"That higher salary should be paid him because of his great skilfulness." (M. A.)

289. Group of 4 figures: — "Woman with spinning wheel, well dressed man to accompany this woman, one woman with a bird cage and a man holding a bird in his hand. To this belongs a woman sleeping and a man standing next to her." Of these it is said that "they belong to a group of 6 figures with a tree and ornamented pedestal." (M. A.)

290. Loc. 1344, Vol. XVIIIᵇ, P. 16; Vol. XVIIIᵃ, P. 164; Vol. XIX, P. 48, 50, 516; Loc. 1346, Vol. II, P. 5.

291. Loc. 1344, Vol. XX, P. 223 and M. A.

292. Rudolstadt, Wallendorf, Monastery of Veilsdorf a. o.

293. From 1764—74 auction sales had brought a profit of 376 474 talers. Loc. 1344, Vol. XX, P. 60 and Vol. XXI, P. 59.

294. Ibid. P. 59f., 99, 181 and 201. The workers by the piece were divided into classes according to their abilities. Those who belonged to the "white brigade" first class had 3 groschen deducted out of each taler, those who belonged to the second class and the girls who were employed for openwork and lace 4 groschen; the painters of the first class 4 groschen, of the second class 5 groschen, of the third class 6 groschen.

295. Vol. XX, P. 498 and Loc. 1345, Vol. XXIII, P. 236. A prohibition for the transit of china as well as for the manufacture and transit of english stoneware and non-saxon fayence had not been issued notwithstanding Marcolini's repeated request. The privy council and the deputation of commerce whose approval of this plan was required thought it inadvisable to issue this prohibition, as they were afraid that counter prohibitions would ensue. Loc. 1345, Vol. XXIV.

296. Loc. 1344, Vol. XXI, P. 56 and Vol. XXII, P. 159.

297. *Ibid. P. 283. The white brigade as well as the I class of the painters received the old prices again. The II class had to agree to a deduction of 2, the III class of 3 groschen in the taler. Several times, especially on Sept. 10th 1777 this lowering of wages caused trouble. Loc. 1345, Vol. XXIII, P. 19.*

298. *v. Heynitz died in April 1779. Loc. 1344, Vol. XX, P. 292 and Loc. 1345, Vol. XXIV.*

299. *Loc. 1345, Vol. XXV, P. 74, Vol. XXVIII, P. 187 and Loc. 1346, Vol. XXXI.*

300. *Helbig died on August 29th 1775.*

301. *Although Poerner suffered some pecuniary loss, as a great number of the tickets remained unsold, still the factory was bene-fited by the sweepstake, because much chinaware that had not been saleable was in this way turned into money. Loc. 1345, Vol. XXVIII, P. 143 f. and Loc. 1346, Vol. XXIX.*

302. *Ibid., Vol. XXXIV and XXXV.*

303. *Loc. 2439, Vol. XXXVIII—XL.*

304. *Loc. 1346, Vol. XXXIII; Loc. 2439, Vol. XXXIX and XL.*

305. *Loc. 1344, Vol. XX, P. 320.*

306. *Loc. 1345, Vol. XXIII and Loc. 1346, Vol. XXXV. His wish to keep Knoefler's professorship at the academy seems to have remained unfulfilled.*

307. *Both temples to-day find a place in the court chamber for silver plate.*

308. *General field marshal Count Nicolai Wasiljewitsch Repnin, born 1732, died 1801. The french representative, Baron Breteuil, who acted in favour of the Saxon politics in Teschen received an artistic table which was inlaid with 145 sorts of Saxon precious stones and pearls set in silver.*

309. *A document in the k. k. Privy court and state chan-cellery in Vienna the copy of which I have to thank the Counsellor Folnesics for, gives the following description of the single groups, by hand of the resident Baron von Metzburg:—"The principal group represents Minerva, the goddess of wisdom, holding in her hand the picture of the ruler of Russia with the inscription 'Catharina II invicta et immortalis' which she looks on with plea-sure and covers with her powerful shield, in her other hand she has a geographical map on which all the countries under the pro-tectorate of Russia — Saxony among them — are drawn. Mars the god of battles accompanies her, he is holding her mighty sword and the crown of the conquerors in his hand and is ready to support her. The lower group represents the god Apollo, as the harmony which makes the whole reign happy. Cybil the goddess of the earth who is accompanied by Ceres and Mercury intently surveys the monarchy. — The second group on the right represents 4 full-grown genii with large wings and with burning flames on their heads; they are standing round a globum terrestrem on which the lands which caused disputes are drawn. They represent the 4 powers Austria, Prussia, Russia and France. The History of Saxony is standing upright under a palm tree on which 4 crowns of immortality are fastened and is writing the following words on the tablet:—Pacta Germania — Teschenensis May 13 MDCC. (?). — The third group on the left represents:—Themis the goddess of Justice is sitting on a square pedestal next to her the Glory of rulers or the Love of peace is embodied in an innocent child which holds up a wreath of pomegranate blossoms — the flowers of justice — and begs justice of peace at present. On one side of the scales she has the goddess of victory on the other the Olive-branch, the latter weighs heavier than the former. The beehive standing by it is a sign of diligence and obedience. Near the goddess a few brave and thoughtful warriors are standing they are holding the russian eagle in the manner of the Romans and are eager to fulfil the commands of the ruler and to fortify her rights. — The fourth group represents the flourishing happiness which the peasant and the citizen enjoy in times of peace. The protecting care of their ruler cause joy to enter their hearts. Those rulers — the foreign russian empress and her successor — are here represented by Ceres and Triptolemus (as teachers of agriculture as well as of culture in general to their subjects at present and in the future). — The fifth group indicates the glorious deeds of Russia on sea and land, on all the four continents and represents the god Terminus with four fold face and an ivy wreath which shows as many views — here it is the likeness of Peter Alexiowitz who has formed his country and created shipping, by his efforts rough rocks have become blooming vales. Over him there is the following inscription:—Peter Alexio-witz, Creator et Legislator. — The sixth and seventh groups form the end of the table, they describe in detail the deeds of Count Repnin as follows:—The first represents Glory descending from the clouds and announcing the deeds of this count; round a pillar in trojan style there is the march from Schwaewitz and the treaty at the Dnestre with Abdul Kerim Pascha of three horse tails, at the base of this the audience of the Great Vizier is seen. The pillar is crowned by a large casque and a herold's rod tied to-gether which — through the inscription 'persuadere' indicate the bravery and the happy result of the mission he was entrusted with. — The second represents Gratitude accompanied by the genius of real honour and good repute, she winds garlands round the following motto which is inscribed by her on a pillar 'Dignissimo Principi Repninio et Belli et Pacis artibus clarissimo'. On the pedestal are represented:—Saxony leaning on its helm and receiving the daughter of Heaven the (?). It is accompanied on one side by the Genius of Happiness with the horn of plenty at his side, on the other side by Count Repnin conquering the Turks. Victory stands by his side on the battle field and adorns him with the order of the Hero."*

310. *In March 1775 Juechtzer completed "a child for the Gellert-monument". As it was his duty at that time to complete what Kaendler had begun, my conclusions are probably correct.*

311. *The first resembles the monument designed by Oeser and executed by Sam. Schlegel and Hesse which was erected in Leipsic in 1774; the second is made by Schlegel after the model for the monument in the Johanniskirche in Leipsic. For details see Graul, "Leipsic Calender" 1909, P. 157 fg., a source which E. Zimmermann drew my attention to. The M. A. speaks of this as follows:— "Gellert's monument consists of three children representing the three graces, two on an antique vase or urn stifling their tears against each other — the second carries a laurel branch. The urn is placed on a fluted column. The third of the graces who attaches the medallion of Gellert to the column has an inscription before her on which is written (memoria C. F. Gellert sacrum) she also holds a branch of laurel and of oak." Of the second:—"Gellert's monument 15 inches high shows two women embodying Doctrine and Religion; they are seated on a tomb decorated with tablets surrounded by laurel wreaths. On them inscriptions dedicated to the glory of the celebrated poet are written. All this is placed on another piece of architecture also ornamented in classic style."*

312. *For what reason this leave of absence on full Meissen pay was granted can not now be fixed. The younger Elsasser seems to have made use of this time for making copper engravings, at any rate in 1792 he sent 176 folios of figures, vases and groups to Meissen. Neither of them returned. The younger became a collector of duties in Herrnhut in 1794, he thereby lost his salary in Meissen, the elder drew it till his death on April 14th.*

313. *This figure had already been made by Matthaï.*

314. *The third figure to the left (J 21) was made by Schoenheit.*

315. *The middle priestess of Vesta in the centre (H 89) was made by Matthaï.*

316. *These were Wieme, Schmal, Schlegel, Kiehme and Groh.*

317. *Here Schiebel and Starcke may be mentioned who helped to work at the group of houris (L15) by Juechtzer exhibited in the academy of arts and the worker in gypsum Daebritz who made the basket illustrated Fig. 193, L60, may be mentioned.*

318. *These were passionate, frivolous and melancholy love.*

319. *The following portraits I found among others:— the Elector and his spouse, the Princes Anton and Max, the Princesses Elisabeth, Karoline, Amalie, the Emperors of Austria, Russia and Turkey, the Kings of Prussia, France and England, the Popes Pius VI and Sixtus, Count Marcolini and his wife, Laudon, Elliot, Lord Hove, Washington, the likeness of Boettger painted in red and brown in 1790.*

320. *In 1781 the following copper engravings were sent to the Meissen factory:—"Oeuvre de Salomon Gessner, 7 leaves engravings incl. title page, figures de l'histoire de France, 3me et 5me Livraison, each book 18 P. engravings, 6 Pages of the family of France, 1 page each Josephus II small, the russian Empress, Hope, by Angelika Kaufmann, Metastasius Romanus, Josephus II, as a husar, view of Vienna, vue des Environs de Bruxelles, d'Anvers, de Bruges, 5 P. 12 Livrs. du Jardin de Monceau, as well as 169 small copper engravings and vignettes.".*

321. *Loc. 1345, Vol. XXIV and XXV; Loc. 1346, Vol. XXIX.*

322. *Kuehn, "History of the Meissen china factory." Manuscript in the court and state archives, Rep. IXb, Div. A, section IV, Let. A, Nr. 1. If the date here given be correct only an amelioration of this colour can here be dealt with, as it had previously been used in Meissen. According to what has been said on P. 64 the first trials were made with it in 1766. Then the M. A. says what follows about painting:—In 1776 "saucers with royal blue" and "cups and saucers for Count Romanzow in royal blue with dainty genii" were painted, as well as "saucers in royal blue with medail. and coats of arms and goblets in royal blue and 1 shield portrait of the king of Prussia in grey" in 1781.*

323. *Loc. 1344, Vol. XXI, P. 201 fg. and Loc. 1345, Vol. XXVII, P. 29.*

324. *Nikolai Repnin-Wolkonski, adopted son of the count mentioned P. 78, born 1778, died 1845.*

325. *Kreishauptmann von Zetzschwitz, Head collector of taxes and Counsellor of mines von Oppel, von Heynitz on Miltitz, Vizerentmeister Bloede and Forstkommissionsrat Zahn.*

326. *Berling, Fayence and stone-ware factory Hubertusburg, P. 14.*

327. *Privy counsellor of finance von Nostitz and Counsellor of mines Freiesleben.*

328. *M. A. Ludwig Richter writes in his reminiscences P. 339 by Schaufuss:—"He copied the Sixtian Madonna innumerable times, the two children at her feet still more often. These copies painted in sepia or on china were always a saleable article and he used to say with selfconsciousness and in acknowledgement of the progress of our time that Raffael had made mistakes which he, of course, corrected." China plaques on which Schaufuss had painted Maria Magdalena and the Sixtian Madonna were exhibited in the Dresden exhibition in 1824 and 1830.*

329. *Loose, a. a. O., P. 46 f.*

330. *On the Dresden exhibition in 1830 the factory put up a plaque by the painter Goertz. On it a view of Meissen "after Richter" was painted.*

331. *Reminiscences, P. 337 f.*

332. *M. A. of March 13th 1833.*

333. *These were at first Bendemann, Huebner and Nicolai. In 1853 the place of the two latter was taken by Rietschel and Schnorr von Carolsfeld. (M. A.)*

334. *Here the Meissen factory was awarded the first prize.*

335. *Scheinert reports about this as follows: — "On the whole it is to be noticed that all these paintings executed in Dresden are not done in the good, old Meissen style which is almost always sought after, but are so made that hardly any of them would be taken up in our stock."*

336. *The collection of 900 numbers and of the value of 75000 marks was exhibited in the Albrechtsburg from 1st to 5th February 1862.*

337. *See P. 135.*

338. *See P. 136 f.*

339. *See P. 148 f.*

340. *Here real lace is used. It is saturated with china paste. In the baking the paste remains, while the threads of the lace burn away.*

341. *He died in 1893.*

342. *Loose, a. a. O., P. 5 f.*

REGISTER.